MW01016501

THE "PLACE" OF JUSTICE

EDITED BY THE LAW COMMISSION OF CANADA

FERNWOOD PUBLISHING • LAW COMMISSION OF CANADA

Editing: Eileen Young
Cover design: Larissa Holman
Printed and bound in Canada by Hignell Printing Limited

Published in Canada by Fernwood Publishing
Site 2A, Box 5, 32 Oceanvista Lane
Black Point, Nova Scotia, B0J 1B0
and 324 Clare Avenue, Winnipeg, Manitoba, R3L 1S3
www.fernwoodbooks.ca

Fernwood Publishing Company Limited gratefully acknowledges
the financial support of the Department of Canadian Heritage,
the Nova Scotia Department of Tourism and Culture and
the Canada Council for the Arts for our publishing program.

Library and Archives Canada Cataloguing in Publication

The place of justice / Law Commission of Canada.

ISBN 1-55266-188-1

1. Social justice. 2. Sociological jurisprudence.
I. Law Commission of Canada II. Title.

HM671.P53 2006   340'.115   C2006-900314-9

CONTENTS

CONTRIBUTORS

NICHOLAS BLOMLEY teaches in the Department of Geography, Simon Fraser University.

SIGNA A. DAUM SHANKS is a PhD student in the Department of History at the University of Western Ontario.

LILITH FINKLER is a student in the Interdisciplinary PhD program at Dalhousie University and a Trudeau Scholar.

FIONA KELLY is a PhD candidate and sessional instructor in the Faculty of Law at the University of British Columbia.

MICHAEL MOPAS is a PhD candidate at the Centre of Criminology, University of Toronto.

CARMELA MURDOCCA is a PhD candidate in the Sociology and Equity Studies in Education/Collaborative Women's Studies Programme at the Ontario Institute for Studies in Education of the University of Toronto.

KIRSTY ROBERTSON is a PhD candidate in the Department of Art at Queen's University.

SEAN ROBERTSON is a PhD candidate in the Department of Geography, Simon Fraser University.

PREFACE

This collection stems from the first annual *Nathalie Des Rosiers Audacity of Imagination Award*, an initiative sponsored by the Law Commission of Canada, the Canadian Federation for the Humanities and Social Sciences and the Department of Justice Canada. The award is for graduate students who are actively engaged in original and innovative research in pursuit of masters or doctoral degrees in law or the social sciences and humanities. The goal is to stimulate critical and multidisciplinary discussion and debate about fundamental issues of law and society. Winners are invited to present their papers at the annual Congress of the Humanities and Social Sciences. The theme for the 2004 award was *The "Place" of Justice*.

The sponsors would like to thank the committee members who selected the essays in this collection. They would also like to thank the two anonymous reviewers who provided helpful comments and feedback on an earlier version of the of this collection, as well as all of the applicants to the first annual *Nathalie Des Rosiers Audacity of Imagination Award* who helped make this initiative a great success. Also, thanks to everyone involved in the production of this book: Eileen Young for copy editing, Debbie Mathers for typing the final manuscript, and Beverley Rach for production and design. A special thanks to Wayne Antony at Fernwood Publishing for all of his support and guidance throughout the publication process.

INTRODUCTION:
THE PLACE OF JUSTICE

NICHOLAS BLOMLEY AND SEAN ROBERTSON

INTRODUCTION

The essays collected in this book derive from a graduate student essay competition, entitled "The place of justice," which was cosponsored by the Law Commission of Canada, the Canadian Federation for the Humanities and Social Sciences and the Department of Justice Canada. These two nouns — place and justice — are both rich and suggestive. As we shall see, when conjoined, they take us to many sites — from Saskatchewan and Ontario to the courtroom and the street, as well as to racism and equality. However, place and justice are both conceptually slippery and ethically complex terms. Broadly speaking, the theme of this volume has emerged as a response to recent critical legal and social sciences scholarship that has both sought to contextualize the substantive and procedural aspects of law within society and space and, partially as a result of this "spatial turn," questioned and unsettled the equivalency drawn between law and justice in orthodox liberal thought. In this introductory section, we introduce the relationship between place and justice, and offer a few thoughts on the ways in which the essays variously engage this problematic aspect of justice. We also present a summary of the six papers contained in this collection that further situates them within the socio-legal literature relevant to the theoretical and substantive issues raised by the authors.

PLACE AND JUSTICE

Modern law is a social tradition that draws its credibility from its objective deliberation on the facts and the disinterested application of the rule of law. "Place," to the extent that it denotes the messiness of social life and lived contexts, thus appears set apart from the realm of law. Moreover, to the extent that place denotes space, there is an added dimension to this expulsion. For modern thought has long treated space in a particular way: "as the dead, the fixed, the undialectical, the immobile. Time on the contrary was richness, fecundity, life, dialectic" (Foucault 1980: 70). Human geography is one discipline that has responded to this problem by criticizing the marginalization of space and proposing the outlines of a critical geographical imagination. Edward Soja (1990), in particular, highlights the centrality accorded the historical imagination in modern intellectual thought, both critical and liberal, and the consequent occlusion of a critical spatial sensibility. The political interests maintained in part by the dominant spatial order are obscured, (although perhaps buttressed) in situations where space is unexamined or where it is only thought of as neutral. Thus, in the call for the elaboration of our singular class, gender, and race-specific "geographical imaginations," geographers have proposed a sensitivity to space — for example, nature, landscape, and, quite simply, the role of space in everyday life — through which the practices and representations of the hegemonic spatial order may be critiqued and resisted by those within and beyond academe (Gregory 1994). Edward Said has examined the classic manifestation of the geographical imagination — the West's construction of the Orient (the Middle East) — as a means to reveal the politics inherent in *knowing* the Orient and to reconfigure the West's political and material consciousness of itself (Said 1979). Thinking critically about space is essential not simply for social scientists interested in unpacking spatial representations and practices and getting at the grounds of reality and knowledge, but also for jurists interested in the grounds of law (or the place of justice); jurists need to have an understanding of the law as a social artifact with political force. More generally, thinking critically about the way that space is produced and the way it can potentially be reconfigured and resisted is important for the politics of the everyday.

The concept of justice emerges in the present collection in at least two ways: as a synonym for law and the exercise of judicial authority, and in reference to an ethic of fairness, equality and redress. Frequently, the two combine: thus, for example, in Carmela Murdocca's paper, "National Responsibility and Systemic Racism in Criminal Sentencing," the workings of the legal system are said to produce unfair outcomes. "Place" is also given several meanings, and is used both metaphorically and materially. In most cases, it is used to refer rather generally to space, situation or context. So, for Fiona Kelly, in "Mis-placed Justice: Justice, Care and Reforming the "Best-Interests-of-the-Child" Principle in Canadian Child Custody and Access Law," the problem with liberal legalism is that it is insufficiently attuned to the messy lived realities of parenting. Similarly, for Kirsty Robertson, in "Whose Streets? Our Streets!: Protest, Place and Justice in Canadian Society," the street must be understood as a material site of shared and embodied experience of public demonstration. In Signa Daum Shanks' paper, "Who's the Best Aboriginal? An "Overlap" and Canadian Constitutionalism," place is used in the way that many geographers may recognize it — that is, as a "meaningful location" (Agnew 1987; Cresswell 2004). In this sense, the dense entanglements of human and nonhuman occupants in the traditional territories of the Dene and Inuit are "locales" (that is, material settings for social relations) imbued with a "sense of place," through which people develop subjective and emotional attachments.

Given the multiple meanings of place and justice, we do several distinct and useful things when we bring these terms together. To enquire into the place of justice, firstly, we explore the often precarious and ambiguous ways in which place (whether as space, context "meaningful location") fits within the world of law. Secondly, we explore the impact of the concept of place on legal deliberation and processes. And finally, we consider what difference place makes to justice. In what follows, we will briefly elaborate on each of these in turn.

Kelly's argument that liberal legalism is predicated on a model of justice that is underpinned by formal equality, objectivity and individualism alerts us to the ways in which law has long defined itself as an essentially closed domain, that is both autonomous from, yet immensely important to, a realm that we can, for want of a better word, term "society." Thus, legal interpretation is understood as distinct from social processes, structured by its own logic and rationality, and governed by what Roberto Unger (1983: 320) terms formalism: a commitment to a method of legal justification that "can be clearly contrasted to open-ended disputes about the basic terms of social life, disputes that people call ideological, philosophical or visionary." Law is also imagined as different to the extent that it constitutes a "defensible scheme of human association" (Unger 1983: 322) distinct from extralegal social orderings. By virtue of its distinctive qualities, law is presented as an "autonomous instrument" (Griffiths 1979: 343) that can be brought to bear on society. In all cases, something called "law" is detached from something called "society."

The aspatiality of modern law has affected the institutional workings of law: according to some writers, the Western legal project is underwritten by an organized forgetting of local places, especially as they may affect core principles, such as the rule of law and legal rationality. Thus, as Berman (1983) reminds us, English common law sought to disembed itself from locality (cf. Blomley 1994: 67–105). When Blackstone (1838: 20) instructed the law teacher to consider his course as "a general map of the law, marking out the shape of the country, its connections and boundaries, its greater divisions and principal cities," he also counselled that "it is not his business to describe minutely the subordinate limits, or to fix the longitude and latitude of every inconsiderable hamlet." In so doing, he neatly expressed the tendency of law to erase spatial specificity and local difference in the name of an ordered and apparently coherent unity. In its very constitution, then, law appears to have an important, if negative, relation to space and place. This disembedding still seems very much with us, at least so far as formal legal discourse is concerned. Wes Pue (1990) goes so far as to argue that law is a profoundly anticontextual faith. "Its god is a decontextualised, highly abstracted and depersonalised rationality. Contexts of all sorts — gender, class, religious, cultural, political, historical or spatial — are the enemies of Law. In all its majesty Law is the antithesis of region, locality, place, community" (566).

Not surprisingly then, as an academic discipline, law has also not always given place serious consideration. To the extent that legal writers have engaged with social and political questions, the tendency has been to think in historical terms (Gordon 1984). While this has been immensely productive, only recently have legal writers acknowledged the "spatial turn" within social thought: that is, an acknowledgement that space and place are more than disinterested surfaces upon which more important social processes unfold. Rather, they are themselves produced by, and constitutive of social relations, meanings and hierarchies (Lefebvre 1991). If we accept, as we must, that law is also "social" and "political," we ignore space and place at our peril. A growing body of scholarship — including this volume — has begun to map out this relationship: it is studied both in critical legal studies (Stychin 1998; Sarat, Douglas and Umphrey 2003) and in the social sciences (Blomley 1994; Blomley, Delaney and Ford 2001; Mitchell 2003; Razack 2002; Stychin 1998; Holder and Harrison 2003).

This body of work demonstrates that while law may be hostile to place, it is, at the same time, a deeply spatial enterprise. This is its paradox. Law makes space all the time. It draws boundaries, carves out territories, and imbues them with legal meaning. These spaces are more than secondary backdrops to law; they are a crucial materialization that makes law possible as a form of organized force and rule. Thus, jurisdiction and sovereignty rely upon a territorialization of law, producing a powerful set of spatializations that have subtle, yet important, effects for the ways in which law is put to work in the world (Ford 1999). Real property also relies upon, and is incomprehensible without, a territorial grid. While its geographies frequently go unremarked, they benefit from closer and more careful examination (Blomley 2003a). The concept of "overlap," described in this volume by Daum Shanks as instances where the Crown is faced with a conflict of interest in deciding the fate of competing claims made by First Nations, must be understood as an outcome of a legal mapping that imagines native treaty rights as finite and mutually exclusive, rather than fluid and negotiable. "Overlap," then, is a product of a colonial legal cartography rather than extant local relationships (cf. Borrows 1997).

But law does not only produce space: it is also often attentive to localized difference. Constitutional law, for example, can oscillate between centralization and a recognition of localized contextual conditions and the integrity of community-based forms of law making and interpretation (Briffault 1990). But law must also be conceived as a vital medium and resource for daily life. And given that, generally speaking, we live our lives out in particular places, that process of legal interpretation is localized in some interesting and important ways: this is noted by Robertson in her essay on street protest, when she argues that the embodied experience of protest — the being-together in public space — may generate alternative ethics and legalities. Similarly, in a fascinating series of studies in three U.S. towns, Carol Greenhouse, Barbara Yngvesson and David Engel (1994) reveal "the place of law and the court in the construction of community and hierarchy," noting the ways in which local as well as extra-local conceptions of law and rights are central to the ways in which community and place are constructed. Davina Cooper (1996) also explores the way in which an appeal to "place and belonging," as she puts it, is important to legal struggles in particular areas. Thus, an attempt by orthodox Jews in Barnet, London, to build an "eruv," allowing them to conform to Jewish legal obligations concerning activity on the Sabbath, became the spark for conflict. Cooper traces the way in which this struggle turned on legal and spatial understandings of "insiders'" versus "outsiders'" rights to place, and the construction of "Englishness." There are echoes here of Finkler's account, in her chapter, "Re-Placing (In) Justice: Disability-Related Facilities at the Ontario Municipal Board," of the "community integration" of the disabled in Ontario: in her discussion, she critiques the ways that dominant representations of the disabled may operate to frustrate their attempts to secure housing.

Western law is also integrally spatial to the extent that it relies upon a "constitutive outside" against which it defines itself. This entails the creation of boundaries that distinguish it from its negative image (Darian-Smith 1999; Vismann 1997). Peter Fitzpatrick (1992) documents the ways in which the law of the European Enlightenment reduced the world to European universality. Rather than a multiplicity of legal possibilities, difference was positioned relative to the West. European legal identity, he argues, entails the mapping of the colonial subject as purely negative, from which the positivity of Western law is derived (cf. Peake and Ray 2001; Bhandar 2004). Similarly, Murdocca underscores the ways in which Canadian law relies upon a particular construction of the benevolent and inclusive nation (implicitly set against other, less enlightened places) in its dealings with, and continued constitution of, racialized others.

Law, then, not only produces space: it is itself shaped by extra-legal conceptions of space, such as the nation. For example, Richard Ford (2003) considers the ways in which U.S. regulation of the Internet has been structured by prevailing characterizations of the Internet as a place. Ford worries that this has the effect of inappropriately importing conceptions of land, property and sovereignty, developed in the context of material space: "a metaphysics of space threatens to derail sound analysis and to smuggle in, as inevitable or logically compelled, background rules that should be subject to debate" (177). In a similar vein, in his chapter, "Putting Cyberspace in its Place: Law, the Internet and Spatial Metaphors," Michael S. Mopas explores the degree to which spatial metaphors have structured judicial understandings of the Internet.

However, we must be cautious about making metaphysical distinctions between place and justice, or space and law (Mitchell 2002). There is a tendency to rely implicitly upon a tripartite split, where "law" affects "space," both of which have a relation to something called "society." But on closer examination, the relationship may be a closer one: "'law' and 'geography' do not name discrete factors that shape some third pre-legal, aspatial entity called society. Rather the legal and the spatial are, in significant ways, aspects of each other" (Blomley, Delaney and Ford 2001: xviii). Thus, legal orderings are simultaneously spatial orderings, and vice versa: the "owner" is to "land" as the "citizen" is to "state territory," and so on, such that the two are inseparable. A prison is neither a legal category nor a space, but both simultaneously — a "splice," if you will (Blomley 2003b). This is important when we remember that, unlike many other institutions, the power of law is such that "legal spaces," like Daum Shanks' "overlap," are produced on the ground, having real consequences for social relations and political possibilities.

The essays in this collection are not merely descriptive. To varying degrees, they point out that the place of justice can have ethical consequences. So, for example, Kelly criticizes prevailing conceptions of justice in relation to child-custody law for their detachment from an ethic of care that better accords with the lived and contextual realities of childrearing and parenting. Yet Murdocca condemns programs of restorative justice, which consciously embrace context and difference, as unjust. So what, then, *should* the place of justice be? We will not attempt an answer here, for, as noted above, place and justice are themselves ambivalent and multivalent terms. It is, of course, tempting to criticize law for its failure to recognize context and difference. Thus, Pue (1990) argues that an attention to place can challenge the authoritarian hierarchies of law within the courtroom, legal education and everyday life, and offer a more socially rooted, and thus humane, set of legal possibilities. Pue argues for the critical importance of what he terms "geo-jurisprudence," arguing that the contributions of space are simultaneously ethical, political and analytic. Selznick (2003) argues that if law is to be effective and responsive, it should (and, in fact, often does) maintain a "fidelity to context," responding to the particular norms and constraints of specific contexts. So, for example, rights can take on different meanings and intensity, depending on context. Rights associated with expression clearly vary according to who, or what, is engaged in communication, and within which settings, he notes. An attention to context, he argues, need not mean the abandonment of principles, such as fairness, freedom or empowerment. However, as Murdocca notes, law can be attentive to difference, yet still productive of hierarchy.

Further, law can produce places and spaces that can have political effects. The territory of the sovereign state is one such legal space. The assumed uniformity of rule within the sovereign territory, and the associated distinctions between inside and outside thus produced, can have problematic consequences (Whitaker 1999). Thus, the territorialization of the law in the container of the sovereign state makes possible and helps sustain a distinction between a domestic realm of politics, governed by procedural justice and a search for the common good, and an international realm (that is beyond the territory of any state), characterized by anarchy, force and disorder (Agnew and Corbridge 1995). This distinction can have insidious effects, as exemplified in the history of colonialism in territories "beyond the line" of European public law (Schmitt 2003). Yet, the geographies inscribed in law that close down political possibilities can also be turned on their head. For example, Fran Klodawsky (2001) notes the ways in which the mismatch between international human rights codes, and the diminished realities of domestic social and economic rights protections, has been used by Canadian anti-poverty activists to powerful effect (cf. Pratt 2004).

However conceived, to ask what the place of justice is, and what it should be, is to ask a series of important and productive questions. As these essays reveal, the analytical lens of "place" can unsettle certain core conceptions of law, revealing the ways in which legal practice and interpretation frequently eschew the messy, fleshy contexts of social life. At the same time, however, law is revealed as produced by, and productive of, extra-legal concepts of space and place, including their attendant metaphors. Notably, the law plays a critical role in boundary making and nation building and, by extension, in the determination of insider/outsider status. The place of justice, then, is an uncertain, yet analytically and politically important one.

OVERVIEW OF CHAPTERS

In "'Whose Streets? Our Streets!': Protest, Place and Justice in Canadian Society," Robertson turns our attention to civic protest and investigates the abandonment of public space as the evacuation of the "place" of justice. Robertson questions the current sentiment of anti-globalization protesters that "the future of protest is in litigation," as opposed to the public space of the streets. In view of the chilling effects of the arrests of protest organizers and the potential threat to freedom of expression in anti-terrorism security legislation, such as the *Anti-Terrorism Act* (2001) (formerly Bill C-36), she laments the impending demise of public protest for two main reasons. First, the mass public demonstrations that characterized the meetings of the World Trade Organization at Seattle, Quebec City and Genoa have been instrumental in raising awareness and politicizing the issues surrounding global justice. More important for the purposes of her paper, however, is the latent potential for the embodied experience of protest to inspire an ethics commensurate with redressing global inequities. With the turn away from public space, Robertson fears the abandonment of a space generative of an anti-capitalist ethics. Instead of justice, the body, and unscripted experience being sites for negotiation and responsiveness in the ethical sphere, the retreat from the space of protest signals the stratification of law, visuality, and recorded experience in ways that do not challenge the current distribution of resources in our society.

With reference to post-structuralist thinkers on the body, affect and resistance (notably Brian Massumi, see References, Chapter 1), Robertson describes public protest as an effective methodology of change. In this analysis, public protest is cast as an interruption of the regime of visuality that underpins capitalist society. Drawing from Michel Foucault, Massumi suggests that this regime operates at levels of institutions and the body throughout society. The knowledge produced and circulated therein frames a subjectivity through which the individual comes into being. The regime is so all-encompassing that any revolutionary action or thought finds itself always-already enclosed, appropriated and re-territorialized by its discourse. On the other hand, public protest evokes a broader affect or sensibility that excites hitherto uncharted points of the body/mind and provides opportunities for unscripted acts and thought along the edges of the regime of visuality. During a protest, the sights of the multitude and the police, the smell of tear gas, and the cacophony of drums, music, and chanting stimulate both a confusing disconnect from the everyday and a republican resonance with the other protesters. According to Massumi, this moment of disorientation holds the potential for individuals to form a transitory connectivity across the crowd. Robertson asserts that the prioritization of the rights of the individual and private property rights in the liberal framework of the law sets the terms of a discourse within which the claims of justice of anti-globalizers are incomprehensible. Thus, any retreat from street protest as a methodology of change would represent the truncating of the potential to think about global justice in ways beyond those delimited by conventional judicial and moral discourses. Robertson concludes by suggesting the role that art plays in providing a space for affect and a place for justice through an examination of *Templates for Activism*, a set of art projects that attempts to represent, via non-traditional means of representation, ideas about a range of topics of concern to feminists, such as rape, from outside the dominant frameworks of interpretation.

In "(Mis)Placed Justice: Justice, Care and Reforming the "Best-Interests-of-the-Child" Principle in Canadian Child Custody and Access Law," Kelly takes issue with the rhetoric of justice as an objective in Canadian family law and suggests that it needs to be re-aligned given the exigencies of family disputes. In an argument similar to that used by Robertson, Kelly suggests that justice is currently defined not by an attempt to resolve disputes and address inequality through a holistic appraisal of reality but rather by a liberal framework of rights and obligations that impedes the struggle for substantive equality. The liberal model of justice is underpinned by three assumptions that serve to provide predictability and efficiency in the law. It first assumes that the parties to any dispute are formally equal, irrespective of the actual power that either party holds. Second, the liberal model assumes that decisions can be made by neutral decision makers using objective criteria. Finally, it assumes that justice is best furthered in situations where it promotes each party's individual rights. According to Kelly, when this "ethic of justice" universalizes, abstracts, and depersonalizes legal disputes, a discourse is produced that prioritizes formal equality over substantive equality. This obfuscation of the messiness of reality is of critical importance in the instance of family law, as these disputes are invariably infused with the complexities of relationships, child-care responsibilities, and everyday life. With reference to changes in other common law jurisdictions and feminist legal approaches, Kelly proposes a decision making process that could accommodate greater discretion and subjectivity in reconciling the intricacies of family disputes within the functional requirements of the law. Kelly concludes by looking to three legislative models that illustrate the ways an ethic of care could augment the static and unresponsive ethic of justice. The ethic of care is capable of addressing the actual relationships between parents and children, as well as the realities of the work of care-giving (as opposed to simply "caring for"), and dealing with child abuse and domestic violence.

Kelly focuses on the "best-interests-of-the-child" principle as the site from which to analyze the ethic of care. Recently, fathers' rights organizations have structured their legal arguments for child access and custody within a rights discourse. This rhetoric of formal equality has been well-received by the judicial system. Fathers' rights advocates' claims for equality have arguably resulted in a presumption in favour of shared parenting. It may be further asserted that a rights discourse promoting shared parenting as synonymous with the principle of the "best interests of the child" has emerged. As Kelly argues, the best interests of the child are paradoxically characterized by a decision that treats the parents equally, as opposed to a decision that looks to the rights and needs of the child. The ethic of care is proposed to correct the excessive reliance on formal equality in the pursuit of justice. Carol Gilligan (1982) has identified three elements of an ethic of care supportive of this objective: it arises out of the realities of relationships as opposed to rules; it is contextual; and, it is tied to material relationships, as opposed to abstract notions of the ideal family (i.e., white, middle-class, nuclear, heterosexual). Despite the deep roots of the best-interests-of-the-child principle in Canadian law, Kelly opines that it must be abandoned in order to promote the more nuanced decision making afforded by a "principle of care." Drafting such a broad concept into legislative form necessitates striking a balance between rules and discretion. While acknowledging the importance of the best-interests principle, Kelly concludes by reviewing three legislative formulations of the principle of care; she suggests that a more responsive and interactive justice would be the result.

Whereas Robertson and Kelly optimistically propose a broader notion of justice through the pursuit of an ethics outside the law, in "National Responsibility and Systemic Racism in Criminal Sentencing," Murdocca situates the epistemic position of the disenfranchised and describes how it functions to frustrate any expression beyond the liberal framework. Murdocca queries the efficacy of attempting to redress the systemic racism of the liberal state by considering discrimination as a factor in the sentencing of individuals. Even in circumstances of apparent reconciliation, Murdocca reveals that the voices of the subaltern are nevertheless gendered and racialized as they are re-mobilized by the state's mythology of nation-building.

In *R. v. Gladue* (1999) (see References, Chapter 3), the Supreme Court of Canada construed the alternative sentencing provisions of Section 718.2(e) of the *Criminal Code* (see References, Chapter 3) as follows: In respect of First Nations, it held that the court must consider the impact of discrimination in structuring the social conditions under which the accused committed their crime. In these circumstances, a traditional punitive sentence would potentially exacerbate the conditions of inequality and, therefore, fall short of the principles underpinning sentencing. Section 718.2(e) requires the court to place emphasis on the restorative or remedial possibilities of sentencing, thereby encouraging alternative sentencing, such as conditional sentences served in the community. Although Murdocca recognizes this provision as an attempt at restorative justice, she argues that the court can only recognize the legal personhood of the accused from a perspective that perpetuates the system of discrimination it aims to redress. In other words, while these narratives of racism serve to establish national culpability for discrimination, they also constitute a discourse of a racialized accused and the benevolent nation. Instead of achieving its goal of substantive equality, as Murdocca points out, the law enacts a project of nation-building that continues to rely on the narratives of gendered and racialized others. In this context, Murdocca seeks to explore "the embodied effects of law."

Murdocca's chapter contemplates whether the consideration of systemic discrimination through the optic of class, race, and gender in sentencing not only does not promote restorative justice, but also whether, through the requirements of identity, it insidiously buttresses discrimination. In order for the law to approximate its objectives of fairness and equality, it must examine the effects and meanings produced through its classificatory practices. To be sure, an accused is made comprehensible as a legal person deserving of alternative sentencing only when they present a narrative of race, gender or poverty that is understandable in a liberal rights framework. While this framework moves from formal toward substantial equality in the provision of alternative sentencing, racist and gendered narratives remain essential to the discourse. As Murdocca asserts with reference to the recent sentencing decision of the Ontario Superior Court of Justice in *R. v. Hamilton* (2003, see References Chapter 3), the desired national accountability resulting from the use of a restorative justice framework nevertheless remains limited as an effort by the state to redress systemic discrimination. The law continues to "function as a locus of racialization," as it both perpetuates dominant narratives of citizenship and leaves unquestioned the culpability of the mythology of the state in producing discrimination. We are led to consider the limits of the capacity of the law in a democratic society to redress systemic discrimination.

In Lilith Finkler's chapter, "Re-Placing (In) Justice: Disability-Related Facilities at the Ontario Municipal Board," the resistance to planning applications for housing for the disabled is mapped and evaluated as an illustration of justice, which does not rest in the hands of the judiciary, but lies in the hands of the public. Based on a textual analysis of thirty-two administrative decisions of the Ontario Municipal Board (OMB), the appellate body for planning decisions in Ontario, Finkler outlines the arguments raised by advocates of the disabled and by neighbours resistant to establishing residences for the disabled in their communities. Despite Not-In-My-Back-Yard (NIMBY) opposition to the siting of residences for the disabled, the OMB generally made its decisions in favour of the opposition, declining to approve all but four applications for disability-related housing and services. Finkler critiques the absence of the voices of the disabled and the rhetoric about their putatively broad supervisory requirements contained in the written reasons of the OMB as serving to further stereotypes about the disabled. This is in contrast to the findings of a review of OMB decisions in respect to places of worship: there the perspectives of worshippers were extensively cited in the decisions.

Finkler locates fifteen themes in her analysis of OMB decisions and she critiques their operative assumptions about the disabled. The most popular theme is community integration. The integration of the disabled into the community has faced its greatest challenge in a NIMBYism fuelled by a fear of declining property values. In North America, this fear is related to a strong stigma associated with the disabled, including the inaccurate belief that they present a physical danger to the community. While not one opponent opposed the integration in general of the disabled into communities, they all argued that the disabled not be integrated into *their* community. Another theme isolated by Finkler involves the decisions regarding *minimum separation distances* between group homes or similar types of community facilities. Because group homes are generally intended for use by the disabled, such by-laws effectively limit the number of disabled persons living in a particular neighbourhood. These "people zoning" regulations obfuscate the discriminatory treatment of the disabled in planning.

Finkler concludes by outlining the potential for human rights arguments in disputes with opponents to disability-related facilities. In *Deveau v. Toronto (City)* (2003) (see References OMB cases, Chapter 4), a decision involving minimum separation distances, the advocates for the disabled argued that disability was an analogous ground to the extensive list in the equality provision of the *Charter*, Section 15 (1982). However, the Chair of the OMB held that the minimum separation distances were based in sound city planning and, therefore, were not discriminatory. By drawing an analogy with homeless shelters as emergency facilities, the Chair was able to reframe residences for the disabled as a type of temporary accommodation that the city has a legitimate interest in controlling. This decision ignored the fact that homeless shelters, which are often used by disabled people, frequently house their residents for extended periods of time. Finkler cautions that moves to strengthen the OHRC (Ontario Human Rights Commission) provisions as a means to open the decisions of the ORB (Ontario Review Board) to greater appellate scrutiny may be ill-founded as the costs of litigation render the appeal process an unlikely avenue for economically-disadvantaged groups, such as the disabled.

The discursive analysis of the metaphorical use of space as a means to conceptualize the Internet in Mopas' chapter, "Putting Cyberspace in its Place: Law, the Internet and Spatial Metaphors," sets it apart from the other works in this collection. A discourse has emerged that both describes and constitutes our socio-legal understanding of the World Wide Web (or the Internet) as territory. Although it is essentially a medium for the exchange of data, not unlike the telephone or snail mail, users of the Internet avail themselves of a decidedly spatial vocabulary: they operate (Netscape) Navigator software that permits them to "surf" the "information commons," "visiting" innumerable web pages, or constructing their own "home" page. Mopas traces the cultural phenomenon of thinking about the exchange of data on the Internet as "cyberspace" from its everyday usage to contemporary discussions in Canadian jurisprudence. Rather than take this metaphor for granted, he interrogates the social and legal implications that inhere in its assumptions. Specifically, he explores the ways that spatial metaphors have enabled the privatization of the Internet and posed significant jurisdictional issues before the courts.

The chapter begins with a historical account of the rise of the Internet and the concomitant emergence of geographic metaphors used to describe it. Mopas draws our attention to the ways that metaphor allows us to conceive of something complex in a familiar form. The horizontal, networked "packet-switching" materiality of the World Wide Web is reduced to a more user-friendly lexicon, as a "virtual reality" or "space." Subsequent to the opening-up of the Internet from its academic and military clientele to the general public, it was heralded as the "electronic equivalent of the Western Frontier; it was 'open, free, and replete with endless possibilities.'" Citing the work of Dan Hunter and Mark Lemley, Mopas draws our attention to the ways that spatial metaphors have furthered the commodification of the Internet.

While Mopas is quick to point out that the spatial metaphor does not go unexamined by the public, he nevertheless argues that metaphors also operate to socially construct technology. The establishment of a normative language, or knowledge, about society's relationship to technology enables policy makers, journalists, judges, and commercial actors to deploy meanings about the Internet that further their interests. More than just a shorthand for the technicalities of a system, metaphor plays a central role in a society's regime of signification and understanding. Mopas draws from Actor Network Theory (ANT), and the work of scholars such as Bruno Latour and Michel Callon to further elucidate the way that metaphors and technology perform in culture: he concludes that they should be seen less as self-evident achievements and more as both part of a network and as actors in that network. Following Marianna Valverde's work on incorporating ANT into legal theory, Mopas disassembles the ways that cyberspace is translated into legal reasoning; instead of the law simply absorbing this knowledge, he observes the interactive and heterogeneous relationship between legal and extra-legal (technological) discourses.

Mopas documents the prevalence of the "cyberspace" metaphor in Canadian jurisprudence in order to assess its effects on legal thought. By conceptualizing the Internet as a physical environment, the courts have been willing to classify and enclose cyberspace. The spatial metaphor plays a critical role in the judicial determination of legal fora. If accessing a web site in a particular physical location is understood as being synonymous with publication at that location, the Internet presents the dilemma of exposing its users to the possibility of litigation from around the world. In this instance, the courts' departure from the spatial metaphor signals a sensitivity to the particularities of the Internet. In the decision of the U.S. District Court, *Zippo Manufacturing Co.* v. *Zippo Dot Com Inc.* (1997) (see References, Chapter 5), it was held that jurisdictional analyses should be based on a determination of whether the web site performs an active or passive role. In *Pro-C Ltd.* v. *Computer City*, a decision of the Ontario Superior Court, the approach of the American court was followed. Here, the court considered whether the website remains "out there" in cyberspace or whether there is "a connection established with a particular geographical entity... in the absence of other traditional indicia, for example a physical presence in the state" (2000, para. 117, see References, Chapter 5). The interactivity test was fashioned to clarify whether or not on-line material crosses international boundaries and, thus, whether personal jurisdiction over a non-resident can be established. Rather than being linguistic shorthand, metaphors are a form of knowledge which themselves affect how judges conceptualize property rights and on-line jurisdiction.

Finally, in "Who's the Best Aboriginal? An "Overlap" and Canadian Constitutionalism," Daum Shanks explores the challenges faced by Aboriginal peoples and the Crown in respect to overlapping claims to Aboriginal title, treaty and rights. As an emerging issue in Canadian Aboriginal Law, overlap has thus far received limited treatment in case law. Overlap involves the competing interests of at least two Aboriginal groups pursuing their rights as enshrined in the *Constitution Act* (1982), Section 35. An issue of overlap arises when legislation in favour of one Aboriginal group impinges on the title, treaty rights or activity of another. Since any resolution to a dispute would tend to favour one Aboriginal group over the other, overlap inevitably compromises the Crown's ability to execute its constitutional obligation to protect Aboriginal peoples. Daum Shanks uses the contemporary claims over the Beverly caribou herd along the boundary between the Dene of northern Saskatchewan and the Inuit in (southern) Nunavut as an illustrative place from which to define overlap, outline its historical and constitutional context, speculate on possible outcomes of litigation, and suggest alternative means of resolving overlap disputes. Instead of the territory of either being characterized by exclusive rights to the land, each

Aboriginal group holds a claim over the shifting movements of the main economic and cultural resource, the Beverly herd. However, the founding of Nunavut presents a challenge to this sharing of resources. In this case, the exclusion of the Dene from the land north of the sixtieth parallel, the northern boundary of Saskatchewan, was brought about with the establishment of Nunavut and the conferring of a "right to exclude" by the Federal government.

Daum Shanks explores the "place" of justice where a fluid Aboriginal right is challenged by the fixed constitutional classification of the territory of Nunavut. Daum Shanks locates three legal arguments available to the Dene in order to redress the trumping of their constitutionally entrenched rights by those of the Inuit. First, the performance of the Crown's fiduciary obligation to Aboriginals is analyzed in respect of the government's provision of the Indian Claims Commission (ICC) to address the dispute. Based on case-law, Daum Shanks argues that, although this non-judicial body owed some degree of fiduciary duty to the Dene, it failed in this regard. Second, in the signing of Aboriginal treaties with the Dene, Canada promised that their lifestyle would not change and was not limited to the metes and bounds of the treaties. When cast against the Crown's provision of the territory of Nunavut to the Inuit, we can see that the obligation to protect the patterns of Dene life has not been fulfilled. Finally, recent jurisprudence on Aboriginal rights affords the Dene a line of argument unavailable during the establishment of Nunavut in the 1990s. Rather than arguing for title to the land of the Beverly herd or for a right flowing from a treaty, it may be argued that the hunt is integral to the survival of the Dene and is thus deserving of constitutional status. Faced with the prospect of burgeoning overlap claims and the potential for burdensome litigation, Daum Shanks proposes a number of alternative means to resolving competing claims, such as the joint management of resources and the establishment of an independent tribunal capable of making legally binding decisions based upon traditional indigenous legal norms.

CONCLUSION

This volume focuses on the spatial turn in critical legal and social sciences scholarship. It seeks to problematize the separation of place and justice as analytically distinct categories. Not only is this separation seen as an act of hegemony; the concrete transactions between place and justice have been revealed as hotbeds for political struggle. While it is readily accepted that "justice" is a normatively complex category, capable of many conflicting meanings, "place" can easily appear as inert and pre-political — as something prior to law and justice. These essays alert us to the fact that place is itself produced, in part, through legal and political praxis. As such, place is not simply a backdrop to justice, but can equally be a crucial site — both metaphorically and practically — in which justice is produced, denied and reconstituted: ultimately it becomes a site of struggle. These accounts of place and justice remind us that the law is always-already implicit in the dominant spatial order whether at the scale of the home, region, nation or globe. Thus, the "place" of justice, as a crucial space of law, demands careful and considered attention.

REFERENCES

Agnew, J. 1987. *Place and Politics*. Boston, MA: Allen and Unwin.

Agnew, J., and S. Corbridge. 1995. *Mastering Space: Hegemony, Territory and International Political Economy*. New York, NY: Routledge.

Berman, H.J. 1983. *Law and Revolution: The Formation of the Western Legal Tradition*. Cambridge, MA: Harvard University Press.

Bhandar, B. 2004. "Anxious Reconciliation(s): Unsettling Foundations and Spatializing History." *Environment and Planning, D, Society and Space* 22: 831–46.

Blackstone, W. 1838. *Commentaries on the Laws of England Vol 1*. New York: W.E. Dean.

Blomley, N. 1994. *Law, Space and the Geographies of Power*. New York: Guilford.

———. 2003a. "Law, Property, and the Spaces of Violence: The Frontier, the Survey, and the Grid." *Annals, Association of American Geographers* 93 (1): 121–41.

———. 2003b. "From 'What?' to 'So What?': Law and Geography in Retrospect." In J. Holder and C. Harrison (eds.), *Law and Geography*. Oxford University Press.

Blomley, N, D. Delaney, and R.T. Ford (eds.). 2001. *The Legal Geographies Reader: Law, Power and Space*. Blackwell: Oxford.

Borrows, J. 1997. "Living Between Water and Rocks: First Nations, Environmental Planning, and Democracy." *University of Toronto Law Journal* 47: 417–68.

Briffault, R. 1990. "Our Localism, Part II; Localism and Legal Theory." *Columbia Law Review* 90 (1): 346–54.

Cooper, D. 1996. "Talmudic Territory? Space, Law and Modernist Discourse." *Journal of Law and Society* 23 (4): 529.

Cresswell, T. 2004. *Place: A Short Introduction*. New York: Blackwell.

Darian-Smith, E. 1999. *Bridging Divides: The Channel Tunnel and English Legal Identity in the New Europe*. Berkley, CA: University of California Press.

Delaney, D., N. Blomley and R. Ford. 2001. "Where is Law?" In N.K. Blomley, D Delaney and R. Ford (eds.), *The Legal Geographies Reader: Law, Power, and Space*. Blackwell.

Fitzpatrick, P. 1992. *The Mythology of Modern Law*. New York: Routledge.

Ford, R. 1999. "Law's Territory (A History of Jurisdiction)." *Michigan Law Review* 97.

———. 2003. "Against Cyberspace." In A. Sarat, L. Douglas and M. Umphrey (eds.), *The Place of Law*. University of Michigan Press.

Foucault, M. 1980. "Questions in Geography." In C. Gordon (ed.), *Power/knowledge: Selected Interviews and Other Writings, 1972–1977*. New York: Pantheon Books.

Gilligan, C. 1982. *In a Different Voice: Psychological Theory and Women's Development*. Cambridge: Harvard University Press.

Gordon, R. 1984. "Critical Legal Histories." *Stanford Law Review* 36: 57–125.

Greenhouse, C. J., B. Yngvesson and D. M. Engel. 1994. *Law and Community in Three American Towns*. Ithaca: Cornell University Press.

Gregory, D. 1994. *Geographical Imaginations*. Cambridge, MA: Blackwell.

Griffiths, J. 1979. "Is Law Important?" *New York University Law Review* 54: 339–74.

Holder, J., and C. Harrison (eds.). 2003. *Law and Geography*. Oxford, UK: Oxford University Press.

Klodawsky, F. 2001. "Recognizing Social and Economic Rights in Neo-liberal Times: Some Geographic Reflections." *Canadian Geographer* 45 (1): 167–72.

Lefebvre, H. 1991. *The Production of Space*. Cambridge, MA: Blackwell.

Massey, D. 1994. *Space, Place and Gender*. Minneapolis: University of Minnesota Press.

Mitchell, D. 2003. *The Right to the City: Social Justice and the Fight for Public Space*. New York: Guilford Press.

Mitchell, T. 2002. *Rule of Experts: Egypt, Techno-politics, and Modernity*. Berkeley, CA: University of California Press.

Peake, L., and B. Ray. 2001. "Racializing the Canadian Landscape: Whiteness, Uneven Geographies and Social Justice." *The Canadian Geographer* 45 (1): 180–87.

Pratt, G. 2004. *Working Feminism*. Philadelphia, PA: University of Temple Press.

Pue, W. 1990. "Wrestling with Law: (Geographical) Specificity vs. (Legal) Abstraction." *Urban Geography* 11 (6): 566–85.

Razack, S. (ed.). 2002. *Race, Space and the Law: Unmapping a White Settler Society*. Toronto, ON: Between the Lines.

Said, E. 1979. *Orientalism*. New York: Vintage Books.

Sarat, A., L. Douglas and M. Umphrey. 2003. *The Place of Law*. University of Michigan Press.

Schmitt, C. 2003. *The Nomos of the Earth in the Jus Publicum Europaeum*. Translated by G.L. Ulmen. New York: Telos.

Selznick P. 2003. "Law and Society Revisited." *Journal of Law and Society* 30 (2): 177–86.

Soja, E. 1990. *Postmodern Geographies: The Reassertion of Space in Critical Social Theory*. New York: Verso.

Stychin, C.F. 1998. *A Nation by Rights: National Cultures, Sexual Identity Politics and the Discourse of Rights*. Philadelphia, PA: Temple University Press.

Unger, R.M. 1983. "The Critical Legal Studies Movement." *Harvard Law Review* 96 (3): 320–432.

Vismann, C. 1997. "Starting from Scratch: Concepts of Order in No-man's Land." In J.B. Brady and N. Garver (eds.), *Justice, Law and Violence*. Philadelphia, PA: Temple University Press.

Whitaker, R. 1999. "Sovereignties Old and New: Canada, Quebec, and Aboriginal Peoples." *Studies in Political Economy* 58: 69–96.

Legislation:

Canadian Charter of Rights and Freedoms, Part 1 of the *Constitution Act*, 1982, Being Schedule B to the *Canada Act*, 1982 (U.K.), 1982, c. 11.

CHAPTER 1

"WHOSE STREETS? OUR STREETS!":
PROTEST, PLACE AND JUSTICE IN CANADIAN SOCIETY

KIRSTY ROBERTSON

INTRODUCTION

A comment that I hear with increasing frequency in Canadian activist circles is "the future of protest is in litigation." It is heard alongside myriad other suggestions and discussions of the direction(s) activism might take in coming years, but, with many of the so-called "leaders" of the global justice movement facing punitive bail sentences and upcoming court dates, the future of protest really *can* be said to be in litigation.[1] More practically, it suggests that protest as a methodology of change has become increasingly difficult, given augmented police presence and powers of surveillance, combined with media focus on violence at the expense of in-depth coverage.[2] The question becomes whether the radically open potential of the global justice movement can adapt to, overcome, or circumvent these conditions, and whether knowing the law will help, or merely act as an engine of containment. In this paper, I unwrap this opening sentence, drawing out some of the complex notions of law and justice tied up in global justice protest, and suggesting that a disconnect between perceptions of the two has had significant impacts on the movement, on ideas of freedom and ethics, and also on wider cultural and national spheres.

I examine the disjuncture between codified law and more fluid notion(s) of justice, arguing that the embodied nature of protest opens a space, or place, for a situational ethics that cannot always be contained by written law. In fact, I suggest that, with respect to the protest movement, the two have a contentious relationship, with the law often (though not always) used to contain what are perceived to be transgressive acts, thereby highlighting liberal (and capitalist) notions of individuality above those of collectivity, and affecting varied notions of freedom, dissent and justice. By looking at the visual culture of global justice protest, particularly the way that protest is recorded for artistic endeavour, for news, or for posterity, I problematize the normativizing strategies of law(fulness), decentring the place of easily dichotomized definitions of right and wrong.

VISION AND POWER

For the most part, my work centers on the problematic consequences of "anti-globalization" protest for those who live in the North American neo-liberal environments that have created the conditions for the protest itself.[3] How do place and justice function within the lives of protesters who daily participate in and withdraw from the powerfully normative systems of capitalism that define most lives in the North-Atlantic region? As an art historian, I deal with these issues within a framework of visuality, exploring both the ways that structures of power are tied up with systems of ocular-centrism, or visual bias, while also analyzing the seemingly oppositional use of visual culture by activists to challenge the system. That looking is linked to power has been documented by numerous postcolonial and feminist scholars who have analyzed the gaze and the way that power can be acted out through the symbolic relations that equate seeing with know-ing and possessing (whether that be land, culture or the female body). (For some of the classic texts analyzing the gaze see Berger, 1973; Mulvey, 1989; hooks, 1992.)

Alongside these texts are a number of arguments that link looking with capitalism and highlight visuality as a way of configuring capitalism for consumption (Benjamin 1999; Baudrillard 1998; Buck-Morss 1989; Crary 1999; Debord 1967; Jameson 1991; Marx 1967; Virillio 1994). In particular, the French Situationist, Guy Debord, suggests that sight has become com-modified to the extent that we live in a society of spectacle, one in which an image of reality comes to be seen as somehow more truthful than reality itself (Debord 1967). To simplify this argument, one might take note of the way that capitalism relies on visual advertising to maintain itself. Sorting through the myriad visual information that confronts us daily, the mere act of perception becomes proprietary — to choose to perceive something becomes indistinguishable from perceiving its value.

This is a very brief overview of these theories; in recent years, scholars have added extensive subtlety to such arguments, suggesting that the deni-gration of sight and the body in such writing represents little more than a re-enactment of the gendered relations that posit a male rational transcend-ence versus a female irrational materiality.(See Grosz, 1999 for an analysis of the "corporeal turn.") Using the "corporeal turn," of recent scholarship, I position myself somewhere in between the two viewpoints, suggesting a critical disconnect between the way protest is performed by the body, and the way that it is remembered through a primarily visual matrix.

VISION AND PROTEST

Once halted, rendered static and outside of the context of the embodied experience of the action, images of protest become bounded, and burdened by the ideology of the interpreter. This is as much about manipulation as it is about vision and understanding. Take, for example, two images, photographed in 2001 and 2003 respectively, of black-clad protesters breaking windows. In both, masked protesters, wearing the "uniform" of Black Bloc anarchists, are caught in mid-action. In the first, a black and white image, the protester's foot connects with the glass, which is broken, but not entirely shattered. In the second, a colour image, the protester lifts a road sign over his head, about to throw it through the window, while a female wearing a business suit looks on with an unreadable expression — shock? Fear? Support?

The first image was published in a small book circulated by the Anarchist Press (Negri 2001): *On Fire: The Battle of Genoa and the Anti-Capitalist Movement*, a collection of essays, letters and think-pieces from the perspective of primarily anarchist protesters. Though no specific accolades are given to this particular window breaker, the book outlines the diversity of tactics used by activists, justifying the reasons some might have for the breaking of corporate windows — an attempt to insert an interruption into the easy acceptance of capitalism in everyday life, for example, or an attempt to expose the limited violence of window breaking, versus the perceived wide-scale violence enacted against the world's poor and the environment through corporate greed. In this case, justice is on the side of those willing to risk themselves to expose the injustices of the system.

The second image, by contrast, was taken at protests in Montreal against the World Trade Organization meetings in July 2003, and was published in the *Montreal Gazette*. Coupled with the headline, "WTO foes promise more confrontations," and the caption, "A pedestrian watches in shock as a demonstrator heaves a road sign through the window of the Gap clothing store on Ste. Catherine St. during a violent anti-WTO protest" — and appearing underneath the headline "More than 230 Arrested" — a much different definition of who is on the side of justice emerges (*Gazette* July 23, 2004).

EMBODIMENT, BIOPOWER AND THE RECORDING OF PROTEST

Notwithstanding differing ideologies, the point I am trying to elucidate here acknowledges a cognitive gap between the experience of protest and its later recording. Within the protest itself — and I'm talking here about large-scale protests that are often answered with teargas and rubber bullets — the protester is confronted with an overwhelmingly sensory experience. The acrid smell and taste of tear gas, the sound of songs, of bongo drums, of riot sticks beating on shields, and the measured marching of the police offer a much richer and often overwhelming experience than can be recreated or recorded in the aftermath. In cases where tear gas is used, sight is barely an issue at all, because it can be impossible to see. Take the following description of the front lines of the anti-WTO (World Trade Organization) protests in Seattle in 1999:

The air was filled with the sounds of singing and the powerful rhythms of marchers pounding on makeshift drums made of plastic bottles, garbage cans, cardboard shields, and even the backs of those walking in front of them. Hands and feet served as rhythmic instruments. In the middle of the road, on sidewalks, in parks, what seemed to be spontaneous storytelling and dancing erupted, encouraging everyone to join in. (Leclair 2003: 5)

The writer highlights the embodied and collective experience of the protester, moving through the city streets in a cacophony of sound, movement and vision. But the joy of the communal atmosphere of the protest — called "collective effervescence" by Emile Durkheim — often gives way to a sense of confusion in the wake of tear gas (Goodwin and Pfaff 2001: 289). "I could see smoke trails as the police launched canister after canister of tear gas into the crowd," writes one protester. "Suddenly the tear gas hit. I could not see. I did not know where I was" (Sharpe 2001: np). It is my contention that this confusion, mixed with the sensory experience of protest, and coupled with the collectivity of the crowd, masks a moment of overwhelming experience that is potentially the moment for the greatest possible resistance. Stripped of the disciplinary daily actions of the body, and forced into confrontation with both the explicit and implicit expressions of state and social power, I argue that the subject is compelled to deal with the ensuing cognitive dissonance (Foucault 1990). Though this is a troubling moment, one so outside of daily experience that protesters often re-inscribe the event within metaphoric norms: protest as tourism, protest as a right within accepted definitions of citizenship, protest as a spectacle to be photographed, I also suggest that the experience is marked semi-permanently within the body to be called up at different times in the future.

This is a biopolitical interpretation, one that takes into account Michael Hardt and Antonio Negri's (2000) realignment of Foucault's notion of biopower as immanent to the social field — diffuse, integral and vital to the function of all individuals. Both power and resistance take place in and through the relations between bodies and between subjects. The theory of biopower suggests that surveillance and policing have changed: as society becomes "an open field composed of thresholds or gateways, it becomes a continuous space of passage" (Massumi and Zournazi 2004). In other words, the exercise of power directly affects movement, setting up a series of minute checkpoints through which all citizens must pass. Whereas previously power functioned through broad disciplinary structures and judging was based on moral character, now the process is largely automatic, rendering the category of upstanding citizen obsolete. Philosopher Brian Massumi, who calls this new form "micro-power," argues that it is built up through the ubiquity of unnoticeable checkpoints in everyday life — withdrawing money from a bank machine, paying at a cash register, passing through a border, surfing the Internet. At each stage information is collected, feeding into systems of surveillance, but also into systems of marketing, creating a correspondence between law and commerce, feeding from the bottom up, rather than through the Foucauldian form of panoptical power (Foucault 1995). At first then, this would seem to suggest a lessening of actual police power, but as the large-scale global justice protests have shown, the opposite is in fact the case. The movement and circulation allowed by the diffusion of power still needs to be held in check, allowing for the proliferation of police power and disciplinary structures (such as prisons) (Massumi and Zournazi 2004). The insidiousness of power as a pervasive and rhizomatous system sets up the uncomfortable suggestion that many challenges to the structure actually result in its reification (Foucault 1995; Hardt and Negri 2000: 24).

THE PLACE OF PROTEST

Within the documentary *Tear Gas Holiday*, a compendium of footage from numerous members of the Toronto Video Active collective depicting their experiences at the Summit of the Americas in Quebec City in 2001, a passage from revolutionary moment to social re-inscription appears clear. The activists, primarily students from Ontario universities, board the bus, providing the filmmakers with in-depth political analyses as to why they are traveling to Quebec City to protest. Midway through the film, shots are taken of a number of protesters affected by tear gas, many of them responding emotionally to what they see as a betrayal of the Canadian state's responsibility to protect its citizens. For many, this is a moment of great clarity: faced with the acute pain of tear gas, the overwhelming police presence and the seemingly opposite sense of solidarity and joy of the front lines, many appear to consider the consequences of their actions, reaffirming their belief in the necessity of the global justice movement. At the end of the documentary, however, the students return to Ontario, exhausted by the weekend, but satisfied with the part they had played. One student holds up a small section of the chain link fence that became the famous symbol of the oppression and secrecy of the talks for many protesters. "I'm glad I have it," she says, "It's my souvenir." This protester, like other interviewees, talks about the protest as something that happened, much like a tourist event (Toronto Video Activist Collective 2001; Robertson 2004). In other words, the way that protest is recorded as touristic differs significantly from the manner in which the action itself was experienced by the participants, marking a disconnect between experience and image, and also between event and memory.

In spite of this re-inscription, however, this equation is far from a simple one: it seems to suggest that perhaps a politics of hypocrisy is actually becoming increasingly important, particularly if the residual elements of embodied protest can never be fully erased. The numerous ways that even weekend protesters might incorporate activism into their daily lives are not predictable. Following a biopolitical argument, I suggest that it is through the relations between bodies that the place of protest is defined. This is not a location, or a geographic space, but a mutable meeting point where the radical potential of experiential elements of protest can be relived, in spite of the ensuing re-inscription of numerous protesters in the daily habits of capitalism. Neither definable space nor traditionally locatable place, the virtual place of protest creates communities of shared interest and experience that have potential to grow and spread unpredictably across borders and affinity groups. For global justice protest, place is infinitely mobile, and, while the exchange of images across borders and events can unite (and occasionally convince), they act as prosthetics to the actual, vital experience. Evacuated from, and unwanted in real space, carefully monitored in the virtual space of the internet, it is this often unconscious place of connectivity, I suggest, that keeps the global justice movement vibrant and builds communities where there often appear to be none.

PROTEST, EXPERIENCE AND JUSTICE

I want to use this idea metaphorically, suggesting that the gap between the way protest is experienced, and the way it is recorded and remembered, is similar to the cognitive gap between justice and law, at least as they are experienced within the global justice movement. In this analysis, following Judy Fudge and Harry Glasbeek, I suggest that law, because it accepts the basic principles of liberalism and the resulting emphasis on individual rights, private property and capitalist economics over collective interests, is already a difficult fit for anti-capitalist protesters (Fudge and Glasbeek, as referenced in Sheldrick 2004). Justice, however, is a different matter, and I am drawing here extensively on the work of philosopher Brian Massumi, who in turn uses Spinoza, Bergson, and the French thinkers Deleuze and Guattari to outline a theory of affect. Massumi suggests that hope, imprisoned in goals, end-results and unachievable utopian futures, is a self-defeating impossibility. Instead, he situates hope in a theory of potentials, in the everyday movements and actions of the body, and in the infinite number of decisions one might take in any given momentary context. Within this theory, it is this maneuverability and choice (conscious and unconscious) that constitutes freedom, as in any situation one is never completely trapped. By situating hope in momentary embodied experience, Massumi suggests that the subject is never entirely isolated, but is connected to others through what he calls affective resonance. The discomfort an audience might share watching a particularly nervous speaker, or the exuberant joy that can spread through protests both illustrate this resonance and connectivity (Massumi and Zournazi 2004).

Within Massumi's argument, he makes a distinction between morality and ethics. While morality might be definable, ethics is not, but is that which produces the most choice, the most affective resonance in any given situation. By producing choice any given action can produce hope. Because of this, ethics is always situational, containing no intrinsic good or evil.

Reading through Spinoza and Nietzsche, Massumi suggests that what is "good" cannot be defined by any universal notion of "goodness" but is that which brings the maximum potential or affect to any given situation (Massumi and Zournazi 2004).

For Massumi then, there is no essential notion of freedom, as the social, cultural and even physical constraints of the world around us make it impossible. Freedom, rather, is a "creative conversion" of constraints, rather than a utopian escape from them. A person walking down the street, for example, is constantly playing against the constraints of balance, equilibrium and gravity, throwing herself into a fall before stopping that fall with another step — an action that, applied on a larger scale, defines an ethical logic based on movement, affect and momentary decision (Massumi and Zournazi 2004). Like the global justice movement, which refuses to define its end goals, it is radical openness that is used against the increased closure of the system. And though Massumi's ideas might seem to suggest an extreme individualism, it is the acknowledgement of collectivity, community and interconnectedness, he argues, that differentiates the merely critical from the truly progressive (Massumi and Zournazi 2004).

I have used Massumi's argument extensively because his definitions of affect, ethics and freedom do not allow anything to be definitively pinned down. To pin down, for example, exactly which actions within the protest are acceptable, how people should behave, or even how images of the protest should be interpreted in the aftermath, is to lose contact with the ephemeral and changing contexts of each action. To use a pertinent example, an activist waving a Che Guevara flag at a protest, where this action might set in motion a whole series of other events and individual potentials, has a much higher affective resonance than the display of a Che Guevara poster in a recent exhibition of 1960s art at the Montreal Museum of Fine Arts. In the latter, a politics of looking forces the viewer's eye to engage with the static image only momentarily before moving onto the next item. What protest might offer is a way to play with constraints, so to speak, a way to create what might be termed affective justice, based on situational contexts rather than judicial precedent. Affective resonance, affective justice, situational contexts and interconnectedness come together to create what I referred to above as the place of protest — the virtual yet lasting connections created through the sensory space and experience of the actual event.

PROTEST AND THE LAW

Massumi's argument, and indeed, the argument that I forwarded with regard to the place of global justice protest can be easily dismissed on the basis that there are no tangible results indicating success, no empirical proof that things are getting better (and indeed much proof that they are getting worse). But the question might be, when the terminology of inevitability has been colonized by neoliberalism, what options are open for activists?

The great success of the global justice movement has been its fluidity, its ability to adapt, and the connections that have been created across borders. When optimism is itself radical, perhaps it is small victories that are most important. As a decentralized "movement of movements," the global justice movement applies an anarchistic potential of loose connectivity to sometimes antagonistic parties (labour activists and environmentalists being the most obvious example), making its goals less easy to define, but also less easy to contain.

This is not, however, to advocate optimism at the expense of results. At the moment, affective justice and the defining of situational ethics in the global justice movement clashes head-on with the rule of law. The "keeping of the peace" (a phrase often aimed at arrested demonstrators, illegal picket lines and so on) is possibly the least affective (meant here in the sense of Massumi's definition of affect) means of dealing with dissent — it pins down unlawful action, and defines what is right and wrong through a series of precedents that override context. Thus, while Massumi's ideas are important, and though I will return to them throughout the paper, there is also, in the case of the global justice movement, the fact that bodies blocking the path of the state often end up in jail and in court, in systems that rely on coded rather than situational ethics.

Toronto lawyer Jackie Esmonde marks a difference between classic civil disobedience and what she calls constructive civil disobedience. In the classic definition, civil disobedience is understood as an illegal, public and non-violent act, done by someone who submits to arrest and punishment because s/he believes in the ultimate legitimacy of the state (Esmonde 2003: 327). In turn protest is allowed, but carefully controlled, through marching permits, trespassing laws, arrests and sentencing (Sheldrick 2004: 40). Constructive civil disobedience, on the other hand, undertakes the same illegal and public acts, but under the assumption that the system is illegitimate, and that a truly just and equal society does not exist, at least not yet. For those who believe that an elite controls both the systems of production and of government, disobedience of this sort, which occasionally resorts to violence, might be the only avenue open to use in pressing for change (Esmonde 2003: 329). In this context, because the state is viewed as unjust, going to jail is no longer something the protester will submissively accept (Esmonde 2003: 329).

But how to get this point across? Many protesters engaging in property damage would argue forcefully that such destruction is a specifically political act, incorporating its own brand of ethics and justice. In the following report from long-time British social activist Diego Jones, Jones describes some of the ethical decisions made by protesters in the front lines at the 2001 anti-G8 protests in Genoa, Italy:

> I turned and saw about ten people hitting the windows of a bank, with anything they could get their hands on, with the bank alarm

soon echoing around the street.... After a few minutes the windows began to crack. I looked around for something else to attack — some symbol of wealth, but along the street — I recognized nothing that could be identified as a symbol of wealth — only little shops, chemists, photography shops, tobacconists. (Jones 2001: 10–11)

Jones continues, describing how some of the protesters continued breaking the windows of the bank, eventually emptying as many files as they could on to the street. As the windows are broken, helicopters appear overhead, and the riot police close in, shooting tear gas canisters in front of them. As Jones moves away, he notes:

people began to run in all different directions, as I was walking backward down a street watching the police, one lad threw a brick though a car at the side of the road, which really pissed me off.... I along with others managed to stop another guy from trying to smash up a bus shelter. This was different than the plans I had — that mindless vandalism that affects ordinary people really pisses me off. (Jones 2001: 10–11)

Esmonde accepts this differential, drawing on language similar to that used by Massumi, and noting: "Violence is a strategic and tactical question that must be assessed in each context rather than being dismissed outright: the choice of means should be 'rationally' calculated to promote the limited ends."[4] In a sense, this is affective justice — contextual, situational and resonant — especially in cases where the discretionary power of the police and state have significantly narrowed the space for lawful protest (Esmonde 2003: 330–32). There is, however, an important caveat here. While, for Diego Jones, breaking bank windows might be essentially different from smashing a bus shelter, the image of his boot smashing the glass of the window — and its circulation through various media — does not carry his politics with it.

When denied any meaningful space in, for example, mainstream newspaper and television accounts, grabbing people's attention often becomes both medium and message, generally resulting in a burial of the issue(s). A member of the Black Bloc, reporting on the massive Genoese protests, notes that coverage of protests has had another effect:

there were lots of young people there who had maybe been attracted to the protests by coverage of other similar things they had seen on TV, and they were doing what they'd seen on telly — what they thought you were *supposed* to do during riots. (Anonymous 2001: 49)

What occurs, in this case, is that the circulation of images, outside of the event of their making, appears to have the effect of radically separating figure from ground, protest from issues, experience from image, creating a situation in which this separation is performed by those attending the protest for its spectacle rather than its meaning. In turn, this creates a justification for the separation between law and justice — while for some protesters the issues (ethics) of the protest grants it its own validity, for others the need to break the law becomes the protest's meaning, making it very difficult for activists, already outside of "acceptable" behaviour, to justify their actions.

MOBILIZING ART

While writing this paper, I am looking for a way to bring these ideas together. I want to interrogate the ideas of law and justice, but also the apparatus that allows protest to be rendered as static visual imagery, often leading to marginalization or co-option by the mainstream. The threat of marginalization is obvious (for example in Jones's de-politicized boot smashing through the window), but of co-option not so easily unfolded. What is wrong, for example, with a video game that pits riot police against protesters, a soft drink called "Revolution" that uses Che Guevara's image on its labels, or a series of exhibitions in Canada's authoritative galleries on the 1960s as a nostalgic corollary to current day protest?[5] The problem with co-option is that it erases the political in favour of the aesthetic — Che Guevara as an image to sell soda pop, the 1960s as art and so on. To commoditize protest is to render it ineffective, to pin it down, frame its impact, and set its boundaries. It is the chaotic potential of that moment in the tear gas contained.

Is there a way out of this? Is there a way to use art, without eviscerating the collective and embodied potential of protest? Perhaps through what film historian Laura Marks calls a haptic visuality — a method of seeing that, by drawing on all the senses, subverts the hegemonic logic of vision in a capitalist society (Marks 2000: xi). Further, such haptic (literally, a tactile or "touching" vision) engagement suggests an empathetic response that in turn can challenge the power relations of a biopolitical society. By drawing on all the senses, *Templates for Activism*, a project initiated by Canadian artist C.J. Fleury and legal scholar Elizabeth Sheehy, might be seen as a method of bringing together and questioning what in this essay have been set up as a series of binaries (law versus justice; image versus experience) (www. templatesforactivism.ca).

Templates for Activism is an ongoing collaborative art project that interrogates the separation between the legal community (in this case that of feminist law) and the arts community. Through a series of interdisciplinary projects, artists, law scholars and practising lawyers collaborated in a project designed to question the use of language in the two spheres, by setting up a series of creative projects that would have a lasting effect, documentable in photography, print, on the Internet and through communication between the numerous participants. In *Hearings at the Rape Maze*, a group of ten artists used the language of rape law to question the juridical construction of the "raped woman" as a public/private figure. Set up as a ceramic crossword puzzle/maze of emotions and legal phrases, complete with oversized sculptures of ears (to represent the difficulties of interpretation inherent in listening), and an overlay of white sticks bearing quotes from a variety of feminist writings, visitors were immersed within a dizzying maze that gave an embodied experience of the trauma of the law in such cases — what reporter Connie Higginson Murray calls "the harsh intermingling of intimacy and justice" at the rape trial (Higginson Murray 2003). The project involved a performance section, which included musical components, a video documentation and a guerilla postering action in which paper versions of the maze were pasted in "safe places," such as washroom stalls. *Hearings at the Rape Maze*, the second template of the *Templates* project was initially shown at the Ottawa City Hall, during a 2002 conference on women's rights and the law (Higginson Murray 2002). The project has recently gone through several other phases, collaborative undertakings and templates, including *Slice*, a "slice and dice" video combining footage of legal documents and dramatizations with tap-dancing law students.

Although *Templates* has the obvious appeal of questioning the disjuncture between law and justice, I am less interested in criticizing the actual work of the project than in examining the collaborative impact of such a cross-disciplinary endeavor. The *Templates for Activism* projects, to my mind, instigate an important method of re-embodying activist art, of refusing to allow the image of protest to be manipulated by language, and of encouraging an embodied, haptic response to what cannot be seen as only a visual artwork. The communal nature of the projects, the links across disciplines, and the insertion of art into the coded and framed spaces of the law leads to an affective reaction of the sort outlined by Massumi — one in which the potential for action is never subverted by the twin structures of language and vision. Perhaps this project, though minimal in scope, might be seen as an initial foray into opening up the spaces between image and experience, between law and justice.

In an exploratory argument posted on the web, visual culture scholar Irit Rogoff asks whether collectivities can be built through experiencing art (Rogoff 2005). Beyond the assigned roles of viewer, spectator and critic, argues Rogoff, there are emergent collectivities, and it is in the momentary space of coming together that connections can be made outside of, or in spite of, a lack of shared beliefs. Outside of ideological beliefs, there are instead "low key participations" in not always conscious mutualities, defined through the relationships between viewers and space, rather than individual relationships between viewers and objects (Rogoff 2005). For Rogoff, meaning is produced as much through webs of connectedness as through studying the object — meaning is always in the present. To understand the display of art in this way is to understand it not as object, but as event, with potential that can spread well beyond the bounded analyses of "looking." As with protest, it is often momentary connections that offer potential in situations where justice seems out of reach.

PROTEST, 9/11 AND BILL C-36

Certainly, this combination of artistic (though not necessarily visual) protest with communal and legal action has been present in a number of recent actions, most notably those of the Campaign to Stop Secret Trials in Toronto, centred on what is seen as the unjust imprisonment of Muslim men under post-September 11th security measures.[6]

Before getting to the Free the Five actions, it might be useful here to introduce the security legislation brought about by 9/11 as it impacted both the global justice protest movement, and the lives of those involved in the Stop Secret Trials collective. For many Canadian activists, the December 2001 passage of *Bill C-36* (Royal Assent of *Bill C-36* 2001), the anti-terrorism bill, fast-tracked through Parliament in six weeks, with wide powers of arrest, detention and surveillance, made an inequity between law and justice readily apparent (Basu 2003). Esmonde (2003: 359) points out that it is the new definition of "terrorist activity" that is so controversial. Section 83.01(1) provides that "terrorist activity" includes:

an act or omission, in or outside Canada

(i) that is committed

(A) in whole or in part for a political, religious, or ideological purpose, objective or cause, and

(B) in whole or in part with the intention of intimidating the public, or a segment of the public, with regard to its security, including its economic security, or compelling a person, a government or a domestic or an international organization to do or refrain from doing any act, whether the public or the person, government or organization is inside or outside Canada, and

(ii) that intentionally

(A) causes death or serious bodily harm to a person by the use of violence,

(B) endangers a person's life,

(C) causes a serious risk to the health or safety of the public or any segment of the public,

(D) causes substantial property damage, whether to public or private property, if causing such damage is likely to result in the conduct or harm referred to in any of the clauses (A) to (C), or

(E) causes serious interference with or serious disruption of an essential service, facility or system, whether public or private, other than as a result of advocacy, protest, dissent or stoppage of work that is not intended to result in the conduct or harm referred to in any of clauses (A) to (C).[7] (Criminal Code, Supra not 27 at 83.01(1) b; as quoted in Esmonde [2003]: 359–60)

Pointing out that the police and courts already have a great deal of power over protesters through the use of the bail system (where punitive bail sentences can prevent as yet unconvicted protesters from attending or organizing demonstrations), Esmonde argues that even the threat of potentially applying C-36 to protesters is enough to constitute an attack on civil liberties (Esmonde 2003: 360). The undefined and hazy language of the *Act* certainly allows for its application to protesters, and, even though the language was altered slightly to afford more protection to activists, the threat is often enough for a chilling effect. An action "committed for political purposes," with the intent of intimidation, that causes substantial property damage could certainly be applied to activists, even with the clause exempting protest actions ("anti-globalization" protesters are already considered to be on the wrong side of the law).

Conor Gearty (2003: 190) argues that this is the first breach, "outside of war time, in a previously (rhetorically) unqualified commitment to the equal protection of the laws, and an indication perhaps of future assaults on the whole idea of civil liberties by a rival discourse rooted exclusively in concerns of national security and counterterrorism." Indeed, Bill C-36 has had very real effects on the global justice movement: at the anti-G8 protests in Kananaskis, Alberta (the first large-scale protest since September 11th, and the first since the anti-G8 protests in Genoa that attracted 300,000 and resulted in the death of Carlo Giuliani), the government was able to use C-36 to set up a security zone, perhaps leading to the presence of much smaller crowds than had been seen at previous protests. Many called it the end of the global justice movement, and the end of large-scale violent protests.

A review of some of the writing and coverage of the 1997 protests at the APEC meetings in Vancouver reveals, in a startling way, how easily C-36 came into power, despite numerous arguments for the protection of civil liberties. Running through W. Wesley Pue's edited volume *Pepper Spray in Our Eyes* is an unstated belief that police repression at APEC was an anomaly, and that the alleged PMO (Prime Minister's Office) interference in the RC-MP's security operations was unwarranted (Pue 1999). What could not be foreseen at that time was the influence of September 11th, 2001, although it remains debatable whether such draconian measures would have been instated nonetheless.

In spite of this, the global justice movement has not disappeared, although the large-scale protests of 1997 to 2003 have also transformed into a number of smaller, single-issue oriented actions. The use of Security Certificates and preventative arrests quickly forged links between global justice protesters and movements such as No One Is Illegal (a group that supports struggles against the deportation of refugees). Mahmoud Jaballah's arrest under a Security Certificate, and his seven-month stay in isolation, quickly became a rallying point for protesters, while the massive mobilization against the war in Iraq also drew on organization and tactics learned from protests in Ottawa, Quebec City and Montreal (Carr 2003).

By 2003, there were five men — Mohammad Mahjoub, Mahmoud Jaballah, Hassan Almrei, Mohamed Harkat and Adil Charkaoui — imprisoned under government-legislated Security Certificates. At the time of writing, only Charkaoui has been released (although he is still facing the threat of deportation and torture). Security Certificates (which did exist before 2001) allow arrestees to be held without charge or bail, on secret evidence that neither they nor their lawyers are allowed to see: they thus reverse traditional judicial notions of innocent until proven guilty <http://www.homesnotbombs.ca/secrettrials.htm>. Faced with a lack of intensive media questioning, a lack of commitment from the large (primarily white) crowds present at global justice actions, pervasive public fears for National Security and an inability to act in a media-attracting violent manner for fear of wider retributions, the Campaign Against Secret Trials has instead organized a concerted effort to gain attention through actions that integrate the public into aesthetic/affective performances, attempting, in effect, to trump the law with wider definitions of justice.

With high police presence at nearly all of their actions, the Campaign organizers have instead opted for humour — dropping off a couch at the CSIS offices, left "to help CSIS agents get over their irrational fears of Arabs and Muslims," a Halloween trick-or-treat session, a visit to CSIS from Santa Claus and a number of candlelight vigils (http://www.homesnotbombs.ca/secrettrials.htm). The actions are always colourful and visibly non-violent, perhaps demonstrating that debates over violent or non-violent approaches to protest are, at this moment, debates of the already privileged. Notwithstanding this, the approach, a combination of spectacle, costume, pamphlets, Internet communications and person-to-person communication has been effective, if not in securing trials, then at least in making the detainment of the five men an ongoing news story and concern. Although the media took the easier route of focusing on terrorism, porous borders and the need for security legislation following attacks in Madrid, Bali, Saudi Arabia and London, the mere coverage of the story and the attraction of notable personalities to the cause (including Alexander Trudeau and Naomi Klein) can be read as a minor success. In the wake of the relative lack of coverage of the government hearing into the scandal over the wrongly deported and tortured Maher Arar, however, it is unlikely that mainstream coverage will go beyond the surface. It is my contention that, because of this, the actions organized by the Campaign to Stop Secret Trials offer not only an attempt to put pressure on the government, but also to strengthen and build community links and connectivity among those directly affected and those who are essentially passers-by.

While the effects of the tightening of security under Bill C-36 are obvious in the case of the Five, its effects are somewhat subtler in other areas. What does the establishment of a post-9/11 security complex mean for the global justice movement, as well as for changing notions of law and justice? How does Bill C-36 fit with the Canadian Charter of Rights and Freedoms, and with beliefs in Canadian tolerance and justice?

PROTEST AND THE NATION

The theories of movement and power outlined by Massumi, and by Hardt and Negri, rely on a system of constant global circulation and of globalization that erases national boundaries. I would argue, however, that this is not entirely, or at least not yet, the case. Where justice collides with law, as outlined here in the passage of Bill C-36, there seems to be a structure of nationality that as yet trumps the global currents of the biopolitical model of power. It can be argued in general that the global justice movement in the North Atlantic occurred at a very awkward moment for the playing out of ideas of nationality and post-nationality. While bodies such as the WTO and IMF enact transnational policies, governments fall back on concepts of the state both to explain these new policies to their populations and to police them. An example of this focus on the state might be the protection accorded (at least rhetorically) to Canadian culture during international trade talks (Szeman 2000). In another example, Reg Whitaker argues that the passage of Bill C-36 actually had less to do with security in Canada than it had to do with maintaining Canadian sovereignty. Faced with threats of either a closure of the Canada/U.S. border or a security perimeter proposed by United States Ambassador Paul Celucci just after 9/11 (and endorsed by a number of provincial premiers, the Official Opposition in Ottawa and the influential Council of Canadian Chief Executives), the passage of Bill C-36 appeared as a relatively innocuous compromise (Whitaker 2003: 255). Of course its passage is not so innocuous to those people who are directly affected, including Muslim and South-East Asian populations in Canada.

Rhetoric surrounding the passage of Bill C-36 often constructed it as pro-Canadian. Anne McLellan, then Minister of Justice, was quoted in the *Calgary Herald* just before the Bill was passed:

> Bill C-36 has given us an opportunity to hear the views of Canadians about the tools and laws we need to deal effectively with the threat of terrorism.... Canadians have told us they want laws that identify terrorists and bring them to justice. They have also told us they want assurances that appropriate safeguards are in place that strike

the right balance between the promotion of public security and the protection of civil rights. (*Calgary Herald*: A6)

The corollary to the depiction of Bill C-36 as pro-Canadian might be the construction, in the corporate media, of protesters as "unCanadian." Describing the front lines at the protests against the signing of the FTAA in Quebec City in April 2001, one reporter wrote, "Within minutes, a 50-metre section of the infamous chain-link fence surrounding the conference centre was down and disturbing, unfamiliar photos of Canada were flashing around the globe.... And in an ugly twist on the nation's favourite game, hockey pucks filled the air" (Canadian Press 2001).

The expulsion of those who perform in an "unCanadian" manner from an ideal of Canadian nationality is perhaps not surprising, but takes on an added layer in the threatened deportation of the Muslim immigrants and refugees arrested under Security Certificates since 1999. The actual physical expulsion, potentially to situations of torture, of the arrested Five, at once redefines and reifies the indissoluble borders of the nation-state to the unwelcomed, while securing the apparent safety of a narrowly defined "Canadian" population.

With the identification of security bills as pro-Canadian, protesters as anti-Canadian, and arrestees as not-yet-"Canadian," I would suggest that the idea of biopower and debates over protest and nationality come together in the notion of intangibility. While numerous theorists, including Hardt and Negri have signalled the waning importance of the nation state, following what Arjun Appadurai calls post-nationality — a tern that refers to the nation state after the dissolution of borders through international trade deals, mass migration, and globalized technology — I argue that the nation in fact becomes an important marker of this very diffusion (Appadurai 1996). In this analysis, "the nation" becomes an idea that can be bandied about to serve a variety of purposes. For protesters, the nation should protect their right to protest, for the journalist cited above, the nation is something to which only those who behave appropriately can belong. As bodies become targets for arrest and violence, protesters have little choice but to play with constraints, testing the judicial boundaries of due process.

The most obvious Canadian case is the 1997 PCC (Public Complaints Commission) hearing into RCMP behaviour at the APEC summit. Though initially plagued with problems of bias, and eventually dismissed by activists as too narrow in scope, the Hughes Commission nevertheless does give protesters a precedent-setting inquiry into perceived police violence or arrest (see Pue 2000). Jail solidarity actions and legal clinics have also been present at all of the recent large-scale protests in Canada. In Seattle, protesters used the law itself to challenge their arrests. At the anti-WTO protests in 1999, 600 were arrested, but many refused to give their names. Because of this, the demonstrators could not be released one at a time, thereby gumming up the court system. Though they eventually gave their names, most pled not guilty, refused their right to a speedy trial and requested court-appointed counsel. Ninety-two percent of the cases were dropped as the time for a speedy trial expired, and of the six people brought to court five won acquittals, while the single conviction resulted in a small fine and community service. Similar cases of solidarity have occurred after most large-scale protests, often resulting in lowered sentences and reduction of charges (Olsen 2003: 366). Here protesters were able to play easily with the constraints of law, setting themselves up as defenders of justice and obtaining what they saw as a just settlement.

For the Five, detained for collectively close to 200 months, playing with constraints is not an easily available option, although challenges through the courts have been successful in similar cases in Britain (Frankel 2004: A21).[8] However, for those detained under the seemingly boundless powers of the Security Certificates it might seem that the constraints of the law are exactly what is needed. I bring this up not only to highlight the effects of different access to the conditions of the law, but also because, as opportunities have opened for the two strands of protest (Free the Five and global justice) to come together, most notably in recent protests against George W. Bush's 2004 visit to Canada, channels are opened for collaborative action where, together, actors and participants can challenge seemingly intractable systems. Although the massive candlelight vigil that greeted Bush's visit was broadcast on neither of the nation's two main television stations, I would suggest that, for those who participated in it, it achieved a great affective resonance that will continue to play out in a number of unpredictable ways, possibly eventually securing at least fair trials for the five suspects.

As such, within a performance and collaborative sphere, the impact of protest is less easily halted and manipulated, but plays out in what might be termed a rhizomatous manner, with connections being made where none existed before, thereby resisting the disembodiment of the memory of protest. From the work of the *Templates for Activism* project and the aesthetic/politic(al) actions of the Campaign to Stop Secret Trials, not to mention myriad other creative protest actions, the limits of the law are tested, and potential places/spaces of affective justice opened. Such creative endeavors might be compared to the world social forums — spaces for those involved in the global justice movement to come together to discuss alternative globalization — or, more locally, the cooperative efforts of the Ontario Coalition Against Poverty who have (outside of their more spectacular protest actions) organized a number of successful and non-violent solidarity actions to protect tenants from landlords, women from security guards and the homeless from harassment (Porter 2001). In conclusion then, though the future of protest might be in litigation, the numerous offshoots of the original movement might be found in any number of participatory, performative and community actions, whether local or global. The future is limitless.

NOTES

1. The numerous arrests and bail hearings for global justice activist Jaggi Singh, and OCAP member John Clarke attest to this (see Jackie Esmonde 2003).

2. This was made brutally evident in the 1997 treatment of protesters at the APEC meetings in Vancouver. When President Suharto, accused of perpetrating genocide in East Timor, asked that he not be embarrassed by protesters, the Canadian government and police forces complied, removing protest posters, protesters, and bystanders, cancelling a potentially "offensive" welcoming speech by Musqueam Chief Gail Sparrow, all in the name of profits and increased trade in the Asia Pacific region. The events and consequences of the APEC meetings are described in the essays in Pue 2000.

3. The term "anti-globalization" is a misnomer, applied, primarily by the media, to diverse groups of activists coming together against the consequences of neoliberal government and corporate actions. Activists dislike the term "anti-globalization" primarily because it pre-supposes that protesters are against globalization, while governments are for it. Transnational links between protest groups, and emphases on policies such as fair trade before free trade demonstrate that this is not the case. The term "global justice movement," "anti-capitalism" or "alter(ed)-globalization" are much preferred.

4. Esmonde supports a definition of civil disobedience that reads, "any act or process of public defiance of a law or policy enforced by established governmental authorities, insofar as the action is premeditated, understood by the actor(s) to be illegal or of contested legality, carried out and persisted in for limited public ends, and by way of carefully chosen and limited means" (Esmonde 2003: 330).

5. Revolution Soda Pop was a company run out of Vancouver, B.C.; Riot Police was a video game released by Activision in 2003; there will be seven large scale exhibitions of 1960s art and culture in Canada's museums and galleries between 2003 and 2007.

6. This shouldn't be confused with the Free the Cuban Five Committee, which also has a branch in Toronto <www.freethefive.ca>.

7. "In the end, as mentioned earlier, a five-year sunset clause was included in the Bill, but only for the provisions dealing with investigative hearings and preventive arrest. Aside from a somewhat weakened sunset clause, the government did accept several substantive amendments from the House committee's recommendations. First, the definition of terrorist activity was narrowed to exclude unlawful, as well as lawful 'advocacy, protest, dissent, or stoppage of work.' Second, an element of *mens rea*, or guilty intent, was added to the requirements for criminal responsibility for a terrorist offence. Third, several safeguards were put in place with regard to the issuance of Attorney General certificates, including the subjection of such certificates to judicial review. Fourth, a non-discrimination clause was inserted to clarify that 'political, religious, or ideological' activity would not in itself be considered terrorism and that minorities would not be targeted for discriminatory treatment." (Mazer 2003: 21–32).

8. In December 2004, Britain's highest court of appeal ruled eight to one that suspects could not be held indefinitely without trial. "In a stinging rebuke to Prime Minister Tony Blair's government, the panel ruled 8 to 1 that the provision authorizing the detentions violated European human rights laws and was

discriminatory because it applied only to foreigners. Eleven suspects are being held under the policy, five of whom have been in custody for nearly three years" (Frankel 2004: A21).

REFERENCES

Addario, F., M. Davis Williams and J. Missen. 2003. "Protecting 'Pursuits that Relate to the Culture of the Country': Advocating for the Artistic Merit Defence in Bill C-12." *English Studies in Canada* 29 (Sep/Dec): 3–4.

Anonymous. 2001. "Being Busy." In Antonio Negri (ed.), *On Fire: The Battle of Genoa and the Anti-Capitalist Movement*. Edinburgh: One Off Press and AK Distribution.

Appadurai, Arjun. 1996. *Modernity at Large: Cultural Dimensions of Globalization*. Minneapolis and London: University of Minnesota Press.

Basu, Arpon. 2003. "Anti-terrorism Law Needs Review to Avoid Abuse of New Police Powers: Expert." *Canadian Press Newswire* February 22.

Baudrillard, Jean. 1998. *The Consumer Society: Myths and Structures*. London and Thousand Oaks: Sage.

Bell, Udy. 2002. "Journalists Must be Watchdogs." *Toronto Star* July 26.

Benjamin, Walter. 1999. *The Arcades Project*, Howard Eiland and Kevin McLaughlin, trans. Cambridge, MA and London: Belknap Press of Harvard University Press.

Berger, John. 1973. *Ways of Seeing*. London and New York: Viking Press.

Buck-Morss, Susan. 1989. *The Dialectics of Seeing: Walter Benjamin and the Arcades Project*. Cambridge, MA and London: MIT Press.

Calgary Herald staff. 2002. "War on Terror: How Canadian Leaders have Viewed the Terrorist Threat to Canada Since Sept. 11, 2001." *Calgary Herald* November 14 .

Canada News Wire. 2002. "Minister of National Defence Tables CSE Commissioner's Annual Report." June 12, 2002.

Canadian Press. "Let Chaos Not Hold Democracy Hostage." *Toronto Star* April 21, 2001.

Carr, Nancy. 2003. "Man Held Without Charges, No Chance of Bail because He's Arab Muslim: Lawyer Says." Canadian Press Newswire (Toronto), May 26.

Clarke, John. 2003. "Social Resistance and Disturbing the Peace." *Osgoode Hall Law Journal* 41/2 and 3 (Summer/Fall).

Crary. Jonathan. 1999. *Suspensions of Perception: Attention, Spectacle and Modern Culture*. Cambridge: MIT Press.

Debord, Guy. 1967, 1983. *Society of Spectacle*. Detroit: Black and Red.

Dixon, John, and Stan Persky. 2003. "Making a Bad Law Worse." *English Studies in Canada* 29, 3-4 (Sep/Dec).

Esmonde, Jackie. 2003. "Bail, Global Justice, and the Limits of Dissent." *Osgoode Hall Law Journal* 41/2 and 3 (Summer/Fall).

Fleury, C.J. 2002. "Co-Creative Models of Art and Feminist Law in the Templates for Activism Project." *N. Paradoxa: Rethinking Revolution* 10 (1).

Foucault, Michel. 1990. *History of Sexuality, Volume 1*. R. Hurley, trans. New York: Vintage Books.

_____. 1995. *Discipline and Punish: The Birth of the Prison*. A. Sheridan, trans. New York: Vintage Books.

Frankel, Glenn. 2004. "British Court Deals Blow to Terror Law." *Washington Post*

December 14.

Fudge, Judy, and Harry Glasbeek. 2003. "Civil Disobedience, Civil Liberties, and Civil Resistance: Law's Role and Limits." *Osgoode Hall Law Journal* 41/2 and 3 Summer/Fall.

Gearty, Conor. 2003. "Reflections on Civil Liberty in an Age of Counterterrorism." *Osgoode Hall Law Journal* 41/2 and 3 (Summer/Fall).

Goodwin, Jeff and Steven Pfaff. 2001. "Emotion Work in High-Risk Social Movements: Managing Fear in the U.S. and East German Civil Rights Movements." In Jeff Goodwin, James M. Jasper and Francesca Polletta (eds.), *Passionate Politics: Emotions and Social Movements*. Chicago, University of Chicago Press.

Grosz, Elizabeth (ed.). 1999. *Becomings: Explorations in Time, Memory, and Futures*. Ithaca and London: Cornell University Press.

Hardt, Michael, and Antonio Negri. 2000. *Empire*. Cambridge, MA and London: Harvard University Press.

Herman, Lawrence L. 2002. "Anti-terrorism Law Forces Business to Scrutinize All Dealings." *Ivey Business Journal* 66, 3 (Jan/Feb).

Higginson Murray, Connie. 2002. "Marriage of Law and Art Gives New Gallery an Edge." *Ottawa Citizen* March 8.

hooks, bell. 1992. *Black Looks: Race and Representation*. London: Turnaround.

Jameson, Frederick. 1991. *Postmodernism, or The Cultural Logic of Late Capitalism*. London: Verso.

Jones, Diego. 2001. "Shooting Blanks." In In Antonio Negri (ed.), *On Fire: The Battle of Genoa and the Anti-Capitalist Movement*. Edinburgh: One Off Press and AK Distribution.

Leclair, Louise. 2003. "Carnivals Against Capital: Rooted in Resistance." In Andy Opel and Donnalyn Pompper (eds.), *Representing Resistance: Media, Civil Disobedience, and the Global Justice Movement*. London and Westport, CN: Praeger.

Marks, Laura U. 2000. *The Skin of the Film: Intercultural Cinema, Embodiment, and the Senses*. Durham and London: Duke University Press.

Marx, Karl. 1967. *Capital: A Critique of Political Economy*. New York: International Publishers.

Massumi, Brian, and Mary Zournazi. "Navigating Movements: An Interview with Brian Massumi." *21 Century Magazine*. <http://www.21cmagazine.com/issue2/massumi.html. Consulted April 20, 2004>.

Mazer, Aex. 2003. "Debating Canada's Anti-Terrorism Legislation: What Have We Learned?" <www.studentpugwash.org/halifax2003/papers/mazer.dpf>. Consulted April 20, 2005.

Mulvey, Laura. 1989. *Visual and Other Pleasures*. Indiana: Indiana University Press, 1989.

Negri, Antonio (ed.). 2001. *On Fire: The Battle of Genoa and the Anti-Capitalist Movement*. Edinburgh: One Off Press and AK Distribution.

Nicholls, Liz. 2003. "File Collective's Dossier under 'Various Visions'." *Edmonton Journal* April 22.

Olsen, Frances. 2003. "Legal Responses to Mass Protest Action: The Dramatic Role of Solidarity in Obtaining Generous Plea Bargains." *Osgoode Hall Law Journal* 41/2 and 3 (Summer/Fall).

Pearlston, Karen. 2000. "APEC Days at UBC: Student Protests and National Security in an Era of Trade Liberalization." In Gary Kinsman, Dieter K. Buse and Mercedes Steedman (eds.), *Whose National Security? Canadian State Surveillance and the Creation of Enemies*. Toronto: Between the Lines.

Porter, James N. 2001. "Intentional Disturbances: Making the Toronto Movement Scene." *Public* 22/23.

Pue, Wesley W. (ed.). 2000. *Pepper in Our Eyes: The APEC Affair*. Vancouver and Toronto: UBC Press.

Robertson, Kirsty. (forthcoming). "Taking Quebec City: Protest, Photography and Tourism at the Summit of the Americas." In David Picard, Mike Robinson, Phil Long (eds.), *Journeys of Expression: Tourism, Festivals and Identity*. Channel View Publications.

Rogoff, Irit. 2005. "WE: Collectivities, Mutualities, Participations." Posted to <http://mode05.org/blog/node/145>.

"Royal Assent of Bill C-36: The Anti-Terrorism Act." <http//canada.justice.gc.ca/en/news/nr/2001/doc_28217>. Consulted April 20, 2004.

Sharpe, E. 2001. Publisher's Foreword. In Editorial Committee (eds.). *RESIST!: A Grassroots Collection of Stories, Poetry, Photos and Analyses from the Québec City FTAA Protests and Beyond*. Halifax: Fernwood Publishing.

Sheldrick, Byron. 2004. *Perils and Possibilities: Social Activism and the Law*. Halifax: Fernwood Publishing.

Szeman, Imre. 2000. "The Rhetoric of Culture: Some Notes on Magazines, Canadian Culture and Globalization." *Journal of Canadian Studies* 35, 3 (Fall).

Templates For Activism. <www.templatesforactivism.ca>.

Toronto Video Activist Collective. 2001. *Tear Gas Holiday: Quebec City Summit 2001* (videorecording).

Virillio, Paul. 1994. *Vision Machine*, trans. J. Rose. London: B.F.I.

Weir, Lorraine. 2003. "'Making up Stories': Law and Imagination in Contemporary Canada." *English Studies in Canada* 29, 3–4 (Sep/Dec).

Whitaker, Reg. 2003. "Keeping up with the Neighbours? Canadian Responses to 9/11 in Historical and Comparative Context." *Osgoode Hall Law Journal* 41, 2–3 (Summer/Fall).

CHAPTER 2

(MIS)PLACED JUSTICE:
JUSTICE, CARE AND REFORMING THE "BEST-INTERESTS-OF-THE-CHILD" PRINCIPLE IN CANADIAN CHILD CUSTODY AND ACCESS LAW

FIONA KELLY[1]

INTRODUCTION

While there is not always agreement in Canadian law as to what constitutes "justice," there is a general consensus that justice has, and must continue to have, a significant "place" in the Canadian legal system. For example, it seems to be universally accepted that "justice" is something for which both judges and the legislature should strive. This consensus about the "place" of justice in Canadian law extends to family law, where the language of justice has provided the backdrop against which recent reform proposals in the area of child custody and access law have been measured. The process of reforming Canada's child custody and access law, which commenced in 1997 with the hearings of the Special Joint Committee on Child Custody and Access, has been focused on achieving justice for each of the various competing groups, including children, fathers, mothers and grandparents. While Parliament, through its various committees[2] and reports (Parliament of Canada 1998; Canada 2002) has ostensibly focused first and foremost on children, it has seemed at times that this goal has been lost in the debates about achieving justice between parents and, in particular, justice for non-custodial fathers (Boyd 2003: 130–57). Given the prominence of the notion of justice in the western liberal legal tradition, it is not surprising that throughout the reform process there has been no questioning of the "place" of justice in Canadian custody and access law. It has simply been presumed that justice is our ultimate goal, even if groups differ as to how it might be achieved.

In this chapter, I argue that placing justice at the heart of Canadian custody and access law has ethical consequences. In particular, the detached objectivity of liberal legalism's concept of justice imposes upon families a model of family life that ignores the contextual realities of child rearing and parenting. In such a system, little space is left for recognition of caregiving or the subjectivity of actual family life. Thus, in this chapter, I question the central "place" of justice in Canadian custody and access law and suggest, drawing on a feminist ethic of care, that it is care, not justice, that should form the wider framework within which custody and access decisions should be made. First, I will address what I mean by the terms "justice" and "care" in the context of custody and access law. I will then discuss why the justice paradigm is flawed and why an ethic of care might be a more appropriate paradigm within which to make custody and access decisions. Second, I will consider how Canadian custody and access law might be reformed so that it better incorporates an ethic of care. I will focus in particular on whether the "best-interests-of-the-child" test, which has been at the ideological centre of the recent reform debates, is capable of incorporating an ethic of care. Finally, I consider whether the best-interests-of-the-child test might need to be abandoned in favour of a model less tied to a justice framework.

JUSTICE AND CARE IN CANADIAN FAMILY LAW

Over the past few decades the ethic of justice has come to inhabit a central place within the debates about Canadian custody and access law, largely as a result of the growing strength of the fathers' rights movement (Boyd and Young 2002). Fathers' rights groups have drawn on the language of the ethic of justice — that the law be "objective," universal and rights-driven — to support the various arguments they make in relation to custody and access law reform (Bertoia and Drakich 1993; Kaye and Tolmie 1998a, 1998b). In particular, they have drawn on the rhetoric of formal equality and rights to support their position that Canadian custody and access law should contain a presumption in favour of shared parenting. They have argued that a presumption in favour of shared parenting — because it treats parents as formal equals and protects the rights of both parents — is the only way to ensure that custody decisions are "just." Fathers' rights advocates have also suggested that such an approach is in the best interests of children because it ensures that children have equal access to both of their parents. This linking of the justice agenda of the father's rights movement to the "best-interests-of-the-child" principle has meant that the two have become closely entwined. In fact, Dawn Bourque found, in her review of reported Canadian custody and access cases from 1990 to 1993, that paternal access is treated by judges as paramount to the best-interests-of-the-child test, "supersed[ing] virtually all other considerations" (Bourque 1995: 6).

The success of fathers' rights groups in the area of custody and access law reform can be at least partly attributed to the movement's appeal to the rhetoric of justice and equality, principles which are held in reverence in most western, liberal democracies (Kaye and Tolmie 1998a). Citing statistics that show that mothers are awarded custody more often than fathers, fathers' rights advocates argue that the family law system is biased against them.[3] The presumption is that, because fathers are awarded custody less frequently than mothers, the system must be unjust. This approach is encapsulated in the written submission of Vancouver lawyer and fathers' rights advocate Carey

Linde to the Special Joint Committee on Child Custody and Access:

> Suppose fifty couples — fifty dads and fifty moms — all come into the courts on the same day. In each case both spouses are seeking an order of exclusive possession of the matrimonial home — seeking to have the other parent kicked out of the house, leaving the kids at home. All the dads and all the moms are equally good parents. All one hundred individuals have exactly the same income and same stable jobs. The kids are all around 10 to 12 years old.
>
> If gender equity prevailed in our courts as some would lead us to believe, at the end of the court day 25 men should be ordered out and 25 women ordered out. Half the parents left in the home with the kids should be dads and half moms. If you believe that, you believe in the tooth fairy. (Linde 1998: 5)

Linde's submission draws attention to a basic model of formal equality that removes families from their day-to-day lived realities. It fails to take into account the nature of the parent/child relationships in each family or the gendered nature of caregiving in children's lives.[4] While Linde's de-contextualized approach to "justice" may seem simplistic, Miranda Kaye and Julia Tolmie argue that such an approach can be extremely powerful "because it appeals to deep and commonly held values, and does so by what appears to be simple and obvious logic — if people are treated differently (according to their gender) then by definition they are not treated equally" (Kaye and Tolmie 1998a: 166).

The power of such an approach to justice has ensured that fathers' rights groups have achieved enormous success in swaying the opinions of both the public and politicians. For example, the equality-based arguments presented by witnesses like Linde led to a general endorsement, and implicit acceptance of, a presumption in favour of shared parenting on the part of the Special Joint Committee on Child Custody and Access (though an actual legislative presumption was not recommended) (Parliament of Canada 1998). Arguably, the "best-interests-of-the-child" test has also been understood differently through this simplistic notion of justice, so that it is presumed to be in a child's best interests to have a shared parenting arrangement following parental separation. As one commentator put it, shared parenting laws have become so commonplace that there appears to be a "contemporary cultural consensus" that it is the "ideal custodial arrangement" for children (Kurki-Suonio 2000: 184).

Because of the reverence afforded to this traditional notion of justice, it has become very difficult for women's groups, who favour a more contextualized approach to family law decision making, to oppose it. Explaining the merit of substantive as opposed to formal equality is a difficult task to achieve in a short, timed submission before a government committee. It is much easier to present the kind of straightforward, simplistic arguments made by witnesses such as Linde. And, as Kaye and Tolmie suggest, the apparent logic and fairness of those arguments make them appealing to an audience of politicians who are looking for easy solutions. However, it remains the view of many women's groups that this strict liberal form of "justice" has no "place" in Canadian custody and access law.

Despite its influence within the Western liberal tradition, the ethic of justice is a deeply flawed paradigm within which to make decisions about custody and access. Because it is largely based on objective and universal notions of what amounts to "justice," it is simply unable to adequately deal with the complex realities of family life. It fails to acknowledge the individual relationships within each family, is ill-suited to dealing with situations of child abuse or domestic violence, and ignores the importance of the actual activity of caregiving. Families are not homogenous entities and a "one-size-fits-all" approach will not adequately meet their needs. Furthermore, what is in the best interests of children should not be premised on what is "just" between their parents. Given the problems associated with the ethic of justice, it might be appropriate to supplement or even supplant it with what Carol Gilligan has referred to as an "ethic of care" (1982).

Feminist sociologist Carol Gilligan has suggested that unquestioning support for the liberal "ethic of justice" ignores the complex nature of human relationships and is potentially damaging, particularly for women and children. Gilligan argues that rather than constructing the world solely through an ethic of justice, we need to also take into account the significant role that care plays in our lives (Gilligan 1982). This is of particular relevance in the context of the family which is largely constructed around relationships of care and caregiving.

Gilligan's research arose out of what she saw as problems with Lawrence Kohlberg's theory of "moral development" (Kohlberg 1984). Basing his theory on the study of eighty-four boys whom he followed for over twenty years, Kohlberg identified six stages of moral development, the sixth of which he called the "ethic of justice" (Kohlberg 1958). This final stage involves the subordination of relationships to rules, and the embracing by the individual of a principled concept of human rights, where he or she "identifies morality with justice (fairness, rights...), with recognition of the rights of others as these are defined naturally or intrinsically" (Kohlberg 1973: 29–30). When measured by Kohlberg's scale, women tend to be deficient in moral development. Women rarely move beyond Kohlberg's third stage where morality is conceived in interpersonal terms and goodness is equated with helping and pleasing others.

Concerned that Kohlberg's research was based solely on boys, Gilligan was interested in whether his theory of moral development was truly universal. In conducting her own research, in which she interviewed both men and women, Gilligan began to hear two distinct moral voices, rather than the universal voice of morality upon which Kohlberg's theory was based (Gilligan 1982). Interestingly, she observed this second or "different" voice while interviewing women. Gilligan called the "different voice" she identified the "ethic of care" and compared it with the "ethic of justice" that Kohlberg had identified as the highest stage of moral reasoning. While Gilligan associated the ethic of care with women and traced its development primarily through women's voices, she made it clear that the different voice she described was, "characterized not by gender but theme," and that its association with women was simply "an empirical observation" (Gilligan 1982: 2).

Gilligan explained the "ethic of care" as follows:

> In this conception, the moral problem arises from conflicting responsibilities rather than from competing rights and requires for its resolution a mode of thinking that is contextual and narrative rather than formal and abstract. This conception of morality as concerned with the activity of care centers moral development around the understanding of responsibility and relationships, just as the conception of morality as fairness ties moral development to the understanding of rights and rules. (Gilligan 1983: 19)

In this passage Gilligan identifies three elements of an ethic of care that distinguish it from the ethic of justice. First, an ethic of care arises out of responsibilities and relationships rather than rights and rules. Second, it is contextual. It is tied to concrete situations, rather than being formal and abstract. Third, an ethic of care is expressed as moral activity or the "activity of care." Thus the ethic of care "is not grounded in universal abstract principles but in the daily experiences and moral problems of real people in their everyday lives" (Tronto 1987: 648). In contrast, the ethic of justice that characterized Kohlberg's theory and that dominates western liberal legal systems is concerned with the application of abstract rules from an impartial stance, giving primacy to issues of equality and rights.

Writing several years after Gilligan, Joan Tronto recognized the fundamental value of the ethic of care for feminist theory, but sought to remove Gilligan's "different voice" from the gendered context in which it had developed. Tronto argued that an ethic of care could be an important intellectual concern for feminists, but that the debate "should not be centered in a discussion of gender difference but in discourses about the ethic's adequacy as moral theory" (Tronto 1987: 646). In seeking to look beyond gender for an explanation of Gilligan's findings, Tronto argued that Gilligan's "different voice" may be the product of women's "subordinate or tentative social position" (Tronto 1987: 649). In reaching this conclusion, Tronto considered research that measured moral cognitive development amongst communities that were not white, middle-class or male, and found that the ethic of care was not necessarily *just* the voice of women. In fact, the different voice that Gilligan tentatively attributes to women is consistently articulated by the poor and by ethnic minorities. For example, research conducted in the United States strongly suggests that the moral conceptions of minority groups, such as African-Americans, Latinos and Indigenous Americans, are more likely to be characterized by an ethic of care than an ethic of justice (Coles 1977; Gwaltney 1980; Nobles 1976). What this research suggested is that the voice of care may be a social phenomenon. For Tronto, the possibility that there may be a social cause for the different voice that Gilligan heard "[broadened] the implications of and possible interpretations of research on an ethic of care" (Tronto 1987: 651). Tronto concluded, as Gilligan had in relation to women, that the moral views of these minority groups were not underdeveloped, but "simply not captured" by Kohlberg's categories. In reaching this conclusion she rejected the possibility that the "different voice" articulated by many women was the product of moral inferiority, or an example of women and minorities "proudly clinging" to their moral views even though society deemed them inferior. Rather, Tronto argued that the ethic of care is most often articulated by women and minorities because their position as carers in society provides them with an opportunity to develop this particular moral sense.

Drawing on the work of both Gilligan and Tronto, feminists continue to use the notion of an ethic of care to conceptualize the human condition in a way that challenges dominant understandings of justice. Many feminists who embrace an ethic of care have followed Tronto's lead and do not presuppose that an ethic of care is the "different voice" of women. Instead they employ the ethic of care as an alternative way of seeing things, a perspective that acknowledges the relational dimensions of human life. Somewhat surprisingly, given the focus on caregiving and relationships within the ethic of care, it has only recently found its way into debates about family law (Sevenhuijsen 1998; Smart, Neale and Wade 2001).

For example, in her work on the public debates about child custody in the Netherlands, Selma Sevenhuijsen suggests that the ethic of care might be able to provide new perspectives on the politics of custody law, particularly if it avoids becoming entangled in the controversies surrounding sexual difference in moral reasoning. Sevenhuijsen argues that:

> The ethics of care... is a specific form of ethics which can also imply new types of normativity. This interpretation offers a better approach for mobilizing various ideas from the care ethics debate in public deliberations about child care and custody than thinking in terms of female or male forms of morality, or maintaining that women are better at caring than men. (Sevenhuijsen 1998: 107)

Adopting Gilligan's three criteria of an ethic of care — relationships, the principle of actuality, and the activity of care — Sevenhuijsen suggests that approaching family law through an ethic of care would radically change how we view both care and men's and women's relationship to it:

In a care ethics perspective, instead of guaranteeing men authority rights to protect them from a (potential) dependency on women, the government should see its primary task as enabling men to build intimate and caring relationships with women and children, by making this possible in terms of time, space and material resources. (Sevenhuijsen 1998: 111)

Carol Smart and her colleagues have also attempted to incorporate the ethic of care into family law decision making (Smart, Neale and Wade 2001). They argue that an ethic of care offers a more appropriate way in which to approach custody and access law than the models that have preceded it. They argue that children need to be understood as "social" beings, rather than atomistic individuals or dependants in need of protection, and that incorporating an ethic of care into family law decision-making may be the best way in which to acknowledge the relational lives of children in the decision-making process.

In seeking to incorporate an ethic of care into Canadian custody and access decision making I do not wish to supplant the ethic of justice. Rather, I want to question the central place of justice within family law and ultimately establish care as a value on par with justice. My starting point is Robin West's premise that "justice must be caring if it is to be just, and caring must be just if it is to be caring" (West 1997: 24). Justice should therefore remain an ideal of human communities, but it ought to be an interactive human value; it cannot be achieved through a decontextualized reading of a dispute. It requires actively engaging with the parties and the realities of their lives. In the context of custody and access decision making this might mean that "justice," which is traditionally understood to rely on objectivity, rights and formal equality, might need to be viewed differently so that it is more "interactive," and thus better able to respond to the complex dynamics of individual families.

Justice should remain central to legal decision making; however, in the context of custody and access law, I agree with Virginia Held's view that care and its related considerations are the wider framework within which room should be made for justice (Held 1997: 16). It is inevitable that the ethic of care may sometimes conflict with certain aspects of what we currently understand to be included within an ethic of justice, such as formal equality and rights.[5] When these situations arise I do not think that justice must always yield to care, but we may need to accept that harmony between the two cannot always be achieved. As Sevenhuijsen explains:

The feminist ethic of care... offers a critical perspective on the idea that it is possible to achieve entirely just and harmonious laws in [custody and access decision making]. The emotional bond between parents and children is, after all, so complex that there is no single satisfactory solution. The law should pay attention precisely to the fragility of the relationships between people and to the different situations in which people need the law because they are unable to sort things out for themselves.... There thus needs to be a 'pluriform' law which takes account of different situations and which abstains as far as possible from positing an abstract idea of 'good family life.' (Sevenhuijsen 1998: 118)

Drawing on Gilligan's "ethic of care" — in particular the three points of difference she identified between an ethic of care and an ethic of justice — the remainder of this chapter will discuss how an ethic of care might be incorporated into Canadian child custody and access law.

INCORPORATING AN ETHIC OF CARE INTO CANADIAN CUSTODY AND ACCESS LAW

Incorporating an ethic of care into Canadian family law is likely to be a complex and difficult process. Because of the central place of justice within the current system, and the strength of the fathers' rights movement that draws on its traditions, it is also unlikely to be successfully achieved by making small amendments to the existing regime. Any reform efforts must therefore go to the ideological heart of custody and access law: the "best-interests-of-the-child" principle. As the discussion earlier suggests, the rhetoric of justice, particularly justice for fathers, is ingrained within the best-interests-of-the-child principle. If family law is going to shift towards a care-based framework it may therefore be necessary to rethink the use of the best-interests principle as the basis of custody and access decision making. This might involve replacing the principle with a new decision-making framework that derives from the ethic of care.

The "best-interests-of-the-child" principle has been widely touted as allowing a flexibility in decision making that is appropriate and necessary in a family law context. Even when it is accompanied by guiding principles, as it is in several jurisdictions,[6] it is usually perceived as a malleable concept that permits the court to take into account the individual circumstances of each child's life. It is this very malleability, however, that causes concern.

From the outset, the best-interests principle was criticized for being inherently indeterminate. As early as 1975, Robert Mnookin expressed this view:

> Deciding what is best for the child poses a question no less ultimate than the purposes and values of life itself.... [W]here is the judge to look for the set of values that should inform the choice of what is best? (Mnookin 1975: 260)

In more recent years the best-interests test has been charged with being an "empty category" filled with different meanings and policies at different times, making it particularly vulnerable to political co-opting (Smart 1995:

183–84; Thery 1989: 81–83). In fact, as Smart argues, despite the flexibility of the best-interests test, in the current family law paradigm a very rigid meaning of the concept is discernable in its practical interpretation:

> What parents seem to be finding (and once again I am being tentative here) is that as long as they agree with each other on everything they want to do, they can do what they like within the usual constraints of not actually harming the child. Thus parents can agree that the father will leave and will never see the children again (although they can no longer agree that he should pay them no maintenance). If they agree to this no one will object in practice that this is against the interests of the children.... However, if a mother feels she has reasons to try to restrict a father's contact with her children she will find it almost impossible to implement her wishes.... Because contact is, *a priori*, regarded as in the best interest of the child, her wishes are seen as damaging and obstructive (although a father's wishes not to see his children are not). Thus the prevailing meaning of welfare is only... imposed on those who wish to restrict contact but not on fathers who wish to have no contact at all. [footnotes omitted] (Smart 1995: 184)

Arguably, particular notions of "parenthood," "motherhood" and "family" are also embodied in the best-interests principle. As Susan Boyd argues, "what is viewed as 'best' all too often involves a normative and idealized image of parenting in the white, middle-class, nuclear, heterosexual family, rather than a concrete determination of a child's welfare" (Boyd 2003: 13). Thus any parent, but particularly a mother, who diverges from this normative model of parenthood — whether by virtue of race, class, culture, sexuality or disability — might be viewed negatively by the courts, regardless of her actual relationship with the child.

While Canadian child custody and access law does not currently include a presumption in favour of shared parenting, the very malleability of the best-interests test allows judges to incorporate such assumptions into the decision-making process. For example, Bourque, who reviewed reported Canadian custody and access cases from 1990 to 1993, found that a child's supposed "need" for or "right" to a father, irrespective of the quality or quantity of his parenting, has "eclipsed virtually all other" elements of the best-interests test (Bourque 1995: 6). Similarly, Boyd found that, although Canada has never adopted a presumption in favour of joint custody, the philosophy behind joint custody — that maximum contact is in the best interests of children and that justice requires that both parents should have equal access to their children — "nevertheless influences the broader trends in redefining custody and access" (Boyd 2003: 133; Boyd 1996: 502).

Research also suggests that the presence of factors that diminish the benefits of contact, such as spousal abuse, has little effect on this pro-contact position (Neilson 2000 and 2001; Rhoades et al. 2000: 78–82). For example, in her study on spousal abuse, children and the legal system in Canada, Linda Neilson found that many family lawyers, who obviously have a significant influence on post-separation negotiations between spouses, consider abuse of partners of little importance in access decisions (Neilson 2001). Many of them felt that "bad spouses" do not necessarily make "bad parents" and endorsed the need for children to have "regular access" to both parents:

> However incapable an abusive spouse may be at appreciating the needs and respecting the rights of his former spouse, he is still a parent; a child separated from a parent needs to see, feel and appreciate this half of who he or she is. The need of the child is overwhelming. Furthermore single parents are often 'swamped' by the daily needs and necessities of raising children. They can't do it alone and hope that the abuse will not continue with the kids. They know that they don't own the children and the children need to know the other parent. (Female lawyer quoted in Neilson 2001: note 148)

Neilson also found that partner abuse seemed to have little effect on judges' decisions about access. In fact, her analysis of reported cases and court files indicated that Canadian courts award access to their children to parents who abuse their partners most of the time. The severity of the alleged abuse or violence appeared to have little effect; cases denying abusers access to their children did not differ markedly from cases awarding access. In justifying their views, most judges and lawyers made a distinction between spousal abuse and child abuse, taking the view that only in cases of direct child abuse should there be any limitations on access. This is despite research evidence indicating that patterns of abusive behaviour often indicate poor parenting skill and ability (Jaffe, Wolfe and Wilson 1999), that between 30 and 50 percent of men who physically abuse their partners will also physically abuse their children and that the rates of child abuse increase with the severity and frequency of the pattern of partner abuse (Pagelow 1994).

This research suggests that there is a judicial trend in Canada towards incorporating within the best-interests principle a traditional, liberal notion of "justice." In particular, it appears that the best-interests principle has come to include notions of formal equality and parental rights — particularly a father's right to equal access to his children — despite the absence of any legislative rule to that effect. These presumptions seem to apply even when the parent to whom access is being given has a history of abuse. Given these findings, I have grave doubts about the ability of the best-interests principle to incorporate an ethic of care. It may therefore be necessary to consider whether the best-interests principle should be abandoned.

If the best-interests test were to be abandoned, it would obviously need to be replaced with some alternative. It is my proposal that the test be replaced with a "principle of care" that would include Gilligan's three fundamental components: (a) that the child be placed in a set of relationships and the quality of those relationships be evaluated; (b) that decision making about the child be based on the actual circumstances of the child's life; and (c) that the court prioritize the activity of care.

In the next section I will consider how the principle of care might be developed legislatively, drawing on three possible models (a) the "approximation principle," first suggested by Elizabeth Scott (Scott 1992) and now incorporated into the American Law Institute's *Principles of the Law of Family Dissolution* [the ALI Principles] (American Law Institute 1997) (b) the "status quo" principle discussed by Australian academic Helen Rhoades (Rhoades, Graycar and Harrison 2000) and (c) the "principles and presumptions" model introduced by another Australian academic, Juliet Behrens (Behrens 2002).

REPLACING THE "BEST-INTERESTS" TEST: THE PRINCIPLE OF CARE IN A LEGISLATIVE FORM

Translating the principle of care into legislative language is an enormous challenge, not least because it is a broad-based concept that does not lend itself to the kind of structure that is required by legislation. In putting the principle into a legislative form drafters must chart a fine line between discretion and rules. While the ethic of care narrows decision making by directing judges to focus on certain principles, the principle of actuality and its emphasis on the individual circumstances of each family introduces a certain degree of discretion and indeterminacy. It thus appears that family law legislation based on the ethic of care might need to incorporate a combination of rules and discretion.

(a) The "Approximation" Principle

The "approximation principle" as an alternative to the best-interests test was first proposed in the early 1990s by American legal academic Elizabeth Scott (Scott 1992). Scott's view was that the available array of custody and access rules — the primary caregiver presumption, joint custody and the best interests of the child — was unsatisfactory, because each option created a presumption in favour of a particular family form: given the increasing pluralism of American families, this narrowing of options was considered to be inappropriate (Scott 1992: 617). A legal preference in favour of the primary caregiver discounts the role of the "secondary parent" and reinforces traditional gender and parenting roles. Joint custody accurately describes parental role allocation only when both parents fully participated in child care during the marriage.[7] And the best-interests standard can obscure or dilute the importance of pre-divorce caregiving (and its gendered nature) because it requires the balancing of many factors, of which caregiving is only one.

The problems associated with each of the available tests for custody and access decision making led Scott to propose the "approximation principle." The approximation principle is based on the premise that the optimal legal framework for custody and access decision making is one that "focuses (almost) exclusively on the past relationships between parents and child and seeks to approximate as closely as possible the pre-divorce patterns of parental responsibility in the custody arrangements" (Scott 1992: 630). Thus, the approximation principle "does not choose between parents or split custody of the child but rather seeks to gauge the strength of existing bonds and to perpetuate them through the custody arrangement" (Scott 1992: 632). According to Scott, the approximation principle provides the following benefits: it promotes continuity and stability for children; it encourages cooperative rather than conflictual resolution of custody, thereby ameliorating the destructive effects of bargaining at divorce; and it recognizes and reinforces role change in individual families. In Scott's view, the approximation principle fulfills better than other frameworks the "rhetorical promise" that custody is about children's welfare rather than parents' rights.

The approximation principle has been developed further by American academics (Bartlett 1999) and was incorporated in 1997 into the American Law Institute's "Principles of the Law of Family Dissolution" (American Law Institute 1997).[8] In Katherine Bartlett's discussion of the principle, she has argued that it should serve as the default position for custody and access decision-making, with several provisos.[9] Like Scott, Bartlett was of the opinion that the principle overcame many of the problems associated with the other available tests, and also resolved some of the ongoing tensions in family law, such as those between finality and flexibility, and determinacy and individualized decision-making. Under Bartlett's proposal the approximation principle would not completely abolish the best-interests test; rather best-interests would only be relevant where past caregiving patterns were not determinative or where replicating them would be impractical (Bartlett 1999. Bartlett's views were strongly endorsed in the ALI (American Law Institute) Principles, not surprisingly given that Bartlett was the primary reporter for the chapter of the Principles dealing with child custody and access law (American Law Institute 1997).

In the ALI Principles the approximation principle is set as a "default rule" for custody and access decision making when the parents do not otherwise agree. The reasoning behind adoption of the principle is explained:

> [By] focusing on how the child was cared for previously, the past caretaking rule anchors the determination of the child's best interests not in generalizations about what post-divorce arrangements work best for children, but in the individual history of each family. How caretaking was divided in the past provides a relatively concrete point of reference. (American Law Institute 2001: 7–8)

A number of sections in the ALI Principles qualify the approximation principle. First, unless circumstances exist warranting limited access (such as drug or alcohol use), each parent should be allocated an amount of custodial responsibility that will enable the parent to maintain a relationship with the child, even if this level of responsibility is not supported by the parent's past level of involvement in the child's care. Second, the court should accommodate the preferences of an older child who has firm and reasonable preferences. Third, the court should attempt to keep siblings together if it determines that doing so is necessary to their welfare. Fourth, the court should depart from past caregiving arrangements to take account of a gross disparity in the quality of the emotional attachments between the child and each parent, or in the ability or availability of each parent. Fifth, prior agreements between the parents should be taken into account if the court determines that doing so would be appropriate in the circumstances. Sixth, courts should take account of logistical and relevant factors that make an otherwise appropriate equal allocation of custodial time impractical or harmful to the child's stability. Finally, a catch-all exception requires departure from past caretaking arrangements to avoid substantial and almost certain harm to the child. Also of significance is Section 2.13, which poses substantial obstacles for a parent seeking to obtain custodial responsibility where domestic violence has occurred. It should also be noted that adoption of the approximation principle does not eliminate all consideration of the best interests of the child. Where past caretaking patterns are too complex or unstable to provide a guide to decision making, the best-interests test comes back into play.

It is clear from the discussion above that the approximation principle, particularly as outlined in the ALI Principles, bears a strong resemblance to the ethic of care. The approximation principle emphasizes the importance of the actual activity of care, it relies on the concrete circumstances of each child's life in order to make decisions about post-separation caregiving, and it focuses on the importance of relationships and evaluates the actual relationships that exist between the child and his or her parents. However, there are several elements of the ALI Principles that appear to conflict with an ethic of care. First, the Principles do not sufficiently emphasize the importance of listening to children. Under the ALI Principles, it is only "older children," who have "firm and reasonable preferences," who are accorded a voice, and then only as a qualification to the approximation principle. The ALI Principles also appear to include a "minimum access" provision that applies independently of any actual relationship between the child and parent. Section 2.02(1)(a) of the Principles states that, unless the parent is unfit to care for the child, each parent should be allocated an amount of custodial responsibility that will enable the parent to maintain a relationship with the child, even if this level of responsibility is not supported by the parent's past level of involvement in the child's care. This provision seems to suggest that a "no access" order is not an option under the ALI Principles, except in a few narrow circumstances. Such an approach comes close to an assumption that at least some access is in the child's best interests, even if there is no pre-existing relationship. It also has the potential to diminish the importance of identifying harmful relationships.

The presumption in favour of shared decision-making authority if both parents have been exercising a "reasonable" share of parenting functions is also problematic. Research suggests that shared decision making can be used by some non-resident parents to continue to exercise control over their former partner. For example, in her study on the *Washington State Parenting Act* in 1999 (which includes a presumption in favour of joint decision making), Diane Lye found that a substantial minority of primary custodial parents (usually mothers) reported that their ex-spouses had used the provision to harass or psychologically abuse them (Lye 1999). Similarly in the Australian context Helen Rhoades, Margaret Harrison and Reg Graycar, found that ongoing parental responsibility had become a "new tool of control" for non-custodial parents (Rhoades, Graycar and Harrison 2000: 2).

Finally, the ALI Principles ignore the fact that replicating pre-separation caregiving patterns, particularly when there has been a roughly equal sharing of responsibility, requires a high degree of flexibility and co-operation that may not be appropriate, or even possible, post-separation. In cases where there is high conflict or violence between parents, it may simply be dangerous to replicate earlier caregiving patterns. Limited financial resources can also make it difficult to maintain the two homes necessary for a true shared parenting arrangement.

While there are some flaws in the individual provisions of the ALI Principles, the purpose of this discussion is not to analyze every element of the Principles, but to consider how an ethic of care might be incorporated into a legislative framework. The approximation rule as outlined in the ALI Principles provides a good example of what custody and access decision-making might look like if it were to be premised on an ethic of care.

(b) The "Status Quo Principle"

A proposal similar to the approximation principle has been developed by Helen Rhoades in the Australian context (Boyd, Rhoades and Burns 1999: 250–51). Rhoades has suggested that custody and access decision-making could be based on the "status quo" principle, which focuses on the family's "social reality," including the pre-existing caregiving arrangements for the child, the quality of the relationships between the child and his or her parents, and the effects of any domestic violence. Like the approximation principle, the status quo principle would necessarily take into account the activity of care, the principle of actuality, and the relational circumstances of children's lives. In determining the family's "social reality," it would also be necessary to listen to the views of the children involved.

The status quo principle already operates in Australian family law at the interim hearing stage where there is a general rule that pre-separation caregiving patterns be maintained until a final hearing. Maintenance of the status quo is premised on the need to promote stability and continuity in children's lives. It is presumed that stability will be achieved by "continuing the existing caregiving arrangements unless there are "strong or overriding indications to the contrary," such as evidence that the children would be harmed unless the arrangements are varied" (Boyd, Rhoades and Burns 1999: 251). Thus, as Rhoades argues, unlike the primary caregiver presumption, such an approach is ultimately child- rather than adult-focused.

An application of the status quo principle is likely to satisfy many of the elements of the ethic of care, though it is possible that the strong presumption in favour of contact, found in Australian family law, may ultimately override the principle. In fact, Rhoades, Graycar and Harrison found that in practice, the presumption in favour of contact, particularly at the interim stage, seemed to take precedent over the status quo principle, even in cases of abuse (Rhoades, Graycar and Harrison 2000: 75–80). It might also be the case that the language of "caring about," particularly when invoked by fathers, carries more weight than the "caring for" emphasized by the status quo principle.

While generally endorsing the status quo principle, Rhoades does express some reservations. She argues that despite its individualized focus, it still prescribes a "static" model of pre- and post-separation family constellation. Like the primary caregiver presumption or a presumption in favour of shared parenting, the status quo principle presumes that a certain post-divorce model is the best one — in this case, a model based on previous caregiving arrangements. In Rhoades' view, this "static" model of justice (that pervades most current models of family law decision-making) must be replaced by a more "dynamic" conception of justice that is capable of recognizing and providing for a diverse range of family arrangements and relationships. She does not speculate as to what such a model might look like, but states that "existing caregiving arrangements" would remain an important consideration.

(c) The "Principles and Presumptions" Model

The final, and most promising, model to consider is that proposed by Australian legal academic Juliet Behrens, which incorporates an ethic of care into family law decision making through a system of "principles and presumptions" (Behrens 2002). Critiquing Carol Smart and Bren Neale's view that custody and access decision-making should avoid presumptions about children by focusing on individualized decision making (as demanded by the principle of care), Behrens argues that custody and access legislation should include a combination of both principles and presumptions, with principles stating the broad value (for example, the ethic of care), and presumptions indicating some of the (value-based) outcomes. Behrens explains her reasoning:

[I]n my view we need more than just principles. I argue this for four reasons. First the principles as I envisage them would be very general and some of the value choices which need to be made in this area can only be made through more precise, outcome-oriented provisions. Second, principles only avoid making very general value-based decisions in each case. They do not carry with them the efficiency benefits of making some of the outcome decisions in advance. Third, the importance of ideology, and the strength of ideology irrespective of form, mean that outcomes need to be specified so as to influence the ideology and conversations consistently with the principle. Fourth... a major role for legislation is to work towards addressing power imbalances that will affect private negotiations. Legislation is more likely to do this if it is reasonably specific about the source of those power imbalances. (Behrens 2002: 409–10)

Behrens proposes incorporating the ethic of care into Australian family law at the level of principle, while simultaneously introducing rebuttable presumptions that qualify the discretion and flexibility inherent in a principle-based system. In practice this might involve replacing the best-interests principle in family law legislation with the three elements of an ethic of care — relationships, the principle of actuality and the activity of care — and directing judges to consider these elements, giving equal weight to each, when making custody and access decisions. For example, legislation might state:

When making custody and access decisions the court shall consider:

(a) the importance of maintaining relationships between children and their carers when it is safe and positive to do so;

(b) the individual circumstances of the child's life and their family arrangements; and

(c) the history of caregiving for the child, including the physical, emotional and social tasks of parenting.

Legislation based on Behrens' model would also include a series of presumptions. For example, Behrens suggests the inclusion of the following presumptions: (a) that a court cannot make an order in favour of a parent who has engaged in violence directed towards the other parent or child; (b) that where there has been a primary caregiver, the child will live with that caregiver; and (c) that a court will not interfere with a decision made by a primary caregiver concerning the children (including a decision to relocate). Each of these would be *rebuttable* presumptions, and the principle of care would provide a basis from which to assess whether or not the assumption should be rebutted. Thus, under Behrens' model there would be no way in which a particular ideology — such as the view that contact is in a child's best interests even when there is abuse — could creep into custody and access decision-making.

The combined "principles-and-presumptions" approach should still be able to maintain the ideal of individualized decision making as proposed by Smart and Neale, while also addressing the inherent indeterminacy of such a system. Behrens' model is also the only one that explicitly aims to redress power imbalances within family law, such as those between mothers and fathers. By including rebuttable presumptions that will often force the stronger party to justify his or her claim, it seeks to address some of the historic inequalities between men and women, particularly those that stem from the use of violence as a means of control. Such an approach might ultimately be the best way in which to incorporate an ethic of care into custody and access decision making.

While there is little political will to reform or abolish the best-interests principle, it is clear from the discussion above that a growing number of critics are suggesting that the ethic of care must play a greater role in family law decision making. The approximation principle, the status quo principle, and the "principles-and-presumptions" model all offer realistic alternatives to the best-interests test. Each of the models places care at the centre of custody and access decision making, and avoids the current propensity to place assumptions about children's needs above the actual circumstances of the child in question. Unlike the approximation and status quo principle, however, the "principles and presumptions" model also addresses the complex question of whether an entirely discretion-based system of decision making is desirable.

A RADICAL RETHINKING OF FAMILY LAW?

Incorporating an ethic of care into custody and access decision-making, particularly if it is achieved through the abolition of the best-interests principle, would necessarily involve a radical rethinking of family law. However, while the abolition of the best-interests principle may appear to be a radical proposal, a growing number of family law academics are suggesting that such a step be taken (Eekelaar 2002; Herring 1999; Reece 1996; Goldstein, Freud and Solnit 1979). For example, Reece has argued that the best-interests principle (or "welfare" principle as it is referred to in the U.K.) should be abandoned because, while it rests on solid consensus, the principle has a questionable rationality (Reece 1996: 268). Reece points out that there is no doubt that the welfare principle is firmly ensconced in child custody law in the U.K. and elsewhere.[10] It has, at various times, been described as the "golden thread" running through the *Children Act* 1989 (U.K.) (Mackay 1989), the "bedrock of the [Children] Act,"[11] and the "cornerstone of the current [family] law" (Bromley and Lowe 1992: 294). And as Martha Fineman argues, "[a]sserting that a position... conforms to, or is advanced in a manner designed to advance, the best interests of the child has become the rhetorical price of entry into the debate over custody policy" (Fineman 1989: 36). However, according to Reece (1996), the general consensus over the best-interests principle is fundamentally flawed for two reasons. First, because of its inherent indeterminacy, the best-interests principle allows value-laden, arbitrary, and even capricious assumptions to "smuggle themselves" into family law decision making. For example, in cases involving lesbian or gay parents, the best-interests test can be construed to incorporate assumptions about "good parenting" and "good families" that are based on the judge's individual beliefs about homosexuality, rather than any notion of the "best interests" of the child (Boyd 1998). Second, Reece argues that the best-interests principle is irrational because it pretends that only children's interests are at stake in custody and access disputes. It ignores the interests of other parties, such as parents, and fails to recognize that the child's welfare is often linked to the welfare of other parties. In light of these flaws, Reece concludes that "[t]he paramountcy principle must be abandoned, and replaced with a framework which recognizes that the child is merely one participant in a process in which the interests of all participants count" (Reece 1996: 303).

In another recent critique of the best-interests principle, British legal academic John Eekelaar (2002) also recommends its abandonment: he presents several reasons for taking such action. First, there is what he refers to as the "lack of transparency" objection: that the best-interests test might "fail to provide sufficient protection to children's interests because its use conceals the fact that the interests of others, or, perhaps untested assumptions about what is good for children, actually drive the decision" (Eekelaar 2002: 238). The second criticism is what might be termed the "lack of fairness" objection, which resonates with the arguments made by Reece. The "lack of fairness" objection is based on the argument that the best-interests principle, because of its exclusive focus on the child, prevents proper consideration of the interests of participants other than the child.

In proposing an alternative to the best-interests principle, Eekelaar sought to retain its virtues, while at the same time ensuring that the alternative would adequately recognize the interests of both children and adults, and that it would prevent the concealment of political interests within it. Eekelaar suggested that this might be achieved by eliminating the notion of "interests," which can too easily be used to cover anything someone else thinks is good for you, and by adopting the more nuanced notion of "well-being." While there is no universal conception of what constitutes "well-being" he makes the following suggestions:

For these purposes, I would summarise a person's well-being as being indicated by the degree of success achieved in realising the person's significant goals in life.... This would include the physical and mental health of the person necessary to achieve those ends; the opportunity to maintain and establish important personal relationships; the ability to benefit from educational, social and economic activity and to integrate into society; the ability to develop abilities and interests and to realize life goals. It will be clear that these include moral, or other-regarding, components, for success in relationships and integration in society cannot be easily achieved without them. It will also be clear that there is an important element of self-determination, since, as Joseph Raz put it 'a person's well-being can be promoted only through his [sic] willing acceptance of goals and pursuits.' However, it is equally evident that this is not synonymous with the mere pursuit of desires or superficial, transitory, contentment. (Eekelaar 2002: 243)

In the context of family law decision making, Eekelaar's proposal would mean adopting a course of action that avoids inflicting the most damage on the well-being of any interested individual.

CONCLUSION

Both Reece and Eekelaar recognize the difficulties involved in abandoning the best-interests test, especially if it is to be replaced with a principle that seems more complex or unrealistic. As Eekelaar explains:

The [best-interests] test is too ingrained to be easily displaced. Certainly one could not imagine the judiciary easily abandoning it. It is easier and more comforting simply to say that we are all doing what we think is best for the child. But the very ease of the [best-interests] test encourages a laziness and unwillingness to pay proper attention to all the interests that are at stake in these decisions. (Eekelaar 2002: 248)

However, Eekelaar goes on to suggest that displacing the best-interests test may not seem so "unthinkable" if a reasoned and structured alternative is presented at the same time. It has been my argument throughout this chapter that the ethic of care might provide such an alternative. A growing number of family law commentators support a greater role for the ethic of care in family law decision making, and an increasing number of legislative reform proposals are drawing on elements of the ethic of care. There is also some evidence of a willingness to incorporate certain elements of the ethic into family law decision-making in several jurisdictions.[12] At the same time, a number of family law commentators have begun to question the central "place" of justice in family law decision making and in the best-interests test in particular. Thus while it might sometimes seem that the best-interests principle is too ingrained in Canadian family law to be displaced, the prospect of a viable alternative, in this case the ethic of care, might be the first step in a long and complex process of change.

NOTES

1. Ph.D. candidate, University of British Columbia. B.A. (Melb), LL.B. (Melb)(Hons), LL.M. (UBC). I wish to acknowledge and thank Professor Susan Boyd for her comments on an earlier draft of this chapter. I would also like to thank the two anonymous referees for their invaluable comments. Any errors or omissions, however, are entirely my own.

2. Special Joint Committee on Custody and Access (Parliament of Canada 1998); Federal-Provincial-Territorial Family Law Committee (Canada 2002).

3. Submission of Malcolm Mansfield of Fathers Are Capable Too, 11 March 1998, *Proceedings of the Special Joint Committee on Child Custody and Access*. Ottawa: Public Works and Government Services [*Proceedings*]; Submission of Heidi Nabert of the National Shared Parenting Association, 11 March 1998, *Proceedings*; Submission of Paul Miller of the Men's Educational Support Association, 29 April 1998, *Proceedings*.

4. Despite Linde's suggestion that mothers and fathers share the responsibility for both caregiving and paid labour, the fact remains that, in the vast majority of Canadian families, women, whether involved in paid labour or not, remain the primary caregivers and homemakers both during and after marriage (Boyd 2003: 158–59).

5. Some feminists have suggested that care and justice need not conflict. For example, Jhappan argues that our concept of "justice" could be revisioned so that it is not in permanent binary opposition to "care" (Jhappan 1998: 83–85).

6. See, e.g., *Family Law Act 1975* (Cth), s. 68F.

7. Interestingly, even when joint custody is awarded, most children live primarily with their mothers, and many couples "drift" back towards arrangements that reflect their pre-divorce patterns of care (Mnookin 1990: 67).

8. Thus far, Ch. 2 of the ALI Principles has only been adopted by the West Virginia state legislature: W. VA. CODE §§ 48-11-101-604 (Supp. 2000). However, the Chief Reporter for the ALI Principles project has suggested that Chapter 2 (the chapter dealing with custody and access) may soon be adopted more widely.

9. Bartlett's provisos were: (a) that a guaranteed minimum amount of post-divorce access by parents who have acted as responsible parents, even when they have not spent a significant amount of time providing caretaking functions for their children; (b) that the "firm and reasonable preferences" of older children be taken into account; and (c) that the child's welfare be protected when there has been domestic abuse or when there is a gross disparity between the parents in terms of the quality of emotional attachments with their children or their parental abilities that does not conform to past caretaking patterns (Bartlett, 1999: 83).

10. In fact, a recent Canadian study found that 99 percent of lawyers surveyed thought that the best-interests test should be retained (Paetsch, Bertrand and Hornick 2001).

11. *Re B* [1993] 1 F.L.R. 543 at 552 (*per* Butler-Sloss L.J.).

12. See, e.g., the application of the status quo principle in interim hearings in Australian family law, and the adoption of the ali Principles' "approximation principle" by the state of West Virginia (W. VA. CODE §§ 48-11-101-604 (Supp. 2000)).

REFERENCES

American Law Institute. 1997. *Principles of the Law of Family Dissolution: Analysis and Recommendations*. Philadelphia: Executive Office, American Law Institute.
_____. 2001. "Principles of the Law of Family Dissolution: Analysis and Recommendations." *Duke Journal of Gender Law and Policy* 8, 1.
Bartlett, Katharine. 1999. "Improving the Law Relating to Postdivorce Arrangements for Children." In R. Thompson and P. Amato (eds.), *The Postdivorce Family: Children, Parenting and Society*. Thousand Oaks, CA: Sage.
Behrens, Juliet. 2002. "The Form and Substance of Australian Legislation on Parenting Orders: a Case for the Principles of Care and Diversity and Presumptions Based on Them." *Journal of Social Welfare and Family Law* 24, 401.
Bertoia, Carl, and Janice Drakich. 1993. "The Fathers' Rights Movement: Contradictions in Rhetoric and Practice." *Journal of Family Issues* 14, 592.
Bourque, Dawn. 1995. "'Reconstructing' the Patriarchal Nuclear Family: Recent Developments in Child Custody and Access in Canada." *Canadian Journal of Law and Society* 10, 1.
Boyd, Susan. 1996. "Is There an Ideology of Motherhood in (Post)Modern Child Custody Law?" *Social and Legal Studies* 5, 495.
_____. 1998. "Lesbian (and Gay) Custody Claims: What Difference Does Difference Make?" *Canadian Journal of Family Law* 15, 131.
_____. 2003. *Child Custody, Law, and Women's Work*. Don Mills, ON: Oxford University Press.
Boyd, Susan, Helen Rhoades and Kate Burns. 1999. "The Politics of the Primary Caregiver Assumption: A Conversation." *Australian Journal of Family Law* 13, 233.
Boyd, Susan and Claire Young. 2002. "Who Influences Family Law Reform? Discourses on Motherhood and Fatherhood in Legislative Reform Debates in Canada." *Studies in Law, Politics and Society* 26.
Brinig, Margaret. 2001. "Feminism and Child Custody Under Chapter Two of the American Law Institute's Principles of the Law of Family Dissolution." *Duke Journal of Gender, Law and Policy* 8, 301.
Bromley, Peter, and Nigel Lowe. 1992. *Bromley's Family Law*. London: Butterworths.
Canada. 2002. "Final Federal-Provincial-Territorial Report on Custody and Access and Child Support: Putting Children First." Ottawa: Department of Justice Canada.
Coles, Robert. 1977. *Eskimos, Chicanos and Indians*. Boston: Little, Brown & Co.
Eekelaar, John. 2002. "Beyond the Welfare Principle." *Child and Family Law Quarterly* 14, 237.
Fineman, Martha. 1989. "Politics of Custody and Gender: Child Advocacy and Transformation of Custody Decision Making in USA." In Carol Smart and Selma Sevenhuijsen (eds.), *Child Custody and the Politics of Gender*. London: Routledge.
Gilligan, Carol. 1982. *In a Different Voice: Psychological Theory and Women's Develop-*

ment. Cambridge: Harvard University Press.

Goldstein, Joseph, Anna Freud and Albert Solnit. 1979. *Beyond the Best Interests of the Child*. New York: Free Press.

Gwaltney, John Langston. 1980. *Drylongso: A Self-Portrait of Black America*. New York: Random House.

Held, Virginia. 1997. "Liberalism and the Ethic of Care." Legal Theory Workshop Series, Faculty of Law, University of Toronto.

Herring, John. 1999. "The Welfare Principle and Parents' Rights." In Andrew Bainham, Shelley Day Sclater and Martin Richards (eds.), *What is a Parent? A Socio-Legal Analysis*. Oxford: Hart Publishing.

Jaffe, Peter, David Wolfe and Susan Wilson. 1999. *Children of Battered Women*. Newbury Park, CA: Sage.

Jhappan, Rhada. 1998. "The Equality Pit or the Rehabilitation of Justice." *Canadian Journal of Women and the Law* 10, 60.

Kaye, Miranda, and Julia Tolmie. 1998a. "Discoursing Dads: The Rhetorical Devices of Fathers' Rights Groups." Melbourne University Law Review 22, 162.

Kaye, Miranda and Julia Tolmie. 1998b. "Fathers' Rights Groups in Australia and their Engagement with Issues in Family Law." Australian Journal of Family Law 12, 19.

Kohlberg, Lawrence. 1958. "The Development of Modes of Thinking and Choices in Years 10 to 16." Ph.D. Dissertation, University of Chicago.

_____. 1973. "Continuities and Discontinuities in Childhood and Adult Moral Development Revisited." In *Collected Papers on Moral Development and Moral Education*. Moral Education Research Foundation, Harvard University.

_____. 1984. *The Psychology of Moral Development: The Nature and Validity of Moral Stages*. San Francisco: Harper and Row.

Kohlberg, Lawrence, and R. Kramer. 1969. "Continuities and Discontinuities in Child and Adult Moral Development." *Human Development* 12, 93.

Kurki-Suonio, Kirsti. 2000. "Joint Custody as an Interpretation of the Best Interests of the Child in Critical and Comparative Perspective." *International Journal of Law Policy and the Family* 14, 183.

Linde, Carey. 1998. Brief to Special Joint Committee on Child Custody and Access. Available at <www.divorce-for-men.com/JOINTCOM.doc>. (Accessed July 25, 2005.)

Lye, Diane. 1999. *Washington State Parenting Act Study*. Report to the Washington State Gender and Justice Commission and Domestic Relations Commission.

Mackay, Lord. 1989. "Perceptions of the Children Bill and Beyond." *New Law Journal* 139, 505.

Mnookin, Robert. 1975. "Child-custody Adjudication: Judicial Functions in the Face of Indeterminacy." *Law and Contemporary Problems* 39, 226.

_____. 1990. "Private Ordering Revisited: What Custodial Arrangements Are Parents Negotiating?" In Stephen Sugarman and Herma Hill Keys (eds.), *Divorce Reform at the Crossroads*. New Haven: Yale University Press.

Neilson, Linda. 2000. "Partner Abuse, Children and Statutory Change: Cautionary Comments on Women's Access to Justice." *Windsor Yearbook of Access to Justice* 18, 115.

_____. 2001. *Spousal Abuse, Children and the Legal System: Final Report for the Canadian Bar Association, Law for the Futures Fund*. Fredericton: Muriel McQueen Fergusson Centre for Family Violence Research, University of New Brunswick.

Nobles, Wade. 1976. "Extended Self: Rethinking the So-called Negro Self-Concept."

Journal of Black Psychology 2, 15.

Paetsch, Joanne, Loren, Bertrand and Joseph Hornick. 2001. *Consultation on Child Support Guidelines and Custody and Access*. Federation of Law Societies of Canada and Canadian Research Institute for Law and the Family.

Pagelow, M. 1994. "Effects of Domestic Violence on Children and their Consequences for Custody and Visitation Agreements." *Mediation Quarterly* 7, 347.

Parliament of Canada. 1998. *For the Sake of the Children*. Ottawa: Report of the Special Joint Committee on Child Custody and Access.

_____. 1998. *Proceedings of the Special Joint Committee on Child Custody and Access*. Ottawa: Public Works and Government Services.

Reece, Helen. 1996. "The Paramountcy Principle: Consensus or Construct?" *Current Legal Problems* 267.

Rhoades, Helen, Reg Graycar and Margaret Harrison. 2000. *The Family Law Reform Act 1995: the First Three Years*. Sydney: University of Sydney and the Family Court of Australia.

Rosnes, Melanie. 1997. "The Invisibility of Male Violence in Canadian Child Custody and Access Decision-Making." *Canadian Journal of Family Law* 14, 31.

Scott, Elizabeth. 1992. "Pluralism, Parental Preference, and Child Custody." *California Law Review* 80, 615.

Sevenhuijsen, Selma. 1998. *Citizenship and the Ethics of Care: Feminist Considerations on Justice, Morality and Politics*. London: Routledge.

Smart, Carol. 1995. "Losing the Struggle for Another Voice: The Case of Family Law." *Dalhousie Law Journal* 18, 173.

Smart, Carol, and Bren Neale. 1999. *Family Fragments?* Cambridge: Polity Press.

Smart, Carol, Bren Neale and Amanda Wade. 2001. *The Changing Experience of Childhood: Families and Divorce*. Cambridge: Polity Press.

Sudermann, Marlies, and Peter Jaffe. 2000. *A Handbook for Health and Social Service Providers and Educators on Children Exposed to Woman Abuse/Family Violence*. Ottawa: Health Canada, National Clearinghouse on Family Violence.

Thery, Irene. 1989. "'The Interest of the Child' and the Regulation of the Post-Divorce Family." In Carol Smart and Selma Sevenhuijsen (eds.), *Child Custody and the Politics of Gender*. London: Routledge.

Tronto, Joan. 1987. "Beyond Gender Difference to a Theory of Care." *Signs: Journal of Women in Culture and Society* 12, 644.

West, Robin. 1997. *Caring For Justice*. New York: New York University Press.

CHAPTER 3

NATIONAL RESPONSIBILITY AND SYSTEMIC RACISM IN CRIMINAL SENTENCING:
THE CASE OF *R. V. HAMILTON*

CARMELA MURDOCCA

On February 20, 2003, the Ontario (Canada) Superior Court of Justice released *R. v. Hamilton,* a decision that judicially considered and recognized the impact of systemic racism against the Black community in Canada in the sentencing hearing of two Black women, Marsha Alisjie Hamilton and Donna Rosemarie Mason, both of whom had pleaded guilty to illegally smuggling cocaine into Canada from Jamaica. Justice Casey Hill reduced the sentences for both Hamilton and Mason based on his view of how systemic racism had impacted their lives and their crimes. In his decision, Hill borrowed directly from the legal precedent set by the Ontario Court of Appeal just over a week earlier on February 10, 2003 in *R. v. Borde*, where Justice Marc Rosenberg wrote the reasons for a unanimous three-person panel. In *R. v. Borde*, Rosenberg instructs judges to consider the impact of systemic racism on the lives of Black Canadians in sentencing decisions. In his analysis, Rosenberg followed the legal precedent set by *R. v. Gladue* (1999): in this case the Supreme Court reasoned that the demand of section 718.2(e) of the *Criminal Code* required that Canadian judges who sentence Aboriginal offenders must recognize the historical and systemic disadvantage that First Nations communities have endured and that they, therefore, must consider remedial or restorative justice principles in the application of alternative sentencing. While Rosenberg explicitly noted a similar need to take into consideration "systemic racism and background factors" in the sentencing of Black youths, such systemic factors did not operate to reduce the sentence of Quinn Borde, an eighteen-year-old Black male charged with "possession of a loaded restricted weapon, aggravated assault and using a firearm in the commission of an indictable offence," because Rosenberg noted that his crimes were "too violent" for such considerations to affect the sentence. In particular, Rosenberg concluded: "systemic racism and background factors faced by Black youths in Toronto are important factors and in another case I believe that they could affect the sentence" (*R. v. Borde* (2003), 172 C.C.C. (3d) 225 (Ont. C.A.) at 2). To be sure, the other case that

Rosenberg anticipates is *R. v. Hamilton*.

In this chapter, using *R. v. Hamilton*, I argue that the application of section 718.2(e) of the *Criminal Code* of Canada constitutes a practice of nation building, in which the negotiation of past injustice in the context of criminal sentencing brings into view how the law produces legitimate citizens and by extension how it legitimates national history, through culturally and racially codifying non-white subjects before the court. I show how the application of section 718.2(e) in *R. v. Hamilton* is contingent upon invoking and enacting historical racial narratives, both for the particular subject before the court (and, as a consequence, for the racial community to which they belong) and for the court, as the (moral) arbiter of the nation. I argue that these racial narratives serve a dual function for the project of law and nation building: by circumscribing their claims to personhood along racial and cultural lines, they invite the subject before the court to participate in the universal core values of "human rights"; at the same time these racial narratives function to inscribe (legal) notions of national responsibility for past injustice. In particular, I suggest that while the application of section 718.2(e) is an instance of anti-racist jurisprudence, its application must be understood in terms of its normative role in establishing the contours of legally codifiable claims to national responsibility as well as its role in the production of national subjects. In effect, the application of section 718.2(e) must be understood through its role in producing both white citizens and non-white citizens: this is accomplished by the invocation of appeals to responsibility. In examining the application of section 718.2(e) in *R. v. Hamilton*, I follow scholars who argue that the law relies upon national narratives for meaning and that, in turn, through such national narratives, the law constructs categories that determine certain historical "truths" and appeal to particular forms of justice (see for example, Barkan 2000; Razack 1999: 159–85 and 2000: 183–211). My objective, in the context of *R. v. Hamilton*, is to situate the application of section 718.2(e) at the interface of narratives that appeal to the nation and its history through the law.

I treat the application of section 718.2(e) as one example of negotiation of compensation, that is currently confined and organized through criminal sentencing. Past injustices in Canada were perpetrated in the name of a state that was founded upon, and organized on and through, ideas about racial difference.[1] This chapter represents an attempt to address the implications of culture-claims and cultural-difference explanations for racism that operate in compensation narratives in the law. As a consequence, this analysis borrows and turns on the argument that the legal recognition of what the nation identifies as past injustice, and its connection to identity (and identity-making practices) in criminal sentencing, is carved out of, and relies upon, cultural-difference explanations: these explanations function through a legal paradigm that determines worthiness.[2] Extending this argument further, I will explore how the use of racial-cultural comparison, and its gendered implications (highlighted by the [possible] extension of race-based sentencing to groups other than Aboriginal), raises questions about the efficacy of anti-racist platforms that are rooted in social identity claims and structured by appeals to cultural difference. The race-based sentencing initiative at work in section 718.2(e), as applied in *R. v. Hamilton,* is rooted in a jurisprudence that, on its face, attempts to address the relationship between race and (in)justice in Canada. Inclusion and compensation for past injustices along racial lines may serve to assuage national (white) accountability; however, the "rights talk" at work in *R. v. Hamilton* also serves to circumscribe the historical narrative of racial injustice that frames contemporary understanding of that subject in Canada. As Elazar Barkan points out, "despite the dissimilar temporality and rationality, there is an overlap between historical injustice and contemporary discrimination" (Barkan 2000: xxxi). In essence, I aim to contribute to the development of an historically situated legal framework — one that identifies the reality of past injustice experienced by racialized communities, as well as one that investigates this "overlap" and recognizes the meaning of the injustice and its contemporary implications both for the perpetrators and the victims. Using *R. v. Hamilton* then, I consider the following questions: How are national racial groups constituted through *particular subjects* found guilty of *particular crimes* in a *particular* historical moment? How does the legal notion of past injustice and systemic racism produce particular *national* subjects? How is "national responsibility" conceptualized through criminal sentencing?

In addressing these questions, I begin with a brief examination of the political and legal technologies and apparatuses, required by the state, in order to constitute individual citizen/subjects: in effect, the nation relies upon individuals who constitute, through their performance, invocation and/or subjection to particular legal technologies, legal identities that produce the racial state order of the nation. I then trace the discourse of racial subjectivity and nation as it is rendered legally comprehensible in *R. v. Hamilton;* I then show how the legal formation of the connections between past injustice and contemporary racism contain a politics of historical identification which is grounded in racial hierarchies operating to circumscribe legitimate claims to "rights." Finally, addressing some of the implications of *R. v. Hamilton,* I suggest how the production of legal subjects, through a paradigm of national responsibility in criminal sentencing, ultimately works to sustain the nation's complicity in colonial violence and racism, while, through the recognition of past injustice, simultaneously promoting a national investment in compensation measures.

Legal discourse offers a critical background through which to investigate the national narratives that are central to the production of Canadian nationalism. In legal discourse, symbolic and material strategies of recognition that operate through a paradigm of inclusion/exclusion become the very process through which citizens are constituted within, and outside of, national narratives. As Lauren Berlant maintains "alongside public iconography and popular narrative is an official story of 'citizenship:' the juridical discussion of what membership in the nation implies and requires" (Berlant 1991: 11). The "juridical discussion of what membership in the nation implies and requires," as embodied through the application of section 718.2(e) in *R. v. Hamilton*, is the conceptual framework that grounds this chapter.

RACE, BIOPOLITICS AND SUBJECTIVITY: THE SUBJECTS THAT ENACT LAW'S RULE

The inquiry that this chapter proposes is to consider how the materiality (the presence) of certain bodies in the courtroom racially scripts national narratives through the implementation of criminal sentences that are "restorative" in their intention but account for the contemporary experience of systemic racism.[3] In particular, I argue that this practice serves to produce legitimate citizens through a consideration of national responsibility for past injustice. Janna Thompson argues that the idea "that individuals ought to be recompensed for the injustices they have suffered is a basic moral and legal idea" in modern states (Thompson 2001: 114). How does this moral and legal idea function to produce subjects — both the subjects (the racial others) of the legal claim and white subjects (of the court and naturalized citizens) in liberal democracies? David Goldberg insists that the racial state requires for its functionality political and legal technologies and apparatuses that constitute individuals.[4] In turn, the historical connections that are legally drawn, linking race and nation, can only be accomplished, by manufacturing people, producing particular subjects in the service of nation-building. Michel Foucault (1990) suggests that manufacturing subjects in the service of state and nation requires a dual process of the operation of what he calls biopower. Biopolitics or biopower refers to the various processes through which bodies of subjects come to constitute modern state order.[5] Biopower is exercised on the body, through disciplinary and regulatory controls (indeed, section 718.2(e) is one such regulatory control), so that individual subjects get constituted as members of a population that are connected with issues of national policy. The dual operation of biopower operates through technologies of governance (or governmentality), bringing together both the disciplinary effects of state practices as well as the interpolative consequences for individual subjects. First, biopower operates directly on the body of individual/subjects in order to classify and constitute individual subjects as a *population* in accordance with state practice. Secondly, biopower operates through what Foucault describes as "technologies of the self." These are the interpolative consequences of governance: they refer to the range of practices through which individuals constitute themselves within and through the systems of power which regulate their bodies, their thoughts and their conduct. The goal, then, is to understand the embodied effects of law, by examining individual subjects of law, through historically produced and constituted/contested identities as exemplified through the application of section 718.2(e) in *R. v. Hamilton*.

To maintain that the modern state depends upon the productive and constitutive powers of law suggests that the production of subjects before the law propel the very interpretive practices of law.[6] While the kind of governance at work in the application of section 718.2(e) is aimed at certain populations (and thus constitutes certain populations), as "national racial groups," implementation through legal decision-making is almost solely directed at individuals constituted in and through their racial group affiliation. In the context of individual "rights-based" legal imperatives, Goldberg suggests that "subjects assume value, then, only in so far as they are bearers of rights; and they are properly vested with rights only in so far as they are imbued with value" (Goldberg 1993: 37). My goal, in what follows, is to track the particular biopolitic at work in the operation of section 718.2(e) in *R. v. Hamilton*, and to show how Marsha Hamilton and Donna Mason accrue legal value — attain legal personhood — which entitles them as *deserving* of the benefits of section 718.2(e) through the invocation and performance of racial narratives particular to their racial and cultural identities. More critically, as I illustrate, the kind of "rights-applicability" at work in *R. v. Hamilton* creates a jurisprudence of national responsibility which only emerges through legal inscriptions of racial/cultural degeneracy on individual subjects and subject populations.

RACE, PAST INJUSTICE AND SENTENCING

Canada has a history of organizing policy responses to the colonized condition of Aboriginal peoples in which certain legal signifiers are employed to explain particular legal interventions: this policy continues to the present day. Section 718.2(e) emerged as a response to high Aboriginal incarceration rates: it includes the ideas that Aboriginal peoples continue to live according to a "fundamentally different worldview" than Europeans in terms of their conceptions of the world and justice, and that they have "traditional cultures," are "uncivilized," "desperate," or are inescapably "dead Aboriginals" (Royal Commission on Aboriginal Peoples, 1996), a conception that entrenches and justifies even further white settler claims and culpability.[7] These cultural (difference) explanations of Aboriginal over-incarceration rates led Canada to officially recognize through its Royal Commission on Aboriginal Peoples that the "history of colonialism" continues to structure every aspect of Aboriginal people's lives. The abstract concepts of "history of colonialism" and "historical injustice," employed in this context in criminal sentencing, are not simply ideological or national justifications for colonialism, they also function as a significant filter through which to investigate the ways in which historical colonial violence and (contemporary) racism are reproduced in law in a contemporary context through demarcations of racial/cultural difference (Royal Commission on Aboriginal Peoples 1996: 309).[8] These signifiers, that are effectively naturalized in law, and that operate as explanations of Aboriginal and Black Canadian disadvantage and "dysfunction," highlight how history gets transformed in law and by law, how cultural difference explanations are offered in place of recognition of the impact of colonial violence and racism, and how rights claims, in the name of social justice, mask the very historical conditions they aim to contest.

In Canada, taking systemic racism into account in sentencing decisions did not begin on February 10, 2003 with *R. v. Borde*. Legal scholars have noted that the relationship between race and sentencing historically developed not only as a consequence of the Royal Commission on Aboriginal Peoples: it also emerges as a result of the federal government's overhaul of the *Criminal Code* — in particular, the addition of section 718.2(e) in 1996 (Daubney and Parry 1999). This subsection of the *Criminal Code*, which conceptually links race and culture in the law, states: "A court that imposes a sentence shall take into consideration the following principles:... (e) all available sanctions other than imprisonment that are reasonable in the circumstances should be considered for all offenders, with particular attention to the circumstances of aboriginal offenders" (*Criminal Code* (R.S. 195, c. C-46). It was not until 1999 when the Supreme Court of Canada released *R. v. Gladue* that the meaning of this particular subsection of the *Criminal Code* was interpreted judicially, and thus acquired the status of legal precedent. As Jonathan Rudin, the Program Director of the Aboriginal Legal Services of Toronto explains:

> In the context of aboriginal offenders, *Gladue* provided an opportunity for judges, with the assistance defence counsel, Crown attorneys and community agencies, to work together to fashion sentences that would not simply perpetuate the revolving door from the street to the jail and back again. (Rudin 2003: A21)

In *R. v. Hamilton*, Justice Hill relies upon the legal precedent set by *R. v. Gladue* and *R. v. Borde* in order to account for the "reduced sentences" given in *R. v. Hamilton*. In *R. v. Gladue* the Supreme Court of Canada reasoned that the historical overrepresentation of Aboriginals in Canada's penal system warranted the practice of "creative sentencing" in order to remedy incarceration rates for Aboriginals.[9] In *R. v. Hamilton*, Justice Hill applied this reasoning to the context of the Black Canadian experience of systemic racism.[10] In particular, Justice Hill maintains that the applicability of the impact of systemic racism and "historical disadvantage" on the Aboriginal community in Canada in the context of sentencing, as outlined in *R. v. Gladue*, demanded a similar approach to "other definable groups" who "shared these attributes or history." Justice Hill noted that this "restorative justice" approach should include a consideration of both the particular use of incarceration and its duration. As Justice Hill explains in *R. v. Hamilton*:

> I understood the Crown to take the position that the statutory reference to aboriginal offenders was included in part on the basis

of aboriginal Canadians' estrangement from the Canadian criminal justice system and their special and long-standing views respecting traditional sentencing objectives. In turn, it was submitted by the Crown that other definable groups were not meant to be included in a similar analysis unless they too shared these attributes or history. Whether or not for other groups s. 718.2(e) permits, or compels, a similar approach to that articulated in *Gladue*... respecting aboriginal offenders, the purposes and principles of sentencing and the exercise of sentencing discretion in accordance with *Charter* values commands consideration of systemic factors in this case insofar as they are related to the commission of the offences for which the accused have been convicted. This is the essence of equity and individualized sentencing. (*R. v. Hamilton*, [2004] O.J. No. 3252 [Q.L.] (Ont. C.A.) at 185)

Justice Hill categorically suggests not only that section 718.2(e) of the *Criminal Code* requires that systemic racism be taken into account in sentencing, but that the *Charter of Rights and Freedoms* also demands a consideration of systemic factors in *R. v. Hamilton*. In effect, the reasoning at work in this excerpt suggests that racialized bodies are and have been judicially marked through the process of their interaction within the legal-juridical context of discretionary power and sentencing. Judgements that rely upon the application of section 718.2(e) identify this link and rest upon the legal connection between past injustice and contemporary racism. In the following section, I examine the ways in which Marsha Hamilton and Donna Mason attain legal personhood (and legal "value") through the invocation and performance of racial narratives particular to their racial and cultural identities.

R. v. *Hamilton*
Marsha Hamilton and Donna Mason risked their lives and their liberty by traveling to Canada after swallowing pellets of cocaine in Jamaica. Both were arrested. Ms. Hamilton nearly died from cocaine leaking into her bloodstream. The offenders, black women and single mothers of three children, pleaded guilty to unlawfully importing cocaine. What remains for the Court is the imposition of a just sentence. (*R. v. Hamilton*, [2004] O.J. No. 3252 [Q.L.] (Ont. C.A.) at 1)

R. v. Hamilton is a sentencing decision by the Ontario Superior Court of Justice concerning two Black Caribbean women, Marsha Hamilton and Donna Mason. The decision is significant because the Ontario Superior Court of Justice, in determining the sentence for each woman, took into consideration the impact of systemic racism on Black Canadians. The impact of this consideration of the part of the court was that both Hamilton and Mason received what have been called "reduced" sentences. Marsha Hamilton and Donna Mason pleaded guilty to cocaine importation. As a consequence of such a plea, *R. v. Hamilton* deals solely with the issue of the "appropriate" sentencing for them. In the course of the hearing and in the decision, the admission of details about their personal lives reveals the process through which the "face" of cocaine importation is racially marked and gendered. In addition, details related to their social location, citizen status, parental status, and employment provided the framework through which Justice Hill ultimately rendered and reasoned (rationalized) his decision. I offer some details pertaining to Marsha Hamilton and Donna Mason as they were presented in the decision in order to show how the racialized and gendered logic at work in *R. v. Hamilton* circumscribes their claims to personhood along racial and cultural lines. *R. v. Hamilton* reveals the manner in which the "meaning" of past racial injustice in Canada comes to be represented through the contemporary legal recognition of systemic racism.

Marsha Hamilton

On November 9, 2000, Marsha Hamilton arrived in Toronto from Montego Bay, Jamaica with her one-year-old son. A Canada Customs Officer, believing that Hamilton looked "suspicious," detained her for further investigation. As a consequence of her being detained, Hamilton acknowledged to having swallowed ninety-three pellets containing cocaine before leaving Jamaica. She was then admitted to hospital, where traces of cocaine were found in her urine. At this point, a physician concluded that her medical condition was critical. As part of his rationale for sentencing, Justice Hill noted that Hamilton, a Canadian citizen, was twenty-six years of age at the time of her arrest and was twenty-eight at the time of sentencing. Admitted in the context of the trial as evidence, it was noted that Hamilton is also a single mother of three children, with no prior criminal record. She attained a Grade 9 education and supports her family on social assistance. In her hearing, Marsha Hamilton addressed the court only in the context of displaying remorse for her actions. Hamilton explained: "All I have to say is I'm sorry, I'm truly sorry, but I made mistakes, some mistakes in the past, and I look forward to getting a job and taking care of my kids now" (*R. v. Hamilton*, [2004] O.J. No. 3252 [Q.L.] (Ont. C.A.) at 60).[11] Justice Hill sentenced Hamilton to twenty months of house arrest, noting that a two to three year sentence was the customary sentence given for the offence that she committed (*R. v. Hamilton*, [2004] O.J. No. 3252 [Q.L.] (Ont. C.A.) at 185).

Donna Mason

Donna Mason arrived at Pearson International Airport in Toronto from Kingston, Jamaica on May 14, 2001. As occurred with Hamilton, a Customs Officer felt that Mason was a "suspicious" traveller because her plane ticket was paid for in cash by a third party. The Customs Officer detained her for further investigation. After a personal search in which she expelled nine capsules of cocaine, Mason was arrested and transported to a hospital where she excreted a total of eighty-three capsules. Mason was thirty-one years of age at the time of her arrest and was thirty-three at the time of sentencing. The decision also notes that Mason is single mother with three children and that she attained a Grade 12 education and supports her family through full-time employment supplemented by welfare assistance. The decision makes clear that Donna Mason is not a Canadian citizen, but rather a Jamaican citizen with "permanent resident" status under the *Immigration and Refugee Protection Act* (2001). Her children are Canadian citizens. Like Hamilton, Mason addressed the court solely in the context of displaying remorse of her actions. Mason explained: "I just wanted to say I'm very sorry.... I'm just asking that you just give me a second chance to better my life with my children and that I can show the court that I can do better in life" (*R. v. Hamilton*, [2004] O.J. No. 3252 [Q.L.] (Ont. C.A.) at 69). Justice Hill sentenced Mason to twenty-four months less a day of house arrest, noting that he granted this sentence (instead of the two or three year sentencing normally given for such an offence) due to the fact that Mason would have faced deportation as a "permanent resident" under Canadian law if her sentence exceeded two years (*R. v. Hamilton*, [2004] O.J. No. 3252 [Q.L.] (Ont. C.A.) at 235–37).

PRODUCING NATIONAL SUBJECTS THROUGH CLAIMS TO NATIONAL RESPONSIBILITY

In his decision Justice Hill included a section entitled "Social Context and Sentencing" where he outlined the social and systemic factors, as well as the legal precedents, that he took into consideration in the sentencing of Hamilton and Mason. Justice Hill maintained that "in [his] view, systemic and background factors, identified in this case... should logically be relevant to mitigate the penal consequences for cocaine importers conscripted as couriers" (*R. v. Hamilton*, [2004] O.J. No. 3252 [Q.L.] (Ont. C.A.) at 224). In light of these "systemic and background factors," Justice Hill granted sentences that were otherwise an exception to the historic sentencing patterns for such offences. Borrowing from *R. v. Gladue* (and setting out what has become known as the *Gladue* test in sentencing hearings) he specified his rationale for weighing the systemic factors and other background factors present in the lives of Hamilton and Mason by framing his rationale around the following questions:

> What combination of systemic of background factors contributed to this particular offender coming before the courts for this particular offence? How has the offender who is being sentenced been affected by, for example, substance abuse in the community, or poverty, or overt racism, or family or community breakdown? (*R. v. Hamilton*, [2004] O.J. No. 3252 [Q.L.] (Ont. C.A.) at 188)

Furthermore, borrowing from an Irish Law Reform Commission's Report (Law Reform Commission (Ireland). 1996), Hill reasoned that a "just" sanction for Hamilton and Mason requires a consideration of how society bears a responsibility for the social and past historical conditions that played a role in the commission of an offence. Quoting from the Commission's report, Hill concurs:

> society bears a responsibility for such conditions and as a corollary, has obligations towards offenders whose personal history or whose offence suggests a link between the offending conduct and the presence of such conditions.... We are not suggesting that society's ills can be cured by the adoption of a socially-concerned sentencing policy.... All we are saying is that retribution on its own can rarely afford sufficient justification for the imposition of a particular sentence. Society must bear a degree of responsibility for the incidence of crime, and this responsibility does not end upon a finding of guilt at the close of a criminal trial. (*R. v. Hamilton*, [2004] O.J. No. 3252 [Q.L.] (Ont. C.A.) at 192)

The framework that Hill proposes in assessing a just sentence operates through a legal optic that contains a politics that links history (past injustice producing society's contemporary "ills") and systemic discrimination directly to the subject before the court. I suggest that this legal optic not only produces a national "identity" for the "offending subject" before the court, but also, more significantly, produces the dominant subject that is the court, and by extension, the legitimate citizen — the core of a liberal democracy. What emerges from this jurisprudential practice is an assessment of racial justice that is both individual and nationally/historically accountable. Assessing the application of "socially-concerned sentencing" where "retribution can rarely afford sufficient justification" suggests that national responsibility of injustice comes into the purview of legal accountability relative only to the historical and social conditions that have brought the subject before the courts. Therefore, subjects can only become legally comprehensible relative to the material conditions they experience (systemic racism), as well as the *symbolic* legal inscriptions those conditions enable. National responsibility too, can only become legally comprehensible relative to the racial identities that are deployed in order to ground legal claims. As a consequence, the negotiation of national accountability through criminal sentencing necessarily requires that "contending narratives shape the identity of both perpetrators and victims, as each side is invested in a particular interpretation of historical events" (Barkan 2001: xxvi). It should be stressed that these normative national investments are both racial and material.

In the case of *R. v. Hamilton*, the interlocking systems of race and gender frame the material conditions that mitigate the application of a just sentence. Justice Hill maintains that:

it would be unfortunate if combining the discussion of race and gender in this case obscured the importance of either issue.... It is apparent that women, and especially African Canadian women, like the offenders here and so many others, are virtue tested by drug operation overseers deliberately preying on their social and economic disadvantage.... Each of the offenders in this case has three young children. Each is a single mother with no financial assistance from their children's fathers. Each requires welfare to survive. In Canada, the feminization of poverty is an entrenched social phenomenon with a multiplicity of economic barriers faced by women. (*R. v. Hamilton*, [2004] O.J. No. 3252 [Q.L.] (Ont. C.A.) at 194-6)

Here, Justice Hill attempts to point to the interlocking nature of race and gender in the lives of women of colour. He does so in order to suggest that both race and gender, as interlocking systems, structure the lives of Hamilton and Mason. Hill makes the necessary link between the systemic and the individual by contextualizing their lives within the larger framework of the reality of both gender and racial bias in society and in the criminal justice system. This passage reveals the manner in which the lives of women of colour are used as a productive legal platform: here discourses linking racial bodies to crime and poverty frame the legal recognition or assessment of social/national responsibility. The particular marking of "African Canadian women," to be sure, inscribes citizenship/immigrant status as a primary marker through which such claims are made. The legal reasoning in *R. v. Hamilton* works to inscribe "outsider" status upon racial bodies: in effect, Hamilton and Mason become circumscribed within an account of Black women who are conscripted as drug couriers. The result is that Hamilton and Mason (and, as a consequence, any other woman of colour who comes before the court for a sentencing hearing) are only legally comprehensible as subjects within terms that link their Blackness to poverty, crime, and indeed to abhorrence: these conditions require "national" consideration.[12] Therefore, their claims to personhood before the courts are scripted and organized along these lines. In an effort to summarize the cumulative effects of the systemic and background factors which led to the commission of their crimes Justice Hill produces a succinct narrative, linking race, gender, motherhood, poverty and crime — the only narrative basis through which Hamilton and Mason can emerge as recognizable legal subjects. Justice Hill further elucidates her decision as folllows:

Offenders like those before the court are subject to both the systemic economic inequality of women caring on their own for young children and the compounding disadvantage of systemic racism securing their poverty status. These individuals, almost inevitably without a prior criminal record, are in turn conscripted by the drug distribution hierarchy targeting their vulnerability. Poor, then exploited in their poverty, these women when captured and convicted have been subjected to severe sentences perpetuating their position of disadvantage while effectively orphaning their young children for a period of time. (*R. v. Hamilton*, [2004] O.J. No. 3252 [Q.L.] (Ont. C.A.) at 198)

The racialization described in this excerpt has an impact on the Black female body, which effectively becomes the discursive object through which criminalization and victimization are legally linked. Furthermore, Justice Hill itemizes a five-point legal calculation which together justifies his application of section 718.2(e) to the sentencing of Hamilton and Mason. His five-point legal calculation includes the following facts: they both pleaded guilty, they are both first offenders and single mothers of three children, they demonstrated real remorse and they spent four days in custody.

Justice Hill articulates that the recognition of individual autonomy (and criminality) comes into the legal purview relative to a social/historical context which operates to produce an idea of social/national responsibility:

> We believe in individual autonomy and that individuals must bear responsibility for the exercise of their choice, including a choice to break the law. We do however believe that the exercise of choice is often influenced by social factors, and in its treatment of offenders, including its sentencing policy, society should recognize some responsibility for the social environment in which much crime is committed. (*R. v. Hamilton*, [2004] O.J. No. 3252 [Q.L.] (Ont. C.A.) at 192)

The application of section 718.2(e) then, operates through a legal calculus where the legal notion of responsibility emerges through the combination of individual autonomy (circumscribed through race and culture in *R. v. Hamilton*) and a legal notion of past or systemic injustice (the need to account for "some responsibility for the social environment"). As a result, even though the question at issue is the legal recognition of the effects of past injustice and systemic racism on the lives of Black women in a sentencing hearing, the construction of Canada as a nation that is accountable for such racial injustice is remarkably absent in his legal synopsis of the case before the court. As a consequence, national responsibility is not only rendered legally absent but, as other scholars have pointed out, a kind of national innocence for past injustice emerges: the nation comes into legal purview as benevolent, and Justice Hill's job as the legal purveyor of such benevolence is to assess the compassionate or humanitarian grounds under which legal decisions are to be made.[13] However, when the meanings of race, gender and nation are articulated in such a way as they are in *R. v. Hamilton*, through the language of "restorative justice," or a kind of "humanitarian sentencing," the racism at the core of such legal reasoning implicates the very meaning of national responsibility. Sherene Razack identifies a similar line of racial legal reasoning in the context of refugee hearings which involve gender persecution cases: here "the racist construct of the benevolent, generous First World... extending a helping hand... is masked by the language of humanitarian values" (Razack 1999: 90). As a consequence, the recognition of systemic racism as institutionalized in the law does not take full account of the connections between the material practices in the law that work to ensure the subjugation of people of colour and Aboriginal peoples, the narratives that circumscribe the claims to personhood in the court *and* the national story of innocence that underscores the ideological impetus behind the legal redress of racial injustice.

CULTURE CLAIMS AND RESPONSIBILITY: *HAMILTON* AT THE COURT OF APPEAL

On August 3, 2004 *Hamilton* was overruled by a unanimous bench of the Court of Appeal for Ontario. The decision was critical of a number of aspects of the trial judge's decision.[14] For the purposes of this chapter, and in order to highlight the operation of national responsibility in criminal sentencing, I will focus on the Court of Appeal's contention that the trial judge erred in reducing Hamilton and Mason's sentences: this was based on the argument that there was no evidence "to suggest that poor black women share a cultural perspective with respect to punishment that is akin to the aboriginal perspective" (*Hamilton* C.A., at 99). I examine this contention and the terrain of culture claims and cultural recognition as it is articulated in the decision as well as in the facta by the community legal interventions (which included the African Canadian Legal Clinic, the Native Women's Association of Canada and Aboriginal Legal Services of Toronto). In addition, I briefly examine the Court of Appeal's view that their crimes were "too serious" to allow for mitigation, and I cast these explanations alongside culture and responsibility claims articulated in the decisions. The court began by stating:

> Sentencing is not based on group characteristics, but on the facts relating to the specific offence and specific offender as revealed by the evidence adduced in the proceedings. A sentencing proceeding is also not the forum in which to right perceived societal wrongs, allocate responsibility for criminal conduct as between the offender and society, or "make up" for perceived social injustices by the imposition of sentences that do not reflect the seriousness of the crime. (*Hamilton* C.A., at. 2)

In its attempt to curtail the use of section 718.2(e) beyond Aboriginal peoples, the court goes so far as to contest the basic premise that Blacks are in fact overrepresented in Canadian prisons. The court noted: "[I]t is not apparent to me that any inference can be drawn from a single statistic indicating that black women make up six per cent of the female penitentiary population and only about two per cent of the general population" (*Hamilton* C.A., at. 77). Justice Doherty, writing for the court, then goes on to provide his own (conveniently unreferenced) statistic indicating that the percentage of Black women in prisons has dramatically dropped over the last eight years (*Hamilton* C.A., at 77). The overrepresentation of Black peoples in prisons in Canada, as elsewhere, is well documented (Report of the Commission on Systemic Racism in the Ontario Criminal Justice System1995: 65, 69 and 75; Davis 2002: 61–78). Studies have also shown that Black women conscripted as drug "mules," like Hamilton and Mason, account for a high percentage of Black women incarcerated in prisons (Sudbury 2004: 173–87).

COMPETING CULTURES[15]

The court was bent on distinguishing Black peoples from Aboriginal people, by organizing possible and competing claims to both historical disadvantage and systemic discrimination, such that Aboriginals are deemed deserving of the application of section 718.2(e) while Black Canadians are understood as not eligible for its possible application. The court's distinction between Aboriginal peoples and Black Canadians is grounded in the reasoning that Aboriginal peoples have historically endured systemic discrimination which continues to the present day; as well they have culturally-specific justice models that together warrant the consideration of alternative sentencing. Black Canadians, the court reasoned, experience systemic racism, but they do not have *culturally-specific* justice models, akin to those in Aboriginal communities. The court therefore construed the application of section 718.2(e) to be dependant upon the presence of cultural practices within Aboriginal communities; it argued effectively, that a kind of cultural justice system was required in order for the application of section 718.2(e) to be warranted. A cultural explanation, then, comes to stand in place of the need for restraint in criminal sentencing. This distinction between systemic factors and cultural factors as applied to Aboriginals versus Black Canadians situates racial subjects within a legal paradigm of culture and worthiness (and a particular idea of Aboriginal culture) which in turn frames the consideration of national responsibility in criminal sentencing.[16]

The court's reluctance to extend the *Gladue* principles (and the application of section 718.2(e)) likely stems from the view that allowing another racial group to benefit from the sentencing principles would result in the unwieldy opening of doors to all peoples who experience racism. There is, of course, no evidence to support the "floodgates" argument; in fact, much has been written about the under-use of *Gladue* even in the context of Aboriginal peoples (see Roach and Rudin 2000: 355–88). Recognizing that Black Canadians share characteristics and circumstances with many members of the Aboriginal community are supportive of a wide judicial interpretation of section 718.2(e) that bring them into more frequent contact with the criminal justice system. The submission by Aboriginal Legal Services of Toronto (ALST) at *Hamilton* states:

> ALST will argue that the trial judge did not err in his interpretation of s. 718.2(e).... Systemic discrimination is a relevant circumstance and it is an error to conclude that s. 718.2(e) only applies to African Canadian offenders if their individual circumstances are similar to those of Aboriginal offenders.

Furthermore, ALST insisted:

> While the Court in *Gladue* did recognize that 'one of the unique circumstances of aboriginal offenders is that community-based sanctions coincide with the aboriginal concept of sentencing and the needs of aboriginal people and communities,' the Court was nevertheless clear that the aims of restorative justice apply to all offenders: 'The aims of restorative justice as now expressed in paras. (d), (e) and (f) of s. 718 of the Criminal Code apply to all offenders, and not only aboriginal offenders. (*Gladue*, paras. 70, 74)[17]

Nonetheless, in order to narrow the sentencing paradigm of section 718.2(e), the Court of Appeal construed section 718.2(e) to the contrary view, implying the need for a particular tradition of restorative justice, or other cultural specific justice models, in the offender's ethnic, cultural or religious life in order to justify a similar sentencing approach.

This argument is flawed for a number of reasons. The court asserted that "there was no evidence in the mass of material adduced... to suggest that poor black women share a cultural perspective with respect to punishment akin to the aboriginal perspective" (*Hamilton* C.A., at 99). This may well have been quite simply because neither the parties nor the trial judge expected this to be a necessary part of the *Gladue* test. Curiously, the court relied on the testimony of a single counsellor employed by the Jamaican Canadian Association in *R. v. Spencer* [2004] O.J. No. 3262 (Ont. C.A.)[18] to emphasize the heterogeneity of the diasporic Black community in Canada and to determine that Hamilton and Mason were more like the majority of Canadians than Aboriginals. The counsellor testified:

> that the black community was a diverse group with a broad range of cultures and beliefs. She also testified that to her knowledge, the Jamaican community did not have a different view about sentencing and personal responsibility for criminal conduct than did other Canadians. (*Hamilton* C.A., at 99)

Following this line of reasoning, the court emphasized the heterogeneity of the Black community as a persuasive explanation for Black exclusion from section 718.2(e). However, in *Gladue*, the court conceded to reasoning in line with the reality of the diversity and heterogeneity of Aboriginal communities.[19] Furthermore, the court made no attempt to address the argument raised by the intervener, the African Canadian Legal Clinic (ACLC), that the devastating impact of slavery in Canada and Jamaica would have destroyed culturally specific legal practices or institutions:

> Slavery in Canada was not abolished until 1834. The history of African Canadians is one of de-facto segregation in housing, schooling, employment and exclusion from public places…. The Courts and the justice system re-enforced these racist practices and perpetuated the exclusion of African Canadians from participation in society, keeping [them] "in their place": at the bottom of the socio-economic ladder in the service of the dominant culture. (Factum of African Canadian Legal Clinic: 2)

Like colonialism, the effect of slavery has deep-seated and far-reaching implications for every aspect of Black cultural life. Here, the ACLC utilizes what can be understood as a simultaneous insertion of the history of slavery and its relationship to contemporary racial relations, as well as a kind of assessment of the litigation performance of the culture. Forestalling the application of section 718.2(e) for Hamilton and Mason, the court responds to this insertion of racial history and culture by offering an explanation that effectively transforms the very meaning of national responsibility and compensation in criminal sentencing. Responsibility is warranted relative only to the presence of, and performance of, cultural justice models in particular communities. This legal demand amounts to nothing more than the fulfillment of descriptive and normative racial and cultural typologies for indigenous and racialized peoples. Culture, therefore, suffocates the moral pull of national benevolence.

Even if one were to engage the court and assume that it was correct in its cursory conclusion that Blacks do not share a cultural perspective, akin to Aboriginals, on punishment, the case law is unambiguous in its assertion that the concept of restorative justice is part of the new Canadian sentencing regime (see R. v. Gladue [(1999) 1 S.C.R. 688] *at* 46). Restorative justice has featured prominently in proposals to reform the Canadian criminal justice system in the last decades of the twentieth century (Hughes and Mossman 2002). While the impetus for restorative justice processes in Canada may have originally derived from concerns about the application of Eurocentric ideas of crime and punishment to First Nations offenders and communities, the racial logic that underpins a restorative justice framework suggests that the model relies upon a particular moral logic that requires identity-making practices on the part of defendants.

THE CRIME IS TOO SERIOUS

Another interesting feature of the analysis of section 718.2(e) lies in the court's decision to forestall its application for serious offences. Similar to the Supreme Court of Canada that refused Jamie Tanis Gladue the benefit of section 718.2(e), the Court of Appeal dismissed the appeals of Marsha Hamilton and Donna Mason on the ground that the offences were sufficiently serious and that, as a consequence, imprisonment would be the only reasonable response, regardless of the ethnic or cultural background of the offender (*Hamilton* C.A., at 100). The Court of Appeal justified its decision as follows:

> The use and sale of cocaine kills and harms both directly and indirectly. The direct adverse health effects on those who use the drug are enormous and disastrous. Cocaine sale and use is closely and strongly associated with violent crime. Cocaine importation begets a multiplicity of violent acts. Viewed in isolation from the conduct which inevitably follows the importation of cocaine, *the act itself is not a violent one in the strict sense.* It cannot however, be disassociated from its inevitable consequences. (*Hamilton* C.A., at 104, emphasis added)

The *Criminal Code* does not make a distinction between serious and non-serious crimes, and there is no legal test for determining what should be considered "serious" (Pellitier 2001). Disallowing the application of s. 718.2(e) for "serious" offences essentially renders the provision useless. Section 718.2(e) is meant to direct judges to consider alternative sanctions to incarceration. Offenders who have committed offences that the court does not consider "serious" would likely not be given a sentence of incarceration in the first place.

Furthermore, the new Canadian sentencing legislation contains a conditional sentence option (section 742.1) that diverts cases from the justice system where, in the opinion of the investigating officers and other authorities, it is appropriate (*Criminal Code*, s. 742.1).[20] In *Hamilton*, the Court of Appeal was concerned that the conditional sentences imposed by the trial judge would not have a sufficiently denunciatory or deterrent effect.

> The recruitment of young black poor women with no criminal records to carry cocaine into Canada from Jamaica could be encouraged by a sentencing policy that treats the very factors which make them attractive as couriers as justifying a non-custodial sentence.... The conditional sentences imposed on these respondents can only reinforce in the minds of drug overseers the wisdom of their recruitment philosophy. (*Hamilton* C.A., at 147)

It is highly unlikely that the sentences of Marsha Hamilton and Donna

Mason will have any impact on the activities of the drug overlords in question.

The gravest consequence of the judicial creation of a new category of "serious" offences will be the disproportionate impact on racialized people and Blacks in particular. The war on drugs has already been documented as having a devastating effect on Black communities in the both the U.S. and Canada. "Throughout the drug war, African Americans have been disproportionately investigated, detained, searched, arrested and charged with the use, possession and sale of illegal drugs: this policy has resulted in the phenomenon of "mass incarceration"(Nunn 2002). Similarly, African Canadian men and women have experienced significant increases in prison incarceration, in particular between 1986 and 1993 when there was an exponential increase in the numbers of African Canadians in Toronto prisons on trafficking and importing charges. The *Report of the Commission on Systemic Racism in Ontario* (1995) notes that Canada's drug combat strategy emphasizes pursuing small-time users and dealers — often found in the Black community — rather than pursuing drug overlords or attempting to prevent and treat drug abuse. "Enforcement against street dealers and couriers is much easier [and] brings quick success in the form of convictions and imprisonment" (Report of the Commission on Systemic Racism 1995).[21] The war on drugs has a differential impact on Black peoples: prison admissions have increased threefold since 1970, but the brunt of this policy has been borne by low income Black women (Boyd 2004). The drug war is a prominent example of the central role that both race and the definition of (serious) crime play in the maintenance of subjugation and oppression. The demarcation of certain crimes as "serious" masks racial oppression by allowing it to be represented as a legitimate response to wrongdoing. The contention that drug importation is closely associated with violent acts and thus deserves more serious punishment is reasonable only if this logic is extended to all illegal acts with violent consequences.[22] The politics of defining a crime is merely one example of the ways in which the racial marking of crime serves to limit a consideration of national responsibility. Finally, although the use of sentencing as a means of addressing race-based discrimination is consistent with the policies that underlie Canada's sentencing procedures, the terrain of and strategy of "competing cultures," as evidenced in both the judicial interpretation and the community legal interventions, raises questions about the efficacy of culture claims in the field of compensations politics.

PAST INJUSTICE AND THE MAKING OF LEGITIMATE CITIZENS

The racialization at work in *R.* v. *Hamilton* is apparent on its face, and is signalled by the discourses of race, gender, citizenship, community, crime and poverty that together construct Hamilton and Mason as abhorrent, disenfranchised and categorically "suspect." In addition, the recognition of systemic racism in the lives of Black women is institutionalized, and even legitimized in *R. v. Hamilton* — the decision sets a legal precedent that criminal legal decisions must be cognizant and take judicial notice of systemic racism in Canada. That legal decisions, sentencing and otherwise, recognize the impact of past injustice and systemic racism in the lives of Aboriginal people and people of colour is indeed, an anti-racist legal practice. However, beyond the fact that such legal practices can be considered anti-racist, since the recognition of systemic racism and past injustice is codified in law, how does such a practice reproduce the idea of "national innocence" with the idea of the legitimate, moral citizen forms at the narrative core? Taking judicial notice of past injustice and systemic racism merely normalizes racial inequalities while engaging in a jurisprudential practice that suggests that the law and the nation are somehow detached from the very historical and political processes that both construct and sustain racial subjugation. Naming and codifying "past injustice" and "systemic racism" in the law does not address the racial/colonial practices of dislocation and assimilation, for example, that operate to sustain racial inequalities. In effect, treating the recognition of past injustice and systemic racism as a case of recognizing individual rights under the law does not take into full account the connections between the material practices in the law that work to ensure racial subjugation (through codifying the contours of permissible racial narratives that invite a consideration of "just sentences") and the ideological consequence that exonerates national accountability.

Unless the legal and historical record is advanced to consider both the *material* practices of discrimination in the law and their connection to identity-making processes of racialization, that enable the nation to position itself legally as the moral arbiter of "just sanctions," articulations of national responsibility will remain caught within a legal and historical framework, where "naming" injustice, rather than understanding the ways in which such a naming serves to assuage national accountability, will continue to reinscribe the liberal contention that the law is somehow detached from the historical processes that both construct and sustain it. The ramifications of this approach mean that legal analyses remains caught within a discrimination (under-the-law) framework that does not take into consideration the historical and ideological links between race-thinking and legal practice.[23] More particularly, this approach as outlined in *R. v. Hamilton* does not take into account how the negotiation of past injustice produces subjects, both legitimate (white) Canadian subjects and non-white subjects and ultimately, obscures the understanding of legal inscriptions through their "relationship to identity as well as to justice," as Razack asserts. In liberal democracies, legal subjects come into view relative to the particular conception of justice. As Sheila Dawn Gill explains in an examination of how the articulation of racism operates in legal and parliamentary discourse in Manitoba, the law must be understood as a "privileged and empowered system of moral praxis (that) contributes to the making of normative Canadian subjects" (Gill 2002:

162). When the reality of racism is named publicly, that naming disrupts fundamental precepts of the nation and who "we" know ourselves to be. Gill adds:

> 'We' know ourselves by identifying and separating ourselves from that which 'we' are not, and according to the dominant Canadian mythology, 'we' are not racist... the vast majority of these 'moral' normative subjects remain unmoved in the face of deeply distressing evidence of injustice. More critically, we are unwilling to know ourselves as benefactors and perpetrators of contemporary colonial relations of dominance. (Gill 2002: 62)

More perilously, I would add, the naming of injustice or racism also works to consolidate national innocence by promoting the idea of a nation that names injustice and racism and furthermore, facilitates the legal ability to amend and compensate for past injustice even in the face of criminality. The consequent institutionalization of systemic racism, as outlined in *R. v. Hamilton*, merely serves to demarcate the connection between past injustice and contemporary racism. Moreover, such a jurisprudential practice is entwined and inseparable from universal core values of "human rights" that ultimately work to promote a particular version of national accountability.

In setting out his reasoning in *R. v. Hamilton*, Justice Hill proclaims that "judging in a multicultural society necessarily recognizes the importance of perspective and social context in judicial decision-making" (*R. v. Hamilton*, Ontario Superior Court of Justice (20 February, 2003) at 179). Significantly, national responsibility in a multicultural society materializes only relative to categorical racialized and culturalized inscriptions on subject populations in sentencing decisions. In this way, *R. v. Hamilton* works to uphold such inscriptions by instituting seemingly anti-racist gestures in law. As a consequence, "systemic racism" becomes a legally quantifiable contemporary reality in Canada, abstracted from historical and political processes. The discursive transformation of the "story" of cocaine importation, for example, into one that is organized around (and against) the recognition of systemic racism in the law, through the invocation of certain populations such as "criminal," "offender," "substance abuser" and "racial minority," thus encodes the discourse of citizenship (or "worthy" citizenship) into the discourse of law and order. The racialization at work in this context obscures the way the law itself produces categories and meanings that encode race through legal signifiers, such as past injustice. Furthermore, national responsibility for past injustice — documenting instances of genocide, eviction or border policing — cannot become recognizable within a criminal legal framework that merely itemizes inequality through the invocation of circumscribed racial and cultural identities.

CONCLUSION

I maintain that the narrative about the application of a fair and just sentence as it is recounted in *R. v. Hamilton* is specifically a story about race and the nation. Following the contributions made by other scholars, I argue that regulating bodies of colour in the context of the application of section 718.2(e) is part of the historical manufacturing of the myth of Canada as a white settler society, with a social hierarchy that is ultimately maintained through a methodical, ordered, structured and controlled disciplinary system of racial value.[24] Indeed, *R. v. Hamilton* constitutes only one episode in a historically sustained effort where the law functions as the locus of racialization in Canada and as a primary site for the policing and regulation of political, racial, sexual, cultural and economic membership in the nation.

The Superior Court of Justice's decision and the Court of Appeal's decision in *R. v. Hamilton* reveal a number of insights into the ways in which the logic of national responsibility is currently being deployed in Canadian law. What I demonstrate in this chapter is that the application of section 718.2(e) sets out a kind of legal metrics for assessing national responsibility. This calculus of governance produces particular legal/national effects, whereby national responsibility is warranted only relative to the combined legal operation of: 1) taking judicial notice of past injustice or systemic racism experienced by the subject, and the community to which they belong, before the court; 2) circumscribing claims to personhood (and therefore, "worthiness") through race and culture and inscribing degeneracy on racialized populations; and 3) maintaining that national responsibility is warranted relative only to the presence of cultural justice models in the cultural or racial communities of the defendant. The national and cumulative effects of this legal operation are three-fold. First, for racialized populations, legal personhood can only be recognizable within cultural/racial frames of reference where the application of remedial sentencing manifestly relies upon the criminalization of racialized populations. Secondly, the recognition of systemic racism in the law is a troubling, unsettling strategy at best — one that, on its face, works to address (but not redress) systemic racism, but in fact merely serves to reinscribe the racialization of certain bodies that are marginalized and deemed degenerate. Finally, the application of this metrics of national responsibility highlights the manner in which mechanisms that structure gendered and racialized membership in Canada are part of evolving political and social practices that determine who is deemed a legitimate and lawful citizen. In essence, I maintain that while the recognition of systemic racism in law is a necessary juridical move, the production of legal knowledge about the impact of systemic racism is central to the sustained manufacturing of legitimate citizens. The racial narratives at work in *R. v. Hamilton* serve a dual function for the project of law and nation building: by circumscribing their claims to personhood along racial and cultural lines, they invite the subject before the court into the universal core values of "human rights"; at the same time, these racial narratives function to inscribe notions of national accountability for past injustice. Furthermore, the legal strategy of attempting to recognize "different differences," as evidenced in this context, is an uneasy one at best. In compensation narratives in the law, the recognition of "different differences" is an uneasy strategy: in order to position itself as multicultural, the nation must perform its past as a singular narrative, telling a legal story of its past in the presence of (and against) subjects circumscribed within a singular and unitary understanding of "cultural difference," that ultimately serves national interest. What results is not an adequate demonstration of multicultural recognition of "different differences" (if that is at all possible), but the story of a unified national (white-settler) culture where the reinvention of Canada as a multicultural nation requires the disavowal of colonial violence upon which the nation and law depends. I have unravelled (some of) the basis of the jurisprudence of national responsibility in *R.* v. *Hamilton* to show how claims to national responsibility come into national/legal purview relative only to the subjects such a practice produces.

In the Canadian context, the production of the nation works to inscribe, through the law and elsewhere, identity-making practices — both individual and national — that are enacted through processes which claim to articulate a kind of national responsibility. Positioning Canada as a nation that facilitates the legal ability to amend and compensate for past injustice is a powerful trope in the story of a nation bent on extolling its liberal virtues to the world.[25] In the context of an historically situated legal framework, it is imperative to analyze the systematically gendered and racialized effects of legal claims to national responsibility and identify inclusions/exclusions that are being enacted through such a legal process. What I have tried to illustrate through the application of section 718.2(e) in *R.* v. *Hamilton* is that, even where the law claims to be compassionate, its application requires coercive legal circumscriptions for particular subjects along racial and gendered lines. In addition, I argue that such inscriptions work to produce subjects, both legitimate (white) Canadian subjects and non-white subjects, while engaging in a jurisprudential practice that suggests that the law and the nation are somehow detached from the very historical and political processes that both construct and sustain racial subjugation. Finally, I suggest that an examination of the contingencies of race and the law should not only operate through a mode of inquiry that is overdetermined by a legal optic that merely assesses individual subjects before the court. Instead, I maintain that investigating legal claims to social/national responsibility should also be examined through a mode of inquiry that is cognizant of the impact of what appear to be anti-racist and/or anti-colonial legal incentives (incentives that identify a nation's own role and complicity in past injustice) and how they ultimately work to consolidate a particular version of the nation that is upheld by the implementation of individual and group justice.

NOTES

1. One need only reference colonization and slavery as founding racist projects from which the West has benefited. As John Torpey (2003: 17) has pointed out, in the context of examining claims to reparations and restitution in North America, Aboriginal peoples and Blacks "share the historical conditions of having been forcibly subjected to white European domination, but here the similarities end. Although indigenes were subordinated as a result of conquest on the home grounds, blacks were subjugated through forced migration and enslavement on lands distant from their origins."

2. Researching empirical data from refugee hearings, Sherene Razack (1998: 88–129) found that the process of culturalization that operates in a refugee hearing (the legal operation of cultural difference as a marker of inferiority) requires a disavowal of the ways in which capitalism and racism work to sustain patriarchal violence.

3. There are a number of critiques of restorative approaches to justice in the context of sentencing. For example, Annalise Acorn (2004: 19) argues that restorative approaches to justice can also be characterized as "compulsory compassion" approaches to justice whereby compassion, and narratives of compassion, forms both the procedural and conceptual structure of restorative justice. Compassion, in this sense, Acorn argues, is utilized as a legal manoeuvre, and inducts all the parties in the legal encounter (judges, defendants and lawyers) to right (actual and perceived) wrongs and injustices. Employing this analysis of restorative justice in the context of criminal sentencing I would ask the following question: In what way does the demand for justice, using restorative justice approaches, contrast with the image of a nation that is profoundly invested in liberal discourses of recognition?

4. David Goldberg (2002) underlines this conception of the constitution of the racial state through a Gramscian understanding of the edifice of hegemony that requires both coercion and consent for full statist expression *and* upon an understanding of the formation of racial governmentalities, in the Foucauldian sense, that requires both programmatic subjection (in the form of disciplinary administrative apparatuses) and the replication of subjection through individual embodiment and performance. Goldberg relies on this Foucauldian conception of subjects within the state in order to show how the law regulates social behaviour and determines the political contours of the state.

5. Biopower functions through state power and is connected to state policies because, as Foucault asserts, certain populations can be adjusted in accordance with state processes involved in the process of nation building. Foucault (1990: 143) defines "biopower as a political technology that brought life and its mechanisms into the realm of explicit calculations and made knowledge/power an agent of transformation of human life."

6. This is congruent to what is understood as the violence of law. The foregrounding of the violence of law in the production and maintenance of modern state racial order is (loosely) reliant upon Jacques Derrida's (2002) work on the violent force of law. Even though the term "violence" is most often used to refer to physical acts directed at particular bodies, Derrida suggests a different genealogy of violence, one whose core structure is both metaphysical and corporeal. Derrida highlights an understanding of the metaphysiclal violence of law: when coupled with Foucauldian understanding of racial governmentalities, law's violence

can (and must) be understood as an empirical historical reality inherent to the structure of law itself. However, in order to begin to unravel the idea of law's inherent violence as a methodological question and as an historical construct central to contemporary state order, it is imperative to historicize colonial violence as constitutive of narratives of progress and linearity that often structure legal interventions in modern nation states.

7. This is both real and imagined. Aboriginal peoples have been and continue to be murdered in the name of the law. Scholars also suggest that liberal democratic nations are now haunted (and obsessed) with the ghosts of Aboriginal peoples and colonial violence. Following these arguments, a "discourse of haunted rationalism" operates through law because the "nation is compelled to return again to an encounter that makes it both sorry and happy, a defiled grave upon which it must continually rebuild" (Bergland 2000: 8 and 22).

8. Furthermore, colonialism has always required cultural narratives in order to accomplish its aims of genocide and exploitation, and these cultural expressions, as Nicholas Thomas (1994: 2) points out, "are not simply ideologies that mask, mystify or rationalize forms of oppression that are external to them; they are also expressive and constitutive of colonial relations themselves" (see also Said 1993).

9. Jamie Tanis Gladue is an Aboriginal woman who pled guilty to manslaughter for the killing of her common law husband and was sentenced to three years imprisonment. Although the Supreme Court of Canada provided the first interpretation of section 718.2(e), Gladue herself did not benefit from the provision because her crime was deemed "too serious" to warrant consideration (*R.* v. *Gladue* [(1999) 1 S.C.R. 688]).

10. *R.* v. *Borde* set out this legal precedent, borrowing at length from the Report of the Commission on Systemic Racism in the Ontario Criminal Justice System (Toronto: Queen's Printer for Ontario, 1995). *R.* v. *Borde*, Court of Appeal for Ontario (10 February, 2003) at 18–24.

11. Many scholars point to the ways in which remorse functions as a disciplinary function in the legal procedure of sentencing hearings. Some argue that subjects *must* appear adequately remorseful in order to benefit from the remedial incentives in provisions like section 718.2(e) (see Weisman 2004: 121–38; Anderson 1999: 303–26). I would suggest that the disciplinary function of remorse operates through a moral and racial logic in a sentencing hearing: remorse functions to inscribe an idea of "worthy citizenship" (worthy of the "rights" secured by citizenship) which are organized along racial lines.

12. The Appeal decision is consolidated and in addition to *R.* v. *Hamilton* it includes *R.* v. *Spencer*. Tracey Spencer, also a Black woman who pleaded guilty to cocaine importation received a college education and had full-time employment as a nurse. In the Crown's facta and in the oral argument at the Appeal hearing it was argued that these factors (education and employment status) did not render Spencer as *deserving* of a "reduced" sentence.

13. There are a number of scholars in Canada who have examined the operation of "national innocence" in Canadian law. For example, Sherene Razack (2002) argues that "white settler innocence" underscores Canadian national mythologies in the law. Constance Backhouse (1999) utilizes the idea of "stupefying innocence" embedded within what she calls the "mythology of racelessness" that together produce national innocence in Canada in her examination of the legal history of race and racism in the first half of the twentieth century.

14. The Court of Appeal was disapproving of the fact that the trial judge had introduced several hundred pages of materials on which the parties were expected to make submissions, substantially broadening the scope of the sentencing hearing, which lasted several months. The "trial judge effectively took over the sentencing proceedings, and in doing so went beyond the role assigned to a trial judge" (*Hamilton* C.A., at 7). Notwithstanding the criticism of the trial judge it is important to note that: (a) s. 723(3) of the *Criminal Code* provides that a court may require the production of evidence that "would assist in the determination of the appropriate sentence" (*Criminal Code*); (b) the trial judge had a judicial duty to inquire into the background of the offenders as per the *Gladue* test at *R.* v. *Gladue* 84–85 (see also *R.* v. *Wells*, (2000), 141 C.C.C. (3d) 368 (Can) at 390–91); and (c) the Crown did not object to the manner in which the proceedings were conducted, but instead fully participated in those proceedings *Hamilton* C.A., at 38. The trial judge is also criticized for using personal observations in determining "the relevance, if any of race or gender to sentencing practices as applied to cocaine importation" (*Hamilton* C.A., at 79).
15. Culture claims in law most often operate through national frames of reference. Seyla Benhabib (2002: 5 and 8), for example, situates her understanding of culture claims within national narratives and frames of reference arguing that what distinguishes her understanding of the culture concept "is the narrative view of action and culture that informs" national ideologies. Maneesha Dekha (2004: 14–53) provides a synthesis of the legal scholarship on the use of culture to frame equality jurisprudence.
16. The idea of "Aboriginal culture" is a slippery concept and is organized through colonial ideologies of racial difference: this has been shown by others for other national and institutional contexts like schooling. Where the cultural argument is employed the "concept is not innocent, but is deeply implicated in the colonial enterprise" (St. Denis 2002: 12).
17. Factum of the Intervener Aboriginal Legal Services of Toronto Inc., at 3, 31.
18. *R.* v. *Spencer* was heard with the Hamilton and Mason appeals.
19. In yet another move to interpret the case from a cultural perspective, the Supreme Court of Canada clearly held in *Gladue* that, despite the fact that Jamie Tanis Gladue lived off the reserve, suggesting her potential distance from her "authentic" Aboriginal heritage, she was entitled to benefit from section 718.2(e) in order to fulfill Parliament's mandate to rectify the overincarceration of "all offenders, with particular attention to the circumstances of aboriginal offenders."
20. A conditional sentence is a sentence of less than two years that is served in the community subject to the conditions prescribed in the order. A conditional sentence is not available where the offence provides for a mandatory minimum term of imprisonment such as, murder. A conditional sentence is generally ordered where the court is satisfied that serving the sentence in the community would not endanger the safety of the community and would be consistent with the fundamental purpose and principles of sentencing in s. 718 to 718.2 of the *Criminal Code*.
21. The Commission on Systemic Racism in the Ontario Criminal Justice System was established in 1992 by the New Democratic Party of Ontario to enquire into and make recommendations about the extent to which criminal justice practices, procedures, and policies in Ontario reflect systemic racism. The inquiry examined three major components of the criminal justice system: the

police, courts and correctional institutions. See Canadian Foundation for Drug Policy <http://www.cfdp. ca/ontrac.html>. (Accessed January 23, 2005.)

22. However, not all crimes with violent consequences are labelled as serious and result in prison sentences. In the instance of corporate crimes, such as the violation of environmental or workplace regulations that have resulted in the deaths of hundreds of people, a comparable logic has not been followed. The direct, adverse and often violent health effects of "white collar" crimes do not result in the more serious designation at sentencing. On the contrary, these crimes are distinguished as less serious or quasi-criminal (Glasbeek 2002).

23. Kay Anderson (1991: 19) argues that there are limitations to any analysis of race that operates within a prejudice/discrimination framework. She argues that while "the prejudice concept has informed a long tradition of race-relations research, it is difficult to locate its explanatory value." In effect, she urges scholars "to take a step beyond studying white attitudes, because it is not prejudice that has explanatory power but rather the ideology of racial difference that informs it."

24. For more examples of scholars that examine the colonial foundation of the myth of Canada as a white settler society see Razack (2000) and Anderson (2000).

25. Canada has taken a lead role internationally to address national accountability. In 2000, Canada was the first country to adopt legislation to assist in formally implementing the International Criminal Court. In addition, through the Ministry of International and Foreign Affairs, Canada has begun an International Criminal Court and Accountability Campaign which promotes "Canada's commitment to the International Criminal Court and to international criminal justice" through encouraging other nations to join forces in the International Criminal Court. See Ministry of International and Foreign Affairs Canada, "Canada and the International Criminal Court" <http://www.dfait maeci. gc.ca/foreign_policy /icc/canada-en.asp>. (Accessed May 5 2004.)

REFERENCES

Acorn, Annalise. 2004. *Compulsory Compassion: A Critique of Restorative Justice.* Vancouver: UBC Press.

Anderson, Chris. 1999. "Governing Aboriginal Justice in Canada: Constructing Responsible Individuals and Communities through 'Tradition.'" *Crime, Law and Social Change* 31.

Anderson, Kay. 1991. *Vancouver's Chinatown: Racial Discourse in Canada, 1885–1980.* Montreal: McGill-Queen's.

_____. 2000. "Thinking 'Postnationally': Dialogue Across Multicultural, Indigenous and Settler Spaces." *Annals of the Association of American Geographers* 90, 2.

Backhouse, Constance. 1999. *Colour-Coded: A Legal History of Racism in Canada, 1900–1950.* Toronto: Osgoode Society for Canadian Legal History.

Barkan, Elazar. 2000. *The Guilt of Nations: Restitution and Negotiating Historical Injustices.* New York: Norton.

Benhabib, Seyla. 2002. *The Claims of Culture: Equality, Difference in the Global Era.* Princeton, NJ: Princeton University Press.

Bergland, Renee. 2000. *The National Uncanny: Indian Ghosts and American Subjects.* Hanover and London: University Press of New England..

Berlant, Lauren. 1991. *The Anatomy of National Fantasy: Hawthorne, Utopia, and Everyday Life.* Chicago: University of Chicago Press.

Boyd, S. 2004. *From Witches to Crack Moms: Women, Drug Law and Policy*. North Carolina: Carolina Academic Press.

Daubney, David, and Gordon Parry. 1999. "An Overview of Bill C-41." In David Daubney (ed.), *Making Sense of Sentencing*. Toronto: University of Toronto Press.

Davis, Angela. 2002. "Incarceration and the Imbalance of Power." In M. Mauer and M. Chesney-Lind (eds.), *Invisible Punishment*. New York: New York Press.

Dekha, Maneesha. 2004. "Is Culture Taboo? Feminism, Intersectionality and Culture Talk in the Law." *Canadian Journal of Women and the Law* 16, 1.

Derrida, Jacques. 2002. "Force of Law: The 'Mystical Foundations of Authority.'" In Gil Anidjar (ed.), *Acts of Religion*. New York: Routledge.

Foucault, Michel. 1990. *The History of Sexuality: Vol. 1*. New York: Vintage Books.

Gill, Sheila Dawn. 2002. "The Unspeakability of Racism: Mapping Law's Complicity in Manitoba's Racialized Spaces." In Sherene Razack (ed.), *Race, Space and the Law: Unmapping a White Settler Society*. Toronto: Between the Lines.

Glasbeek, Harry. 2002. *Wealth by Stealth: Corporate Crime, Corporate Law, and the Perversion of Democracy*. Toronto: Between the Lines.

Goldberg, David. 1993. *Racist Culture*. MA: Blackwell Publishers.

_____. 2002. *The Racial State*. MA: Blackwell Publishers.

Hughes, Patricia, and Mary Jane Mossman. 2002. "Re-Thinking Access to Criminal Justice in Canada: A Critical Review of Needs and Responses." *Windsor Review of Legal and Social Issues* 13, 1.

Law Reform Commission (Ireland). 1996. *Report on Sentencing*. LRC 53-1996. Dublin Law reform Commission.

Nunn, Kenneth. 2002. "Race, Crime and the Pool of Surplus Criminality: Or Why the 'War on Drugs' was a 'War on Blacks.'" *Journal of Gender Race and Justice* 6, 381.

Pelletier, Renee. 2001. "The Nullification of Section 718.2(e): Aggravating Aboriginal Over-Representation Canadian Prisons." *Osgoode Hall Law Journal* 39.

Razack, Sherene H. 1999. "Making Canada White: Law and the Policing of Bodies of Colour in the 1990s." *Canadian Journal of Law and Society* 14, 1.

_____. 1999. *Looking White People in the Eye: Gender, Race and Culture in Courtrooms and Classrooms*. Toronto: University of Toronto Press.

_____. 2000. "'Simple Logic:' Race, The Identity Documents Rule and The Story of a Nation Besieged and Betrayed." *Journal of Law and Social Policy* 15.

Report of the Commission on Systemic Racism in the Ontario Criminal Justice System. 1995. Toronto: Queen's Printer for Ontario.

Roach, Kent, and Jonathan Rudin. 2000. "*Gladue*: The Judicial and Political Reception of a Promising Decision." *Canadian Journal of Criminology* 42, 3.

Royal Commission on Aboriginal Peoples. 1996. *Bridging the Cultural Divide: A Report on Aboriginal People and Criminal Justice in Canada*. Ottawa: Minister of Supply and Services.

Rudin, Jonathan. 2003. "Justice, Race and Time." *Toronto Star*. February 17.

Said, Edward. 1993. *Culture and Imperialism*. New York: Vintage Books.

St. Denis, Verna. 2002. "Exploring the Socio-Cultural Production of Aboriginal Identities: Implications for Education." Ph.D. Dissertation, Stanford University.

Sudbury, Julia. 2004. "'Mules,' 'Yardies,' and Other Folk Devils: Mapping Cross-Border Imprisonment in Britain." In Julia Sudbury (ed.), *Global Lockdown: Race, Gender and the Prison-Industrial Complex*. London and New York: Routledge.

Thomas, Nicholas. 1993. *Colonialism's Culture: Anthropology, Travel and Government*.

New Jersey: Princeton University Press.

Thompson, Janna. 2001. "Historical Injustice and Reparation: Justifying Claims of Descendants." *Ethics* 112 (October), 114–135.

Torpey, John. 2003. *Politics of the Past: On Repairing Historical Injustice.* Oxford: Rowman & Littlefield.

Weisman, Richard. 2004. "Showing Remorse: Reflections on the Gap between Expression and Attribution in Cases of Wrongful Conviction." *Canadian Journal of Criminology and Criminal Justice* 46, 2.

COURT CASES

R. v. *Borde* (2003), 172 C.C.C. (3d) 225 (Ont. C.A.)

R. v. *Gladue* [(1999) 1 S.C.R. 688]

R. v. *Hamilton* [2004] O.J. No. 3252 [Q.L.] (Ont. C.A.).

R. v. *Spencer* [2004] O.J. No. 3262 (Ont. C.A.)

STATUTES–

Criminal Code (R.S. 195, c. C-46)

Immigration and refugee Protection Act, S.C. 2001, c. 27.

CHAPTER 4

RE-PLACING (IN) JUSTICE:
DISABILITY-RELATED FACILITIES AT THE ONTARIO MUNICIPAL BOARD (OMB).[1]

LILITH FINKLER

INTRODUCTION

While deinstitutionalization began in Ontario more than thirty years ago (Simmons 1990, 1982; Marshall 1982), disabled persons are still sometimes denied access to homes in residential neighbourhoods. Disability-related facilities such as group homes and nursing homes often meet intense opposition when establishing themselves in residential neighbourhoods (Cork 2004; Stewart 2004; Welch 2004). Although initial concerns may focus on parking and safety, overt expressions of resistance to the presence of disabled persons in the community may also arise (Moloney 2004). Residents' fears of declining property values are often featured prominently in media coverage of local controversies (Da Silva 2004). These conflicts, which focus on the right to place, are often referred to as NIMBY (Not In My Back Yard) disputes. Frequently, such disputes require formal adjudication of the planning controversy. At least one geographer argues that marginalization of disabled persons occurs contemporaneously with NIMBY activities (Gleeson 1999).

This chapter, which utilized Ontario Municipal Board (OMB) decisions rendered between January 2000 and August 2004 to obtain data regarding disability-related facilities, focuses on the ways in which disabled persons are understood and conceptualized in a land-use law context. Scholars investigating land-use law have not considered disability as a social phenomenon. If disability is examined at all, it is within the context of specific building codes that eliminate physical barriers posed by inaccessible environments. Disability analysis, however, requires more than measurements for a ramp. It demands that disability perspectives be integrated within all aspects of intellectual inquiry. Unfortunately, disabled persons' perspectives regarding planning practices are rarely considered as evidence at OMB hearings.

This chapter aims to correct this omission by placing an analysis of disability and disability-related facilities at the centre of critical land-use law discourse. I argue that the OMB re-places the social injustice of segregation by supporting the siting of disability-related facilities in residential neighbourhoods.

Despite vigorous opposition, organizations administering disability-related facilities typically receive OMB approval to locate homes in the desired area. However, the reasoning the OMB demonstrates in arriving at their decisions complicates this reversal of previous injustice. OMB members evince both sympathy for, and condescension towards, disabled persons. The intellectual framework within which the OMB renders its decisions conceives of disabled persons primarily, if not exclusively, as recipients of care. Details mentioned in the decisions suggest that disability-related facilities are subject to a scrutiny which other forms of shelter do not endure. If this is indeed the case, then one can only conclude that the injustice of segregation must be replaced not only within residential neighbourhoods, but within the administrative tribunal itself, within the (in)justice system.

In the first part of the chapter, I briefly describe the Ontario Municipal Board in the context of its structure as an administrative tribunal. In the second part, I outline the analytical framework within which I examine the research data. I describe the social model of disability and its application to OMB decisions. I also elaborate on my research method and the criteria I used to select relevant cases. In part three, I examine the ways in which some OMB decisions have constructed "impairment" (a difficulty with physical, emotional or cognitive function present in a particular individual) and "disability" (a social construct, similar to race, gender and class, which emphasizes physical/mental impairments as categories of social exclusion; also refers to the social and attitudinal barriers that people with impairments experience). By studying legal texts, I interrogate able-bodied bias embedded in land use law. My critical reading of OMB documents emphasizes disability as a category of legal, social and spatial analysis. By examining the arguments used to challenge the siting of disability-related facilities, I hope to expose social constructions of disability that both reflect and reinforce discriminatory attitudes and experiences. I also discuss efforts made by advocates to raise human rights and charter issues at the OMB. By strengthening the OMB's ability to apply the Ontario Human Rights Code (OHRC) to its decisions, it may be possible to limit NIMBY efforts directed at disabled persons. I conclude that the OMB resisted NIMBYism focused on the exclusion of disabled persons, although it did so in a manner which buttressed stereotypic attitudes and oppressive planning practices.

PART ONE: ADMINISTRATIVE TRIBUNALS

Administrative tribunals are quasi-judicial bodies that adjudicate within the framework of a particular legal regime. For example, the Canada Pension Plan Appeal Tribunal determines if applicants qualify for the Canada Pension Plan (CPP) benefits under its disability provisions. The Criminal Injuries Compensation Board (CICB) determines if applicants are victims of crime and, if so, whether they are entitled to a monetary award as compensation for loss of income or pain and suffering. Adjudicators may be lawyers, but they do not have to be.

Tribunals are often more accessible and informal than the courts. Typically, tribunals allow members of the public to represent themselves. Sometimes, legal staff is specifically assigned to assist individuals with the processing of their applications. For example, at the Ontario Rental Housing Tribunal,[2] a duty counsel may assist tenants in asserting their legal rights. Rights Advisors are appointed under the Mental Health Act to provide information and complete applications requesting appeals to the Ontario Consent and Capacity Board.[3] Such opportunities are rarely available at court.

In theory, disabled persons can access administrative tribunals easily. However, since they are disproportionately impoverished as compared with the general population (Lee 2000), they can rarely afford access to higher courts. The physical pain associated with disability or the environmental and attitudinal barriers present in the judicial system increase the frustration that many disabled persons experience (Lepofsky 1995). Lengthy litigation can create additional psychological and physical burdens on already vulnerable people.

Although administrative tribunals are accessible to persons unrepresented by lawyers, there are, nonetheless, still significant power imbalances between decision makers and subjects of a hearing. Some tribunals, such as those constituted by the regulated health professions, require that tribunal members be peers of those under investigation. However, at other tribunals, notions of "expert knowledge" may place tribunal members in direct conflict with the individual(s) about whom they are making a decision. Disabled persons frequently have decisions made about them by those who claim disability-related expertise on their behalf. For example, at Consent and Capacity Board hearings, a three-member panel will include a lawyer, a psychiatrist and a layperson. The psychiatrist is considered a medical expert. However, the very nature of the expertise in question may, for example, put the practitioner in direct opposition to psychiatric patients involuntarily detained in a psychiatric facility. Disabled persons may wish to leave the facility while the doctor usually decides they should remain. Because of the authority accorded to medical professionals, persons with psychiatric impairments may become invisible in the legal proceedings (Arrigo 1993).

The Ontario Municipal Board (OMB)

Land use in Canada is governed by provincial legislation that mandates public participation and efforts at consensus building. In the absence of community agreement, provincial statutes typically permit an appeal to an administrative tribunal.[4] In Ontario, local residents and/or housing providers may appeal municipal decisions to the OMB. The OMB hears parties present their case and then, based on expert evidence and witness testimony, determines whether the proposed use constitutes good planning. Appeals from municipal decisions to an administrative tribunal are allowed in most provinces only when citing errors in law (Epstein 2004). In Ontario, however, appeals to the OMB are heard de novo. Both parties to a proceeding can present their case anew, elaborating on both the facts and matters of law.

The OMB hears appeals pertaining to matters such as zoning by-laws, variances, land compensation, official plans and subdivision plans. The Board operates under approximately one hundred different pieces of legislation, including the *Planning Act* (1990). The tribunal was originally instituted as a municipal and railway authority in 1906. Legislators delegated complex municipal matters to the OMB so they could curtail their own heavy workload (Laskin 1937).

Applicants to the OMB can represent themselves, although retaining a lawyer is considered wise.[5] The OMB process is frequently litigious. Fortunately, staff assistance is available; further guidance to applicants is being contemplated.[6] Forms available on the OMB website guide applicants though the appeal process.[7]

There are no statutory requirements that members of the OMB be planners or architects or belong to designated professions.[8] However, Section 27(1) of the *Ontario Municipal Board Act* provides for specific appointment of experts.[9] OMB members tend to be lawyers, planners, engineers, architects and related professionals (Krushelnicki 2003). Board members consider carefully the testimony of planning experts and quote their comments in the decisions. Disabled persons, even if they are the subjects of the hearing, appear invisible in the cases under deliberation. Their expertise is not considered authoritative. This privileging of professional knowledge reinforces the divide between "experts" and disabled persons who are often the subject of investigation.

One can appeal an OMB decision to Divisional Court if an error in law has been made. The test for an appeal appears in *Toronto Transit Commission v. Toronto (City)* (1990) where Justice O'Brien, citing an earlier decision, stated that

> leave to appeal in these matters [OMB] should only be granted where the court is satisfied there is a point of law of sufficient importance to merit the attention of the Divisional Court and there is some reason to doubt the correctness of the Board's decision. (*Toronto (City)* v. *Torgan Developments* (1990) M.P.L.R., para. 7)

In *London (City)* v. *Ayerswood Development Corporation* (2002), Justices O'Connor, Laskin and Borins stated that

> The proper standard of review was one of correctness or reasonableness, depending on the nature of the particular question of law. Questions of law that engage the specialized expertise of the Board, such as interpretation of its own statute, attract a standard of reasonableness. Questions of law that are of general application

for which the Board has no special expertise are reviewed on a standard of correctness. (*London (City)* v. *Ayerswood* Development Corporation (December 13, 2002), para. 7)

The implications of the above decisions are clear. If the OMB made a decision about an issue directly related to their area of specialization, a court of appeal would examine it and determine if the decision was "reasonable" under the circumstances. However, if the OMB addressed an issue such as an allegation of human rights violations, the decision would have to be "correct" in law. The latter threshold is much higher and consequently is much less likely to survive judicial scrutiny at the appellate level.

Since 1998, there have been only nine OMB cases appealed to Ontario Court of Appeal (OCA) and one Supreme Court of Canada (SCC) case. According to Mark Michaels,[10] counsel for the OMB, 90 percent of the tribunal's cases deal with disputes under the *Planning Act* (1990). Only 10 percent focus on *Expropriation Act* (1990) or other areas of jurisdiction. Since 1998, there have been three appeals under the *Planning Act* (1990).[11] In contrast, there have been three appeals under the *Expropriation Act* (1990),[12] two appeals under the *Assessment Act* (1990),[13] and one under the *Development Charges Act* (1997).[14] The one appeal of an OMB decision heard by the Supreme Court of Canada addressed *Expropriation-Act*-related matters.[15] None of the cases appealed from the OMB to higher courts has dealt with disability-related facilities.

PART TWO: ANALYTICAL APPROACH

The Centrality of Disabled Persons' Perspectives
OMB activities may be viewed as generally peripheral to disabled persons' concerns. Nonetheless, the OMB must address a variety of disability-related issues. Disability-related facilities such as group homes, nursing homes and homeless shelters are the subject of appeals. Individuals and/or citizens' groups opposed to the siting of facilities in their neighbourhood, or housing providers whose development applications have been refused, may challenge a municipality's decision.

Sadly, disabled persons' perspectives are rarely mentioned. Of the thirty-one cases examined for this study, disabled peoples' voices are referred to in only one decision[16] and quoted directly in only one.[17] This invisibility in the Canadian land use law context mirrors the invisibility that disabled persons have experienced in the professional planning arena. The disregard for disabled persons' concerns appears in sharp contrast to OMB decisions regarding other NIMBY-related conflicts. For example, a separate review of OMB decisions addressing places of worship,[18] found that the perspectives of worshippers were frequently included in the decisions (Finkler 2002).

The evidence highlighted within OMB decisions and court judgments usually emphasizes the opinions of "qualified planners," professional experts who may not appreciate the lived reality of disabled individuals. Planners, representing local ratepayers' associations, municipalities and housing providers, present conflicting information about proposed developments. Housing providers' perspectives and those of their opposition typically dominate the text.

Unless groups advocating on behalf of disabled persons can afford legal costs or, alternatively, qualify for legal aid,[19] they are unable to obtain representation at a hearing. However, even when disabled persons do retain lawyers and obtain party status, as they did in an appeal initiated by the Cabbagetown South Association (*Toronto (City) Official Plan Amendment No. 244* (Re) [2003], O.M.B.D. No. 792), their voices are still not included in the decisions rendered. In thirty-one decisions reviewed for this study, only one group home resident is quoted (see *Newmarket (Town) Official Plan Amendment No. 20* (Re) [2004], O.M.B.D. No. 41, paragraph 27): Mr. Tom Hanly[20] indicated that "he likes the responsibility of living without staff." The OMB, however, frowned upon the idea of unsupervised housing and denied the operator's application for an amendment to the *Official Plan*.

It is a central premise of this paper that disability-centred perspectives must be integrated into an analysis of land use law. Such perspectives would ensure the active participation of disabled persons, integrate the views of disabled persons and ally itself with the goals of the Disability Rights Movement (DRM) (Charlton 1999; Deegan 1992; De Jong 1979).[21]

The Social Model of Disability and its Application to OMB Decisions
The word, "disability" is generally interpreted within a "medical model" framework. This approach understands disability as a limitation located within the body or mind of an individual and is often characterized as an "affliction" and/or "tragedy" (Michalko 2002). Such language locates the social problem of disability within the confines of medicalized bodies and minds, negating capacities, sensibilities or agency.

Among disability studies scholars, however, the language used reflects entirely different analyses. "Impairment" refers to difficulties with physical, emotional or cognitive function. "Disability" describes social and attitudinal barriers that people with impairments experience (Oliver 1990). For example, wheelchair users have a physical impairment. They are, however, disabled by the architecturally ubiquitous staircase. The physical environment planned, created and maintained by the able-bodied population reflects the needs of those who conceived it.

This analysis, referred to as the social model, argues that inaccessible environments create more obstacles than impairments themselves (Barnes, 1998). The social model insists that disability is not an individual impediment, but like gender, race and class, a social construction to be dismantled. Many articles in the spatial literature reproduce able-bodied perspectives by emphasizing the relationship that persons with impairments have to their local care-giving institution (Parr 2000; Gleeson 1998; Philo 1997;

Radford and Park 1993). Disabled persons are rendered invisible outside the institutional context in which they previously resided. Describing socio-spatial relations solely through institutionally based relationships reinforces disabled persons' roles as recipients of care rather than as independent agents resisting an oppressive society. By describing disabled persons almost exclusively in relation to facilities which they would inhabit, I risk reproducing the above problematic paradigm. Nonetheless, I hope to challenge portrayals of disabled persons in OMB decisions within the context of a social model analysis.

Method of Study: Case Selection Criteria

This chapter examines decisions rendered by the OMB between January 2000 and August 2004. Only those cases that focused primarily, if not exclusively, on facilities for disabled persons were included. Senior citizens' facilities were incorporated due to the implicit connection between seniors and Alzheimer's disease or senile dementia (National Advisory Council on Aging 2003). Homeless shelters are also included in this paper as disability-related facilities. Studies have consistently confirmed a high correlation between psychiatric impairment and homelessness (Bridgeman 2003; Mayor's Taskforce on Homelessness 1999). Psychiatric survivors,[22] therefore, constitute a high percentage of the population using homeless shelters as a form of housing.

I used a variety of case selection criteria. A search of all OMB decisions was conducted on the database Quicklaw.[23] Key words such as "disabled," "mentally ill," "group home," "halfway house" and "homeless" were used to locate OMB decisions involving disabled persons. Searches conducted using terms such as "shelter," "ramp" and "patients" yielded hundreds of cases I did not peruse. A more thorough investigation may, therefore, yield a higher number of cases.

I reviewed all cases for their relevance to the subject under investigation. First, I determined whether the appeal involved a disability-related facility. Second, I ensured that the facility was the primary issue under dispute. Ten cases addressed a disability-related issue but were otherwise deemed irrelevant. These cases focused on financial matters rather than on the facility or dealt with individual homeowners wishing to modify the structure of their houses. Two cases focused on redevelopment plans proposed by disability-related institutions. Although the latter disputes contained compelling narratives that pitted former inhabitants of the institutions against current administrations, these cases also did not fit the strict NIMBY-focused case criteria.

Two factors limited the number of decisions which were available on the database. First, only those cases that led to a full hearing are sent by the OMB to Quicklaw. According to recent annual reports, approximately 1800 cases are opened each year.[24] It is unclear, however, exactly what percentage of opened files actually proceed to full hearing.[25] In addition, some NIMBY cases were not appealed to the OMB, but rather, were heard in another legal venue. For example, *Lighthouse Niagara Resource Centre v. the Corporation of Niagara Falls* (2003) was originally heard in front of the Superior Court of Justice. The City of Niagara Falls argued that the words "community building," as defined in the city's zoning by-law, did not refer to a shelter for homeless youth. On appeal, the court held that, in fact, a shelter for youth did comply with the meaning intended in the zoning by-law and therefore, plans for the shelter could proceed.[26] Because of the OMB focus of this research, I did not examine NIMBY cases which were not heard originally by the tribunal.

PART THREE: FINDINGS

After reviewing cases associated with the original keywords, I noted thirty-one relevant decisions. Fourteen contested sites were located in the Greater Toronto Area (GTA) and seventeen others were in smaller towns and cities. One group home was located in a rural area. As noted in Figure 4.1, potential neighbours opposed the developments in sixteen cases. In nine situations, the municipality refused the housing application; in these cases, the developer appealed. In six cases, there was a hearing focused on procedural matters. However, despite sometimes significant controversy, the OMB approved all but three proposed applications for disability-related housing and services. Disabled persons may well be invisible within the legal planning context. However, the OMB appears to have successfully subverted attempts to deny disabled individuals their rightful place in community spaces.

Figure 4.2, which illustrates the nature of the contested facilities and the type of intended occupants, points out that 58 percent of proposed sites provided services or housing to psychiatric survivors or homeless people. Seniors' facilities were group homes or nursing homes. Only five contested sites provided housing for developmentally disabled persons. This is a relatively small number when considering the many group homes administered by Associations for Community Living across Ontario (organizations that provide residential services for developmentally disabled individuals across Ontario). The Toronto Association for Community Living (TACL) alone administers fifty-one group homes, none of which have been the subject of an appeal to the OMB in the time frame covered by this study (Toronto Association for Community Living [TACL] 2004).

Figure 4.1
Appeals to the OMB and their outcomes

Opposition and Result (by year)	2000	2001	2002	2003	2004	Total for 4.5 year period
Neighbours' Appeal	4	5	2	4	1	16
Housing Provider Appeal	2	0	2	2	3	9
OMB Approval of Project	6	5	3	6	2	22
OMB Denial of Project	0	0	1	0	2	3
Procedural Matters	0	3	0	2	1	6
Total Number of Cases in Year	6	8	4	8	5	31

Figure 4.2
Contested Facilities 2000–2004 by proposed occupant and nature of site

Proposed Occupant	Psychiatric Survivors	Homeless Persons	Addicted Persons	Seniors	Developmentally Disabled Persons
Number and Percent	10 = 32%	8 = 26%	1 = 1%	7 = 23%	5 = 16%
Nature of Site		Homeless Shelter			
	Group Home	Soup Kitchen		Nursing Home	
			Small Farm Residence		
	Apartment Building	Drop-In Centre		Group Home	Group Home

THEMES EMERGING FROM THE DECISIONS

At least fifteen themes emerged from the OMB decisions. They are presented in order of declining frequency in Figure 4.3. The most common themes were community integration, compatibility with neighbourhood, safety, supervision of residents, visual buffering and minimum separation distances. These themes can be viewed relationally and interpreted as responses to one another. For example, psychiatric survivors (persons with a psychiatric history) are perceived as "dangerous"; hence, safety concerns are raised by opponents to a development. In order to reassure potential neighbours, housing providers discuss strict supervision of group home inhabitants. The themes of safety and supervision, therefore, function in response to one another.

Figure 4.3
Themes Present in Ontario Municipal Board (OMB) decisions

Themes Present in OMB decisions	Frequency
Community integration	14
Compatibility with neighbourhood	12
Safety, crime	11
Supervision of residents, staff	11
Visual buffering	9
Minimum separation distance	8
Parking and traffic	8
Place undesirable facility elsewhere	7
Declining property values	6
Relationship to residents-business impact	6
Bad faith negotiations	4
Noise	4
Hierarchy of disabilities	3
Accommodation for disabled persons★	2
Heritage preservation	1

★ "Accomodation" is used in this context to discuss human rights legislation that requires agencies to accommodate disabled persons up to the point of undue hardship.

COMMUNITY INTEGRATION AND COMPATIBILITY WITH NEIGHBOURHOOD

Community integration was the theme mentioned most often. The OMB frequently commented that disabled persons must be integrated amongst able-bodied persons. Typically, local citizens would concur, but simultaneously argue that the proposed development was not compatible with their area and should, therefore, be placed elsewhere. No one argued that disabled persons should not be integrated. Instead, opponents insisted that disabled person should not be integrated with *them!* This expression of general support for community integration by group home opponents must be viewed cautiously. A study conducted in Montreal by Piat (2000) noted that, in fact, many group home opponents were vehemently opposed to integration of formerly institutionalized persons. It may be that, in a legal forum, opponents chose not to articulate such views.

Takahashi and Dear (1997: 89) suggest that increased exposure to disabled persons may increase, rather than decrease, opposition to human service facilities:

> Lower acceptance rates among respondents living in metropolitan areas suggest that continuous or long term exposure to client groups

is not necessarily associated with greater acceptance for facilities. Continuous exposure, perhaps resulting from facility saturation or from increasing the size and dispersion of the client population, may in fact, be one catalyst igniting the NIMBY syndrome across socio-economic, class and racial divisions.

In this context, how are we to understand reluctance to accept disability-related facilities in residential areas? Given that 58 percent of OMB cases in this study focused on facilities for psychiatric survivors or homeless people (acknowledging that approximately one-third of homeless people are psychiatric survivors as well), one must ask what it is about psychiatric survivors that is so distasteful to the able-bodied population?

The stigma associated with "mental illness" is well documented in the Canadian literature (Arboleda-Flórez 2003; Angermeyer, Beck and Matschinger 2003; Teschinsky 2000). It is evident in both large cities and smaller towns. In one situation, opponents to an affordable housing project in Toronto argued that their neighbourhood was incompatible because there were no parks (Gillespie 2001). Presumably, psychiatric survivors require park space while able-bodied persons do not. The logic in such comments was not evident from the article.

In another situation, neighbours appealed the rezoning of a former ecclesiastical residence. The Ottawa building, which originally housed twelve nuns, was being rezoned to provide shelter to thirteen homeless women.[27] There were to be absolutely no changes to the exterior. Only minor changes to the interior were planned: the building function would continue to be exclusively residential. Nonetheless, local residents expressed opposition to the change in inhabitants and appealed to the OMB. At the hearing, opponents to the development requested an adjournment which was refused. The OMB ruled in favour of the affordable housing project (*Ottawa (City) Zoning By-Law No. 205-2000* (Re) O.M.B.D. No. 381).

One could attribute the unreasonable behaviour demonstrated above to conceptions that link psychiatric survivors and violence. However, after reviewing over one hundred studies conducted in North America, psychiatrist Dr. Arboleda-Flórez concluded that "mental illness" is no more likely to be causally linked to violence than a range of other factors (Arboleda-Flórez, Holley and Crisanti 1996).

Geoffrey Reaume, a medical historian, reflected on this phenomenon in his book about the history of patients at the Ontario Hospital for the Insane (now known as the Centre for Addiction and Mental Health):

> The vast majority of psychiatric patients were not and are not, violent. It is important when researchers write about the minority of people with mental disorders who were and are abusive, that they deal with this issue by avoiding the stereotypes that only perpetuate the myth of the violent mental patient. This stereotype has

been used too often throughout history and in oral tradition to tar unfairly all patients with the same brush. It is a caricature and an insult to a very diverse group of people. (Reaume 2000: 253)

Safety and Supervision

In eleven cases, opponents to housing developments expressed concerns about their own safety or the safety of their children. Potential neighbours of a group home for eight children in Blenheim were worried about the possibility of increased criminal activity. Although group home opponents worried about youth crime more generally, they also suggested that group home residents specifically had committed illegal offenses. The OMB chair, however, noted the following in his decision:

> The neighbours in the Blenheim proposal expressed concerns with existing area youth related to loitering, trespass, property damage and threats. It was conceded by one resident that existing problems were hard to resolve due to a lack of being able to identify perpetrators. (*Chatham-Kent (Municipality) Zoning By-Law No. 103-2003* (Re) [2003], O.M.B.D. No. 946, paragraph 21)

Ultimately, the OMB approved the group home.

In Sarnia, the town planner opposed the installation of a soup kitchen in a residential neighbourhood. The OMB chair at the hearing cited his words in the decision:

> The introduction of the soup kitchen use would be an incompatible land use... particularly given the subject property's location adjacent to a school where the potential for negative interaction between students and soup kitchen clients would be created (*Sarnia (City) Zoning By-Law No. 118-2001* (Re) [2002], O.M.B.D. No. 250, paragraph 28).... Mr. Williams advised the Board that some of the mitigation measures could include bussing clients to the site; stopping children from using the site in the day and at night; containing the activities within the building itself and generally providing a tightly controlled environment. (*Chatham-Kent (Municipality) Zoning By-Law No. 103-2003* (Re) [2003], O.M.B.D. No. 946, paragraph 40)

While a soup kitchen might not generally be considered a disability-related facility, the church sponsoring the kitchen indicated that "the usual soup kitchen client is either for health reasons unable to prepare meals or resides in boarding homes (a common form of housing for psychiatric survivors) where meals are not provided."[28]

Interestingly, in the Sarnia case, neighbourhood children are portrayed as needing protection. However, in the Blenheim case, children residing in a facility run by a child protection agency are viewed as potential offenders. This contrast illustrates the implicit association of particular forms of housing with criminality, even when residents are children.

Safety issues also arose in a variety of other cases. Rural Keppel Township refused to amend a zoning by-law to permit the establishment of a group home. My Father's Ministries, a Christian organization, wished to create a residential facility for persons addicted to various substances. During the appeal to the OMB, two residents mentioned the slow response time of the local police force. Seven residents testified that they felt a general concern for their own physical well-being or for that of their families and property. Given the strict regimen of the religious organization, its refusal to admit anyone with a history of violent offenses and an institutional commitment to intensive twenty-four-hour supervision, it is unclear what additional reassurances could have been offered. In the end, the OMB approved the proposed group home over strong local opposition (*Keppel (Township) Zoning By-Law No. 119-1992*, (Re) [2000], O.M.B.D. No. 875).

In only one case (out of thirty-one) was there concrete evidence of physical threats to safety. An already established drop-in centre for homeless people submitted a rezoning application to ensure conformity with existing by-laws. The City of Hamilton approved their request. Local residents raised serious security issues in their appeal. Wesley Urban Ministries operated a drop-in for Hamilton's most destitute individuals in the city's downtown core. Many drop-in users were homeless psychiatric survivors with few skills or resources. The drop-in provided food, clothes, bathing facilities and an opportunity to access mental health services. Unfortunately, some drop-in users engaged in

> anti-social behaviour which is very disturbing to the neighbours and the neighbourhood with loud noise, profane language, lewd gestures, rudeness, vomiting, urinating and defecating. This behaviour occurs sometimes in the late hours of the evening and early hours of the morning when residential neighbours are trying to get sleep. It sometimes involves accosting or frightening residents and visitors to the neighbouring buildings. It sometimes involves trespass on to neighbours' properties. (*Hamilton (City) Zoning By-Law No. 97-147* (Re) [1999], O.M.B.D. No. 127, paragraph 9)[29]

Despite compelling evidence of disturbance to neighbours and unsuccessful negotiations with members of the neighbouring cooperative, the OMB insisted that the two organizations work together to resolve their differences. The Chair, in a follow-up hearing, was blunt in his assessment of the situation. He directed both drop-in administrators and drop-in neighbours to "change your attitude." The drop-in centre was not going to be closed. The neighbours should stop insisting it be moved elsewhere. Furthermore, the neighbours had legitimate complaints that must be addressed by the drop-in administration (*Hamilton (City) Zoning By-Law No. 97-147* (Re) [2000], O.M.B.D. No. 411, paragraphs 21–39). After elaborating at some length about the necessary changes in attitude and revising Board conditions, the OMB concluded with a comment questioning the motivation of the parties:

> The Board got the feeling that more was happening lately in terms of dealing with the Board's conditions simply because the Board 'had come to town'.... The Board hopes that the feeling was misplaced; that the more things happening as the Board 'came to town' was a coincidence. (*Hamilton (City) Zoning By-Law No. 97-147* (Re) [2000], O.M.B.D. No. 411, paragraph 30)

It is evident from the above decision that the OMB would not necessarily deny a facility for psychiatric survivors its right to place even when the users of the service did indeed infringe on the rights of others. The OMB did state, however, that in so deciding,

> this was the most difficult and troubling case this Member has had since joining the Board. This Member, therefore, reviewed the evidence again and again and struggled with coming to this decision over an extended period of time. (*Hamilton (City) Zoning By-Law No. 97-147* (Re) [1999], O.M.B.D. No. 127, paragraph 7)

"Supervision" and "Control"

Eleven decisions mentioned the need for supervision and control of disabled persons living in a residence. In Sophiasburgh, a small town near Belleville, the director of the proposed group home stated that "the appellant now has approximately twenty homes in eastern Ontario. In each, there are up to six residents. There is responsible supervision, three staff at night and up to five daily" (*Sophiasburgh (Ward) Zoning By-Law No. 1056* (Re) [2002], O.M.B.D. No. 1060, paragraph 7). In the above-mentioned Sarnia case, the OMB approved the installation of a soup kitchen, but reminded the church that

> The challenge is for the Inn [kitchen's name] to control its own clients in such a way that the Inn's activities operate in a manner which is in keeping with the characteristics of the neighbourhood which is a stable quiet, residential area. (*Sarnia (City) Zoning By-Law No. 118-2001* (Re) [2002], O.M.B.D. No. 250, paragraph 50)

The OMB decisions reveal the tribunal's belief that developmentally disabled persons and psychiatric survivors require control and supervision. Where such supervision was not in evidence, the OMB did not approve the application. John Gaspar, a for-profit group home provider, indicated that some of the residences he administered did not have on-site staff supervision. One proposed group home would be located on a flood plain. The OMB refused permission to establish the facility, concluding, "If some sites have no staff living on site, it is highly unlikely that staff would be able to make plans in the event of a regional storm and ensuing flooding" (*Newmarket (Town) Official Plan Amendment No. 20* (Re) [2004], O.M.B.D. No. 41, paragraph 27). However, depending on the tenants' degree of impairment, it might have been possible for them to deal with a storm or flood independently.

In this study, it is significant to note that cases which mentioned supervision of residents all involved psychiatric survivors or developmentally disabled persons. Cases involving nursing homes did not mention supervision at all. It is clear from the above discussion that safety issues figured prominently among neighbourhood concerns. Housing providers attempted to allay fears of violence by describing sometimes intensive forms of supervision. This response, unfortunately, only served to reinforce the original fears. If such supervision is necessary, neighbours might reason, group home residents must indeed be dangerous. Therefore, by replying within the framework established by the opposition, housing providers merely reinforced, rather than assuaged, local concerns.

Minimum Separation Distances

The term "minimum separation distance" refers to the mandatory minimum distance between group homes or similar types of community facilities. This requirement, a by-law frequently enacted by municipalities, prevents housing for disabled people from concentrating in the same vicinity. As a result, organizations in smaller communities may have difficulty locating their premises within close proximity to local amenities. Residents of some group homes may not, for example, have access to public transportation.

In early 2004, John Gaspar appealed the Town of Newmarket's *Official Plan* amendments, which instituted a minimum separation distance requirement of 300 metres between group homes. Gaspar argued that the minimum separation distance requirements were discriminatory. He stated that there was no inherent logic to minimum separation distance requirements which were applied inconsistently by different municipalities. The OMB did not rule on allegations of discrimination. In the decision rendered, however, the OMB quoted the town planner, with approval:

> It was the evidence of Mr Unger that the Province supports the setting of group homes in residentially designated areas. He stated that integration is best achieved for the residents in areas that do not have an *over-saturation* of group homes. (*Newmarket (Town) Official Plan Amendment No. 20* (Re) [2004], O.M.B.D. No. 41, paragraph 10) (emphasis mine)

In contrast to Mr. Gaspar's lack of success in challenging minimum separation distances, non-profit group home operators who argued against such requirements received exemptions from the OMB.[30]

Minimum separation distances also limit the concentration of institutions such as places of worship and day-care centres. However, the only type of residences to which minimum separation distance requirements apply are residences for disabled persons. Residences for able-bodied people face no such restrictions. Minimum separation distances explicitly limit the number of disabled persons living in one neighbourhood. It is highly unlikely that municipalities would enact a by-law limiting the number of members of a particular religion that could live in a particular area. Minimum separation distances targeting disabled persons should be considered similarly offensive.

Municipalities may argue that minimum separation distances are simply a regulation of land use. However, one could also argue that such by-laws are a form of "people zoning," a phenomenon prohibited by the courts (*Alcoholism Foundation of Manitoba* v. *Winnipeg* (1990) 65 Manitoba Reports (2nd) 81 (Manitoba Court of Appeal). A group home is generally designated as housing for disabled persons.[31] Determining that a finite number of disabled persons can live in a particular neighbourhood appears discriminatory on its face. If there are specific planning concerns such as traffic volume, municipalities can address them directly by, for example, regulating the required number of parking spaces.

Visual Buffering

Opponents to local development, housing providers, as well as the OMB, all spoke frequently of the need for visual buffering. A visual separation of the disability-related facility from the rest of the nieghbourhood was viewed positively by all participants. For example, in a decision regarding an Aurora nursing home, the OMB commented:

> The site has been generously landscaped to provide ample buffering and screening from existing uses. The signage has been altered at the request of the residents. A proposed back lit sign has been replaced by a more traditional less ostentatious sign. (Aurora (Town) Zoning By-Law No. 2213-78 (Re) [2001], O.M.B.D. No. 1156, paragraph 8)

In a case discussing a proposed nursing home in Sarnia, the OMB commented that "12 ft. trees could replace the proposed 8 ft. trees if that was more agreeable to the residents" (*Sarnia (City) Official Plan Amendment No. 30* (Re) [2001], O.M.B.D. No. 759, paragraph 13). In another case discussing a proposed group home in Chatham, the housing provider "confirmed her willingness to share the cost should fencing be requested" (*Chatham-Kent (Municipality) Zoning By-Law No. 102-2003* (Re) [2003], O.M.B.D. No. 946, paragraph 26). In a fourth case which discussed an affordable housing project for psychiatric survivors, the planner for the housing provider stated that "the outdoor amenity space on the rooftop will be screened, i.e. there will be no overlooking views of other buildings" (*McDonald* v. *Toronto (City) Committee of Adjustment* [2001], O.M.B.D. No. 749, paragraph 7(5)). Not only did local residents not wish to see disabled persons. They did not wish prospective disabled inhabitants to see them.

Ostensibly, the purpose of locating disability-related facilities within residential areas is to facilitate community integration. It appears unlikely that integration will take place if efforts are made to separate disabled individuals from their neighbours before they have even moved into their homes. The physical placement of disabled persons within residential areas does not guarantee integration. In fact, visual buffering serves to limit the possibility of relationships between disabled newcomers and those already living in the immediate vicinity.

It is disconcerting that the OMB endorsed the installation of visual buffering in the above cases. The Ontario government closed institutions and initiated community integration of disabled persons (Ministry of Health 1993: Standing Committee on Social Development 1991). The OMB, an arm of that same government, now thwarts the process. By approving the visual demarcation of disability-related facilities, the OMB is complicit in the re-segregation of previously institutionalized individuals.

From the above discussion, it is evident that the OMB adheres to a medical model analysis of disabled persons' struggles. Opposition to homes for disabled persons was interpreted as fear of the unknown rather than systemic discrimination. The OMB addressed such resistance by insisting on scrupulous supervision of disabled persons, the very thing disabled persons themselves wish to escape. OMB approval of visual buffering indicated support for the separation of disabled persons from the surrounding population. The enforcement of minimum separation distance requirements distanced disabled persons living in one residence from those living in another. OMB decisions, therefore, ultimately reinforced the social isolation of disabled persons.

The OMB also reinforced oppressive stereotypes. For example, the OMB consistently portrayed disabled persons as those requiring ongoing supervision. This inaccurate assumption simultaneously infantilized developmentally disabled individuals and encouraged the erroneous link between psychiatric impairment and dangerousness.

The OMB did recognize disability-related discrimination in a planning context and successfully subverted attempts to deny disabled persons their right to place in residential neighbourhoods. However, the oppressive context in which they functioned, and the reasoning they used, ultimately perpetuated the re-segregation of disabled persons in so-called "community" settings.

Resistance to NIMBYism at the OMB

It is firmly established in law that the OMB has jurisdiction to hear arguments pertaining to both the *Ontario Human Rights Code* and the *Charter* (see References, Introduction) (Epstein 2002). One decision, *Grushman* v. *Ottawa (City)*, focused on opposition to a proposed funeral home located in a predominantly Chinese community. Local residents argued that their religious beliefs should be considered in the placement of such facilities. On appeal, Ontario Superior Court Judge O'Leary stated, "The Board in our view knew full well that it had the jurisdiction to deal with *Charter* and *Code* issues" (*Grushman* v. *Ottawa (City)* [2001] O.J. No. 4642).

More recently, in a Supreme Court case, Justice Gonthier confirmed that administrative tribunals do have authority to decide charter issues. He stated:

> From this principle of constitutional supremacy flows, as a practical corollary, the idea that Canadians should be entitled to assert the rights and freedoms that the Constitution guarantees them in the most accessible forum available, without the parallel proceedings before the courts. (*Nova Scotia (Workers' Compensation Board)* v. *Martin; Nova Scotia (Workers' Compensation Board)* v. *Laseur*, [2003] 2 S.C.R. 504)

Unfortunately, it appears that few lawyers have applied the *Ontario Human Rights Code* (1990) (OHRC) disability provisions to restrictions governing the location of disability-related facilities. In one case before the OMB, the Advocacy Centre for Tenants Ontario (ACTO) raised human rights issues on behalf of the Dream Team, a group of psychiatric survivors supporting affordable housing (see *Toronto (City) Official Plan Amendment No. 244* (Re) [2003], O.M.B.D. No. 792; Controneo 2003). Unfortunately, the presiding member mentioned neither the OHRC arguments nor the views of psychiatric survivors. If the Dream Team had not been listed as a party to the legal proceedings, it would not have been evident that the group was represented at the hearing. The OMB decision made no mention of psychiatric survivor perspectives.

In a second case, ACTO argued that homelessness was an analogous ground under the *Charter*. Minimum separation distances applied to homeless shelters were, therefore, a discriminatory practice targeting homeless people (*Deveau* v. *Toronto (City)* [2003] O.M.B.D. 0569). The OMB decision in that case concluded that the minimum separation distance requirements pertaining to homeless shelters did have a sound base in planning and furthermore, did not violate *Charter* section 15. The OMB also insisted that Charter arguments should not have been argued before the Board as the remedy sought by ACTO, i.e. a declaration of invalidity of the by-law, was something available only through the courts.

The most disturbing aspect of the above decision was the inability of the OMB to relate the by-law to the real life circumstances of homeless people. The OMB stated that homeless shelters were not a form of housing but rather constituted emergency shelter in a public facility (*Deveau* v. *Toronto (City)*

[2003] O.M.B.D. 0569, page 30). In fact, many homeless people, particularly psychiatric survivors, live in the same homeless shelter for years. For example, Seaton House, a municipal shelter for homeless men in Toronto, acts as an informal trustee for some residents, managing the money sent to them by social assistance.[32] Such financial arrangements are made precisely because residents live there on a long-term basis. Homeless shelters may not provide permanent housing for all their residents. However, they may well be the only form of shelter on which vulnerable people can rely.

The OMB also decided that minimum separation distances did not constitute "people zoning" but rather served to disperse homeless shelters across the City of Toronto. Such logic is seriously flawed. Homeless shelters should not have to be dispersed. Neither luxury condominiums nor monster homes must comply with such requirements. In fact, zoning for large minimum lot sizes permits wealthy people to concentrate in particular areas; people living on modest incomes cannot afford sprawling homes. However, the presence of large numbers of rich people in one neighbourhood is viewed positively.

The OMB also determined that, because of their size and intensity of use, shelters should be located only along arterial roads. This assumption is based on a particular size and structure of shelter. Homeless shelters, however, do not conform to specific physical configurations. Some might easily fit into residential neighbourhoods.

It is unclear why housing providers and/or disabled persons' organizations generally chose not to raise human rights issues. Some might suggest that NIMBY cases are not appropriate venues for human rights arguments. The OMB focuses primarily on physical, rather than social, aspects of planning. However, in some cases, submissions made on appeal by potential neighbours demonstrated that the developments were unacceptable solely because of the inherent characteristics of proposed occupants.

In the city of Vaughan, just north of Toronto, inhabitants opposed the building of a nursing home. The decision included a lengthy discussion about windows. The director of the facility agreed to frost the windows and include additional visual buffering so that future residents could not look at their neighbours. In the decision, the OMB Chair commented:

> One of the opposing landowners advised that the difference was that they would not know who was looking out of the windows in a nursing home, but with a residential development, they could be friends. This fear of the unknown is a natural human response, but the Board challenges all the residents... to meet these neighbours in the same way. (*Vaughan (City) Zoning By-Law No. 1-88* (Re) [2003], O.M.B.D. No. 382, paragraph 38)

Ultimately, the OMB approved the nursing home application.

In response to a downtown Toronto proposal for supportive housing for psychiatric survivors, neighbours argued "that the residents of the proposed development would be victimized because of their vulnerability in the neighbourhood." The OMB chair responded by stating:

> The Board finds the concern somewhat disingenuous. The proposal is publicly funded and will be under the punctilious scrutiny of the Ministry of Health.... It is our finding that the need for housing for the mentally ill cries out for urgent recognition. It is not a tenable argument to say that because the mentally ill deserve better, one must wait for another building opportunity. In planning, as in life, there is no reason to allow the best to defeat the good. (*Toronto (City) Official Plan Amendment No. 244* (Re) [2003], O.M.B.D. No. 792, paragraph 13)

In cases such as the above-mentioned one, employing human rights arguments could be used to effectively halt an appeal. Advocates could argue that the opposition is motivated solely by discriminatory sentiments. A preliminary motion could then be made to dismiss the case. Discrimination, such as that expressed by some opponents mentioned in this paper, should automatically establish that the case was not brought in good faith. Provisions allowing for a prompt dismissal of such an appeal would shorten the length of hearings, contribute to case management and cost containment at the OMB and limit legal expenses for housing providers. The OMB Rules of Practice and Procedure (Rules 99–107)[33] already allow the OMB to assign costs if the Chair believes that a case is of a frivolous or vexatious nature. Perhaps a phrase could be added to the rules emphasizing that opposition to a project based on discriminatory grounds could also result in the ordering of costs.

One might also argue that Section 2 (h) (1) and Section 51 (24) of the Planning Act, which state that plans "must have regard to" disabled persons' concerns, does not conform to Section 17 (2) of the *Ontario Human Rights Code* (OHRC), which states that agencies providing services must accommodate disabled persons to the point of undue hardship. Given the satutory inconsistency, planners should be held to the higher OHRC standard. Strengthening the OHRC provisions within planning legislation might, however, simply subject OMB decisions to more stringent reviews by appellate courts as the courts consider themselves the experts on human rights matters. Ultimately, embarking on such a strategy may be futile. Human rights arguments may result not only in further appeals but also entail even greater legal costs.

Response of the OMB to NIMBYism
In the majority of cases reviewed, the OMB approved of housing for disabled persons and sometimes reprimanded opponents. The OMB successfully subverted opposition to housing for disabled persons. While opponents of

social housing and disability-related facilities often emphasized the type of tenants that might inhabit such developments, the OMB focused almost exclusively on planning issues involved. Comments directed to the parties emphasized planning policies, structural layout, environmental impact assessments, etc. The nature of the occupants of a proposed development was not relevant to the OMB.

Furthermore, the OMB was not hesitant to directly confront NIMBY sentiments even when manifested by municipalities. In at least two cases, the OMB alleged that municipal officials had negotiated in bad faith with housing providers. In *Eboh* v. *the Town of Markham*, the OMB reprimanded municipal officials and, citing vexatious behaviour, awarded costs to the group home providers (*Eboh* v. *Markham (Town)* [2002] O.M.B.D. No. 85). Counsel for the Town of Markham apparently failed to meet with the housing providers; they directed government officials to a public meeting, rather than discussing issues with them directly. The Chair in *Eboh* stated:

> The evidence presented to the Board revealed one of the most clear and shocking misuses of municipal planning powers this board member has ever dealt with…. Misusing municipal planning powers to the point where the municipality forces a citizen to come to this Board is not an appropriate or legal means for dealing with community concerns…. There was nothing constructive about forcing this matter to hearing, no merit to the hearing and nothing achieved by the hearing. (*Eboh* v. *Markham (Town)* [2002] O.M.B.D. No. 85, paragraphs 13–17)

In a case involving Sagecare Incorporated, the City of Toronto refused an application to build a group home for seniors with Alzheimer's disease. The City instead passed an interim control by-law in order to "assess changes." The OMB Chair concluded:

> The Board believe[s] that the following considerations lead to the conclusion that the by-law was passed simply to stop this particular development proposal and not from any pressing need to deal with land use designations in this area generally or specifically. (*Toronto (City) Interim Control By-Law* [2000] O.M.B.D. No. 530, paragraph 7)

The OMB did not approve the interim control by-law and permitted the group home to go ahead with its development. The Chair stated:

> The Board was asked to accept that community interests should prevail in this circumstance. The Board agrees. The Board finds that, in this hearing, the interest that needs to prevail is the important need for the provision of housing for 16 people living with

Alzheimer's disease. (*Toronto (City) Interim Control By-Law* [2000]O. M.B.D. No. 530, paragraph 4)

The decisions I reviewed were rendered by a variety of Chairs. No single OMB member stood out as an advocate for disabled persons. Despite a conventional approach to land-use matters, OMB members nonetheless viewed NIMBY-related cases regularly and were, therefore, able to identify discriminatory attitudes and/or practices that might not have been readily evident. It is clear that the OMB protected disabled persons' right to place by ensuring that discriminatory attitudes were not an excuse for exclusion.

Unfortunately, the OMB rendered positive decisions within an oppressive medical-model understanding of disability. Disabled persons do not automatically require supervision by virtue of their impairment status. There should not be extensive visual separation between the homes of disabled persons and homes of able-bodied neighbours. Community integration must mean more than physical placement within a residential area. Perhaps most importantly, the voices, perspectives and lives of disabled persons must be present within the decisions. To render silent group home tenants is to render silent the central figures in land use conflict.

CONCLUDING COMMENTS

While this study examined thirty-one appeals regarding disability-related facilities at the OMB, we must exercise caution in arriving at any general conclusions. This study examined only a sample of NIMBY cases that appear in the public record. It is conceivable that other meritorious claims were not pursued due to financial difficulties or due to the vulnerability of disabled persons. As Mosoff (2000) notes in her review of human rights tribunal decisions, severely disabled individuals and those living in institutions are least likely to be able to protest discriminatory policies and practices.

In addition, I relied entirely on the written decision for information about the various appeals. Details about the specific context of opposition are, therefore, unavailable. It is conceivable that opposition to disability-related facilities also involved oppressive attitudes towards other marginalized groups. Racial stereotypes pertaining to alcoholics, for example, may have affected neighbourhood opposition to a proposed group home for persons with addictions.[34]

In communities where large provincial institutions also exist, opposition to group homes might reflect a general resentment directed less at disabled persons and more at government cost-cutting initiatives. As a result of deinstitutionalization, more highly educated newcomers who work in community-based facilities may replace the local institutional workforce. In addition, group home wages may be lower than those offered in institutional settings (Edelson 2000).

Finally, one cannot ignore the economic context in which NIMBY values are articulated. The assumption that one may determine who one's neighbours will become, and exclude those with whom one is uncomfortable, is prevalent primarily among individuals fortunate enough to own a home. Property ownership functions as a badge of entitlement that marginalizes disabled persons and reinforces class divisions. An economic system which values land as a commodity to be bought and sold for profit may easily disregard those persons seen to be of little financial significance. The links between capitalism and NIMBY cannot be underestimated.

Addressing political and social complexities such as those mentioned above is beyond the scope of this short chapter. They may, however, offer fruitful directions for further investigation of the NIMBY phenomenon as it impacts on disability-related facilities.

NOTES

1. Thanks to the Law Commission for their generous support of this research. I offer grateful acknowledgement to Jill Grant and Bill Lahey, professors whose invaluable feedback guided me in this writing. Thanks also to two anonymous reviewers for their helpful comments. Of course, any errors or omissions are my own.

2. "The Tribunal resolves disputes between landlords and tenants, regulates rent increases, and educates landlords and tenants about their rights and responsibilities under the Tenant Protection Act." From the OHRT website <http://www. orht.gov.on.ca/userfiles/HTML/nts_3_5224_1.html>. (Accessed August 30, 2004.)

3. The Ontario Consent and Capacity Board hears applications challenging, among other things, findings of incapacity to consent to treatment and a determination that involuntary detention in a psychiatric facility is necessary to prevent imminent harm to the patient or to a third party.

4. Neither Quebec nor British Columbia have such an appeal body. In those provinces, parties would appeal municipal decisions directly to the courts.

5. See the OMB website <http://www.omb.gov.on.ca/About/OMB_Guide. html#Lawyer>. (Accessed August 30, 2004.)

6. See website of the Ontario Ministry of Municipal Affairs and Housing Consultation Document and Online Questionnaire <http://www.mah.gov.on.ca/ userfiles/HTML/nts_1_17435_1.html>. (Accessed August 30, 2004.)

7. See OMB website <http://www.omb.gov.on.ca/Hearing/checklists.html.> (Accessed August 30, 2004.)

8. Section 5 (2) of the *Ontario Municipal Board Act* states simply that "the Lieutenant Governor in Council shall appoint the members of the Board and shall appoint one member as chair and may appoint one vice-chair or more."

9. "The Lieutenant Governor in Council may from time to time, upon the recommondation of the Board, appoint one or more experts or persons having technical or special knowledge of matters or subjects within the jurisdiction of the Board or in question in respect of any particular matter or subject before the Board to assist the Board in an advisory or other capacity" (Section 27 (1) *Ontario Municipal Board Act*).

10. Personal conversation July 28, 2004.

11. *Shanahan* v. *Russell* [December 19, 2000]; *London (City)* v. *Ayerswood Develop-*

ment Corporation [December 13, 2002]; *Toronto (City)* v. *Goldlist Properties Inc.* [October 14, 2003].

12. *Ministry of Transportation* v. *Tripp* [August 5, 1999]; *747926 Ontario Limited* v. *Upper Grand District School Board* [October 10, 2001]; *Devine* v. *Ontario (Ministry of Transportation)* [March 22, 2002].

13. *Slough Estates Canada Limited* v. *Regional Assessment Officer Commissioner* [January 20, 1999]; *Great Lakes Power Limited* v. *Regional Assessment Commissioner, Region No. 31* [August 5, 1999].

14. *Mississauga (City)* v. *Erin Mills Corporation Limited* [June 25, 2004].

15. *Toronto Area Transit Operating Authority* v. *Dell Holdings Ltd.* [January 30, 1997] 1 S.C.R. 32.

16. *Newmarket (Town) Official Plan Amendment No. 20* (Re) [2004], O.M.B.D. No. 41.

17. *Newmarket (Town) Official Plan Amendment No. 20* (Re), [2004], O.M.B.D. No. 41.

18. *Lindsay* v. *York (City) Committee of Adjustment* [1997] O.M.B.D. No. 1008, paragraphs 44 and 101; *Canadian Islamic Trust Foundation* v. *Mississauga* [1998] O.M.B.D. No. 299, paragraphs 25–28; *Talim-Ul-Islam Ontario* v. *Toronto (City) Committee of Adjustment* [1998] No. 1076, paragraphs 6 and 14.

19. Legal Aid certificates are typically not available for matters heard before the OMB. However, test case litigation funding may be provided to argue equality rights matters before the Board. In the alternative, it is possible that a community legal clinic may be able to represent an eligible party before the tribunal.

20. Mr. Hanley is the only resident of a contested facility mentioned by name in the OMB documents I reviewed. I refer to him in this paper because it is important to make visible individuals who are often relegated to the margins of the historic record.

21. The DRM is not homogeneous. Wheelchair users, for example, wish for architectural accessibility and integration within the able-bodied population; deaf people wish for sovereignty and recognition as a distinct cultural and linguistic group. Despite this heterogeneity in experience and demands, disabled persons collectively support the need for a) services delivered to disabled persons, controlled by disabled persons b) increases in social assistance rates, eliminating poverty and c) acceptance within the community and the elimination of institutions as a form of housing.

22. While the word "mentally ill" locates psychiatric impairment within the individual, the term "survivor" reframes the experience of involuntary detainment and understands psychiatry as a system of oppression. The shift in terminology used to describe psychiatric survivors reflects changing perceptions and analysis during the last century (Reaume 2002).

23. All OMB decisions (with rare exceptions) are sent to the Quicklaw database administrators. There is an approximately three week lag time from date of receipt until date of posting on the database. Personal conversation with Quicklaw staff, August 3, 2004.

24. See OMB *Annual Reports* for 2001–2002, 2002–2003 and 2003–2004.

25. Mathew Blevins, planning assistant OMB, August 16, 2004, e-mail on file with author.

26. *Lighthouse Niagara Resource Centre* v. *The Corporation of the City of Niagara Falls* (February 7, 2003) O.J. No. 3490.

27. Some might argue that I conflate psychiatric disability with homelessness. There

are indeed homeless women who are not psychiatric survivors. Nonetheless, given the statistical correlation mentioned elsewhere in this article and the close association between the two experiences, I wanted to include this example in this section.

28. *Sarnia (City) Zoning By-Law No. 118-2001* (Re) [2002], O.M.B.D. No. 250, paragraph 14.
29. Although this decision was rendered in 1999 and would not ordinarily have been included in this study, a follow-up decision was rendered in 2000: since the cases address exactly the same issues, they therefore really constitute one case.
30. *Hamilton (City) Zoning By-Law No. 97-147* (Re) [1999], O.M.B.D. No. 127; *Hamilton (City) Zoning By-Law No. 97-147* (Re) [2000], O.M.B.D. No. 411; *Sarnia (City) Official Plan Amendment No. 30* (Re) [2001], O.M.B.D. No. 759; *Surex Community Service v. Toronto (City) Committee of Adjustment* [2004], O.M.B.D. No 548.
31. Halfway houses for ex-prisoners administered by social services also experience NIMBY (Correctional Services Canada 2004).
32. I became aware of these arrangements during my work at a local community legal clinic.
33. Full details and a complete Rules of Practice and Procedure are available at the OMB website <http://www.omb.gov.on.ca/Hearing/Rules20of20Procedure/costs.html>. (Accessed August 30, 2004.)
34. For an analysis of the racialization of space in a NIMBY context, see Wilton, Robert (2002), "Colouring Special Needs: Locating Whiteness in NIMBY Conflicts." *Social and Cultural Geography* 3: 3, 303–22.

REFERENCES

Angermeyer, Matthias C., Michael Beck and Herbert Matschinger. 2003. "Determinants of the Publics Preference for Social Distance from People with Schizophrenia." *Canadian Journal of Psychiatry* 48, 10: 663–68.

Arboleda-Flórez, Julio. 2003. "Considerations on the Stigma of Mental Illness." *Canadian Journal of Psychiatry* 48, 10: 645–50.

Arboleda-Flórez, J., H.L. Holley, and A. Crisanti. 1996. *Mental Illness and Violence: Proof or Stereotype?* Ottawa, Ontario: Health Promotion and Programs Branch, Health Canada.

Arrigo, Bruce. 1993. *Madness, Language and the Law.* Albany, NY: Harrow and Heston.

Barnes, Colin. 1998. "A Social Model of Disability: A Sociological Phenomenon Ignored by Sociologists?" In Tom Shakespeare (ed.), *The Disability Reader.* London: Cassell.

Bridgman, Rae. 2003. *Safe Haven: The Story of a Shelter for Homeless Women.* Toronto, ON: University of Toronto Press.

Butler, Ruth, and Hester Parr. 1999. *Mind and Body Spaces: Geographies of Illness, Impairment and Disability.* London, England: Routledge.

Charlton, James. 1999. *Nothing About Us Without Us: Disability Oppression and Empowerment.* Berkeley, CA: University of California Press.

Controneo, Christian. 2003. "Dream Team's crusade is dignity for mentally ill. Group fights for supportive housing." *Toronto Star*, February 16.

Cork, Campbell. 2004. "Few want housing project." *Kitchener Waterloo Record*, July

16.

Correctional Services Canada. 2004. *Community Corrections and the NIMBY Syndrome.*
Available at <http://www.csc-scc.gc.ca/text/pblct/forum/e022/e022h_e.shtml>.
(Accessed August 15, 2005.)

Da Silva, Orlando. 2004. "Well Off Families Deny Poor People Their Dream Home."
Kitchener Waterloo Record, July 14.

De Jong, Gerben. 1979. "Independent Living: From Social Movement to Analytic
Paradigm." *Archives of Physical & Medical Rehabilitation* 60.

Deegan, P.E. 1992. "The independent living movement and people with psychiatric
disabilities: Taking back control over our own lives." *Psychosocial Rehabilitation
Journal* 15, 3: 3–19.

Dorn, Michael, and Deborah Metzel. 2001. "Symposium on Disability Geography:
Commonalities in a World of Differences: Introduction." *Disability Studies
Quarterly* 21, 2.

Edelson, Miriam. 2000. *My Journey with Jake: A Memoir of Parenting and Disability.*
Toronto, ON: Between the Lines.

Epstein, Howard. 2002. "Land Use Appellate Bodies and the Charter." *Municipal
and Planning Law Reports* 29 M.P.L.R. (3d) 29–48.

_____. 2004. "Land Use Appellate Bodies: The Standard of Review Upon Appeal
to the Courts — Comments on Tsimiklis." *Municipal and Planning Reports* 43
M.P.L.R. (3d) 195.

Finkler, Lilith. 2002. "Stressing Sacred Places." Unpublished paper. Available from
the author.

Gillespie, Kerry. 2001. "Housing Plan Runs into Walls: Opponents Fight Project
for Mentally Ill." *Toronto Star*, December 4.

Gleeson, Brendan. 1998. "Justice and the Disabling City." In Ruth Fincher and Jane
M. Jacobs (eds.), *Cities of Difference.* New York, NY: Guilford.

_____. 1999. *Geographies of Disability.* London, Eng.: Routledge.

Krushelnicki, Bruce W. 2003. *A Practical Guide to the Ontario Municipal Board.* Toronto: LexisNexis Butterworths.

Laskin, Bora. 1937. *The Ontario Municipal Board.* Boston, MA: Harvard University,
Unpublished thesis.

Lee, Kevin K. 2000. *Urban Poverty in Canada: A Statistical Profile.* Ottawa, ON:
Canadian Council on Social Development.

Lepofsky, David. 1995. "Equal Access to Canada's Judicial System for Persons with
Disabilities: A Time for Reform." *National Journal of Constitutional Law* 183,
5.

Marshall, John. 1982. *Madness: An Indictment of the Mental Health Care System in
Ontario.* Toronto, ON: Ontario Public Service Employees Union.

Mayor's Taskforce on Homelessness. 1999. *Taking Responsibility for Homelessness; An
Action Plan for Toronto.* Toronto, ON: City of Toronto.

Michalko, Rod. 2002. *The Difference Disability Makes.* Philadelphia, Pennsylvania:
Temple University Press.

Ministry of Health. 1993. *Putting People First: The Reform of Mental Health Services
in Ontario.* Toronto, ON: Ministry of Health.

Moloney, Paul. 2004. "Housing approvals signal a city trend: Council bucks objec-
tions to housing." *Toronto Star*, August 3.

Mosoff, Judith. 2000. "Is the Human Rights Paradigm 'Able' to Include Disability:
Who's In? Who Wins? What? Why?" *Queen's Law Journal* 26, 225: 226–63.

National Advisory Council on Aging. 2003. *Dementia in Canada.* Ottawa, ON: National

Advisory Council on Aging. Available at <http://www.phac-aspc.gc.ca/seniors-aines/pubs/vignette/vig34-50_e.htm>. (Accessed February 27, 2005.)

Oliver, Michael. 1990. *The Politics of Disablement*. London, Eng.: Macmillan

Ontario Human Rights Commission. 2000. Available at <http://www.ohrc.on.ca/english/publications/disability-policy.shtml>. (Accessed August 30, 2004.)

Parr, Hester. 2000. "Interpreting the 'Hidden Social Geographies' of Mental Health: Ethnographies of Inclusion and Exclusion in Semi-institutional Places." *Health and Place* 6: 225–37.

Philo, Chris. 1997. "Across the Water: Reviewing Geographical Studies of Asylums and Other Mental Health Facilities. *Health and Place* 3, 2: 73–89.

Piat, Myra. 2000. "The NIMBY Phenomenon: Community Residents' Concerns About Housing for Deinstitutionalized People." *Health and Social Work* 25, 2" 127–39.

Radford, John, and Deborah C. Park. 1993. "'A Convenient Means of Riddance': Institutionalization of People Diagnosed as 'Mentally Deficient' in Ontario, 1876–1934." *Health and Canadian Society* 1, 2: 369–92.

Reaume, Geoffrey. 2000. *Remembrances of Patients Past: Patient Life at the Toronto Hospital for the Insane, 1870–1940*. Toronto, ON: Oxford University Press.

———. 2002. "Lunatic to Patient to Person: Nomenclature in Psychiatric History and the Influence of Patients' Activism in North America." *International Journal of Law and Psychiatry* 25, 4: 405–26.

Simmons, Harvey G. 1982. *From Asylums to Welfare*. Toronto, ON: National Institute on Mental Retardation.

———. 1990. *Unbalanced: Mental Health Policy in Ontario, 1930–1989*. Toronto, ON: Wall & Thompson.

Standing Committee on Social Development. 1991. *Multi-Year Plan for Deinstitutionalization of Developmentally Handicapped People in Ontario*. Toronto, ON: Legislative Assembly, Government of Ontario.

Stewart, David. 2004. "Charlottetown deputy mayor rejects charge of conflict in shelter vote." *Charlottetown Guardian*, March 2.

Takahashi, Lois, and Michael Dear. 1997. The Changing Dynamics of Community Opposition to Human Service Facilities. *Journal of the American Planning Association* 63, 1: 79–94.

Teschinsky, Ursula. 2000. Living with Schizophrenia: The Family Illness Experience. *Issues in Mental Health Nursing* 21, 4: 387–96.

Toronto Association for Community Living [TACL] 2004. *Annual Report, 2003–2004*. Toronto, ON: TACL.

Welch, Mary Agnes. 2004. "City Hall approves transitional housing: Residents fear complex will attract trouble." *Winnipeg Free Press*, July 9.

Wilton, Robert. 2002. "Colouring Special Needs: Locating Whiteness in NIMBY Conflicts." *Social and Cultural Geography* 3, 3: 303–22.

Supreme Court Cases Cited

Nova Scotia (Workers' Compensation Board) v. *Martin*; *Nova Scotia (Workers' Compensation Board)* v. *Laseur*, [2003] 2 S.C.R. 504.

Toronto Area Transit Operating Authority v. *Dell Holdings Ltd.* [January 30, 1997] 1 S.C.R.32.

Ontario Court of Appeal Cases Cited
Lighthouse Niagara Resource Centre v. *The Corporation of the City of Niagara Falls* [February 7, 2003] O.J. No. 3490.

747926 Ontario Limited v. *Upper Grand District School Board* [October 10, 2001] O.J. No. 3909.

Great Lakes Power Limited v. *Regional Assessment Commissioner, Region No. 31* [August 5, 1999] O.J. No. 2833.

Slough Estates Canada Limited v. *Regional Assessment Officer Commissioner* [January 20, 1999] O.J. No. 2554.

Ministry of Transportation v. *Tripp* [August 5, 1999] O.J. No. 2832

Shanahan v. *Russell* [December 19, 2000] O.J. No. 4762.

Grushman v. *Ottawa (City)* [May 7, 2001] O.J. No 4642.

Devine v. *Ontario (Ministry of Transportation)* [March 22, 2002] O.J. No. 1056.

Mississauga (City) v. *Erin Mills Corporation Limited.* [June 25, 2004] O.J. No. 2690.

Toronto (City) v. *Goldlist Properties Inc.* [October 14, 2003] O.J. No. 3931.

London (City) v. *Ayerswood Development Corporation* [December 13, 2002].

Ontario Divisional Court
Toronto (City) v. *Torgan Developments* (1990) O.J. No. 55.

Toronto Transit Commission v. *Toronto (City)* (1990) O.J. No. 2049.

Manitoba Court of Appeal
Alcoholism Foundation of Manitoba v. *Winnipeg* (1990) 65 Manitoba Reports (2nd) 81.

OMB Cases Cited
Aurora (Town) Zoning By-Law No. 2213-78 (Re) [2001], O.M.B.D. No. 1156.

Canadian Islamic Trust Foundation v. *Mississauga* [1998], O.M.B.D. No. 299.

Chatham-Kent (Municipality) Zoning By-Law No. 102-2003 (Re) [2003], O.M.B.D. No. 946.

Deveau v. *Toronto (City)* [2003] O.M.B.D. No. 0569.

Eboh v. *Markham (Town)* [2002], O.M.B.D. No 85.

Hamilton (City) Zoning By-Law No. 97-147 (Re) [1999], O.M.B.D. No. 127.

Hamilton (City) Zoning By-Law No. 97-147 (Re) [2000], O.M.B.D. No. 411.

Keppel (Township) Zoning By-Law No. 119-1992 (Re) [2000], O.M.B.D. No. 875.

McDonald v. *Toronto (City) Committee of Adjustment* [2001], O.M.B.D. No. 749.

Milton (Town) Official Plan Retirement Community Amendment (Re) [2000], O.M.B.D. No. 1246.

Newmarket (Town) Official Plan Amendment No. 20 (Re) [2004], O.M.B.D. No. 41.

Ottawa (City) Zoning By-law No. 20-2000 (Re) [2000], O.M.B.D. No. 566.

Ottawa (City) Zoning By-Law No. 205-2000 (Re) [2000], O.M.B.D. No. 381.

Sarnia (City) Official Plan Amendment No. 30 (Re) [2001], O.M.B.D. No. 759.

Sarnia (City) Zoning By-Law No. 118-2001 (Re) [2002], O.M.B.D. No. 250.

Sophiasburgh (Ward) Zoning By-Law No. 1056 (Re) [2002], O.M.B.D. No. 1060.

Surex Community Service v. *Toronto (City) Committee of Adjustment* [2004], O.M.B.D. No. 548.

Talim-Ul-Islam Ontario v. *Toronto (City) Committee of Adjustment* [1998], No. 1076.

Toronto (City) Interim Control By-Law [2000], O.M.B.D. No. 530.

Toronto (City) Official Plan Amendment No. 244 (Re) [2003], O.M.B.D. No. 792.

Legislation

Assessment Act, R.S.O. 1990, c. A. 31.
Development Changes Act, 1997, S.O. 1997, c. 27.
Expropriations Act, R.S.O. 1990, c. E. 26.
Ontario Human Rights Code, R.S.O. 1990, c. H. 19.
Planning Act, R.S.O. 1990, c. P. 13.

CHAPTER 5

PUTTING CYBERSPACE IN ITS PLACE:
LAW, THE INTERNET AND SPATIAL METAPHORS

MICHAEL S. MOPAS

INTRODUCTION

> Cyberspace. A consensual hallucination experienced daily by billions of legitimate operators, in every nation.... A graphic representation of data abstracted from the banks of every computer in the human system. Unthinkable complexity. Lines of light ranged in the nonspace of the mind, clusters and constellations of data. Like city lights, receding. —William Gibson (1984)

The above excerpt, taken from William Gibson's 1984 science-fiction novel *Neuromancer*, is frequently cited by academics and Internet enthusiasts as the very first appearance of the term "cyberspace." Although this term was originally coined well before the emergence of the Internet into popular Western culture and the mainstream use of applications like e-mail and the World Wide Web (www), cyberspace now commonly refers to the domain of human activity and social interaction made possible through advancements in computer-mediated communication. Twenty years after the initial publication of *Neuromancer*, the term has become a part of most people's vocabulary and has even made its way into the online version of the *Oxford English Dictionary* (2004), which defines it as:

> The notional environment within which electronic communication occurs, esp. when represented as the inside of a computer system; space perceived as such by an observer but generated by a computer system and having no real existence; the space of virtual reality.

What is clear from this definition and Gibson's description presented above is that cyberspace has no real physical geography; it is not a physically tangible place like a living room or a library. Instead, it is a spatial metaphor that describes the "consensual hallucination" of a "virtual reality" experienced by those using this technology.

In spite of the fact that it cannot be located geographically, the use of the term cyberspace and other references to it "as a place" allows us to ignore the various technical complexities surrounding this new medium.

The language of DNS (Domain Name System) server addresses and TCP/IP (Transmission Control Protocol/Internet Protocol) protocols that is foreign to most is replaced with spatial images that are more familiar and easily understood. But, as Richard Ford (2003: 154) suggests, thinking about the technology spatially will "not *help* us to understand the Internet so much as it will affect the *way* we understand the Internet" (emphasis in original). Moreover, the manner in which we conceptualize the Internet directly shapes the way we approach this new technology. In particular, the form of knowledge that becomes readily accepted and relied upon has immediate consequences for how the Internet may be regulated.

Like in other countries, the courts in Canada have recently faced the challenge of deciding whether or not other nation-states can rightfully impose their laws on Canadian citizens for activities that transpire over the "global" network of the Internet. Given the legal tradition of determining jurisdiction on the basis of territory, the courts are often required to answer the following question: Where in the (physical) world does an activity take place when it occurs "online"? In order to do so, the courts must first establish a general sense of how computer-mediated communication operates. Perhaps not surprisingly, the courts have avoided the use of highly technical jargon and have opted to think about the Internet spatially.

However, the courts' importation of the cyberspace metaphor and other spatial references has transformed it from a way of understanding Internet technology to a legal construct. By taking up and mobilizing this concept of cyberspace, the work of various legal actors has reproduced it as a "real" place within the context of the law. This legal recognition of cyberspace "as a place" figures prominently in the determination by the courts in Canada of legal jurisdiction on the Internet. As a result, one could argue that cyberspace has become less virtual and more of a reality. To use a term from a branch of Science and Technology Studies (S&TS) called Actor-Network Theory (ANT), the courtroom is a site where cyberspace has been "translated." And, much like the translation of text from one language to another, the transportation of cyberspace from a literary to a legal register does not always render a precise reiteration. Thus, the cyberspace that is constructed and produced by the courts is far different from the utopian vision imagined by early Internet enthusiasts.

By examining the various Canadian court judgements where the term "cyberspace" appears, (and utilizing key analytical tools from ANT and S&TS in this examination) this chapter considers how the spatial metaphor of cyberspace is taken up and translated in law. Rather than engaging in the current debate over whether or not the "cyberspace as place" metaphor is an appropriate one (see, for example, Hunter 2003; Lemley 2003), the chapter looks at the ways in which the courts spatially conceptualize and articulate this technology, and the effects that are generated from the formation of these kinds of knowledge. More specifically, I will focus on how the "cyberspace as place" metaphor has been adopted in cases that deal with the question of legal jurisdiction on the Internet, and I will assess the impact this has had on judicial decision making. I will then discuss the ways in which the courts have turned cyberspace from a literary device used to describe the technology of the Internet to a legal "reality." Thus I take a different approach to exploring the nexus between "place" and "justice" than the one used by the other authors in this edited collection. Instead of directly addressing the question of the "place of justice," I consider how conceptualizing the Internet in spatial terms has allowed the courts in Canada to render online disputes, particularly those involving parties from different jurisdictions, "justiciable" or subject to jurisdiction. I begin this discussion by documenting how spatial discourse is currently being used as a way to talk about and make sense of computer-mediated communication.

"BUILDING CYBERSPACE" AND THINKING ABOUT THE INTERNET "SPATIALLY"

During the very early stages of its development, access to the Internet was limited to researchers, those in certain areas of government, and the academic community (See Castells 1996; Gutstein 1999). Not until the invention of the modem in 1978 was network connectivity made available to those outside this select group. With this new piece of hardware, individual computers were now able to directly communicate and transfer files without the assistance of a host system. Further advancements in technology then made it possible to link computers together over regular telephone lines. Computer users, who were not affiliated with a university or research institute and thus excluded from the private network of the Internet, had found a way of connecting with each other on their own.

Yet this new technology created more than just an alternative means of communication. In addition, it allowed for bonding or "communion" among Internet users (Watson 1997: 104). Thousands and thousands of networks emerged to support discussions on topics ranging from politics and religion to sex and research. Howard Rheingold (1993: 5), one of the early "pioneers" of the Internet, views these shared discussions as the primary foundations of the "virtual community," which he defines as the "social aggregations that emerge from the Net when enough people carry on those public discussions long enough, with sufficient human feeling, to form webs of personal relationships in cyberspace." More importantly, many of the early developers held a decidedly American-centric view of this technology and believed it would create a "space" that was far different from the "real" world. This new "cyber" space was the electronic equivalent of the Western Frontier; it was "open, free, and replete with endless possibilities" (Hunter 2003: 443).

Over the last two decades, however, the Internet has undergone a variety of changes. It has grown from a network open only to researchers and academics to a global means of mass communication. Although it was once thought to be inappropriate to utilize the Internet for commercial purposes, users can now purchase anything from groceries to automobiles at the click of a mouse. In North America, dial-up connection to the Internet has almost become obsolete, as DSL (Digital Subscriber Line) technology, high-speed cable access, and wireless networks become the industry norm. But, while the technology and its availability have drastically changed, the ways in which we think about and conceptualize the Internet appear to remain the same.

More specifically, many people still commonly use the term cyberspace to describe the abstract and virtual domain created by the advancements in computer-mediated communication. Indeed, the Internet continues to be heavily dominated by spatial and territorial imagery. Stephen Graham (1998: 166) goes even further, suggesting that the "expanding lexicon of the Internet" is "not only replete with, but actually *constituted* by, the use of geographical metaphors" (emphasis in original). So, for example, by using a web browser like Internet "Explorer" or Netscape "Navigator," one can get on the "information superhighway" and "visit" websites, "surf" the Net or construct "home pages." Furthermore, many cyber-libertarians maintain an Athenian image of the Internet as a new "information commons" and a space for public discourse where "all can speak, all can hear, and all can consider, in a process of open and constructive debate" (Herbert 2000: 101).

Capitalizing on this notion of cyberspace as a new dimension of exploration to market their web browser and computer operating system, Microsoft aired commercials with images from around the world asking consumers, "Where do you want to go today?" Obviously, however, no one really "goes anywhere" when using the Internet. Though we may have the visual or sensory experience of travel, we do not actually leave our physical environment to "enter" cyberspace. A number of scholars have also questioned the appropriateness of the "cyberspace as place" metaphor. Mark Lemley (2003: 524) argues that the "idea of cyberspace as a physical place is all the more curious because the instantiation that most resembles travel to the casual user — the World Wide Web — is in fact much more like a traditional communications medium." People do not actually "visit" websites; instead, they send a request for information to the provider of the website who, in turn, sends back data in the form of a web page (Lemley 2003: 524). Because this process is automatic and almost instantaneous, there is an appearance that the user has actually "arrived" at another page by clicking on a hypertext link. The fact that these pages can come from anyone and from anywhere in the world may push us further into thinking this process is more like travelling and less like communication.

Some critics have argued that spatial metaphors are purposefully used to separate the Internet from other means of communication like the telephone or the television. Jonathan Koppell (2000) explains,

> One reason that cyberspace is described as a place is to avoid downgrading it to the status of a mere medium, and perhaps especially to

avoid comparisons with television. Those who would distinguish the Internet from television point out that Web denizens are not mere passive recipients of electronic signals. That may be (partly) true. But telephones and the postal system are also communications media that allow two-way communication. We don't regard them as places.

He further suggests that thinking of the Internet as a place makes it seem more intriguing, thus providing computer companies and Internet Service Providers (ISPs) with a powerful marketing tool to sell more computers and Internet services. As Koppell (2000) writes, "the various websites, Initial Public Offerings (IPOs), and dot-coms-of-the-day feed on the fervour surrounding our exploration of this strange new land. By morphing the Internet into a destination, cyberspace has become the Klondike of our age."

Regardless of whether or not we "buy in" (no pun intended) to these spatial metaphors, it is important not to discount their value. These metaphors are more than just literary tools that help us colourfully describe what are, in effect, "abstract flows of electronic signals, coded as information, representation, and exchange" (Graham 1998). In addition, they influence the way we think about and understand this technology. As Graham (1998: 166) points out:

> The metaphors that become associated with information technologies are, like those representations surrounding the material production of space and territory, active, ideological constructs. Concepts like the 'information society' and the 'information superhighway' have important roles in shaping the ways in which technologies are socially constructed, the uses to which they are put, and the effects and power relations surrounding their developments. Metaphors also encapsulate normative concepts of how technologies do or should relate to society and social change.

Furthermore, metaphors can be taken up by social actors and deployed to generate particular effects. Policy makers, industry spokespeople, journalists and academics often use these metaphors to promote their own interests by conveying certain images of what the Internet is or should be in the future (Wyatt 2004: 244). Consequently, Wyatt (2004: 244–45) cautions that metaphors "need to be handled carefully" as they can be used to help the imaginary become real or true. Metaphors can thus be understood as both a tool to achieve certain goals and a reflection of the desires and views of those who use them.

Another way of viewing metaphors is to see them as forms of knowledge (see Ford 2003). The use of the term "cyberspace" offers us a much easier way of understanding and conceptualizing how the Internet operates and functions as a means of communication. Rather than thinking about the technical aspects of network connections and packet-switching design, we can reduce the level of complexity by relying on these spatial metaphors as shorthand references. So, instead of describing websites as recombined bits of data that are transmitted from a computer on one end of a network at the request of another, we can simply talk about sites being "put up on the web" or "posted in cyberspace."

The more the term cyberspace gets taken up and used, however, the less we need to think of the machinery that lies behind it. Indeed, it may be fair to say that most Internet users rarely ever consider all of the underlying and intermediary steps that occur when they sit in front of a computer and browse a website or send an e-mail. Instead, cyberspace is thought of as a place (real or virtual) that can be dissociated from the technology by which it is produced. To borrow a term from S&TS, cyberspace becomes "black boxed." As I illustrate later in this chapter, this "black-boxing" process, in turn, produces a common or lay knowledge about the Internet, and how it operates, that can be used in place of computer expertise and technical know-how.

METAPHORS AND ANALOGIES AT WORK IN LAW

Metaphors are generally used to help make sense of the new or unknown by drawing connections to the things we know about. They are constructed by mapping familiar and understandable qualities onto unfamiliar objects; as a result, they can generate new thoughts about how these objects work that were not there in the first place (Hunter 2003: 471). As discussed throughout this chapter, the "cyberspace as place" metaphor lets us think about and understand Internet communication as having the same spatial characteristics as the physical world. Consequently, metaphors are more than just literary or linguistic devices: they can actually "form part of the core of our cognitive conceptual system" (Hunter 2003: 470).

But metaphors can also be analogized to make a variety of inferences. As Dan Hunter (2003: 472) points out, if we accept that cyberspace is a place, then it can be "zoned, trespassed upon, interfered with, and divided up into a series of small landholdings that are just like real world property holdings." What is important to note here is that it is this initial connection between the Internet and space that lets us draw the analogy with the "real world" and make these metaphorical deductions.

As in other areas of social life, metaphors and analogies play a key role in law. Cass Sunstein (1993) suggests that analogical reasoning is the paradigm most frequently used by lawyers and non-lawyers alike to think about legal and moral questions. He describes the four basic steps involved in this type of legal thought as follows:

(1) Some fact pattern A has a certain characteristic X, or characteristics X, Y, and Z; (2) Fact pattern B differs from A in some

respects but shares characteristics X, or characteristics X, Y, and Z; (3) The law treats A in a certain way; (4) Because B shares certain characteristics with A, the law should treat B the same way. (Sunstein 1993: 745)

In order for analogies to work, it is important to know that A and B are "relevantly" similar and that relevant differences do not exist between them. The major challenge, however, is in deciding when the differences between them are indeed particularly relevant and thereby concluding that the analogy no longer applies.

Given the level of complexity surrounding computer-mediated communication, it is perhaps not surprising to see legal actors relying on metaphors and analogies as a way of making "legal" sense of this new technology. Looking at the responses to the Internet in criminal, tort, and constitutional law in the United States, Hunter (2003) has examined the influence of the "cyberspace as place" metaphor and its social and legal consequences, demonstrating, for example, that by adopting the notion of "computer trespass," U.S. courts have taken up the spatial conception of the Internet. He goes onto show how pre-Internet computer laws like the *Computer Fraud and Abuse Act* (CFAA) of 1986 have been used to regulate this new technology.

Under the CFAA, it is a criminal offence to "access" a computer system without permission. But when applied to the Internet, the predominance of the "cyberspace as place" metaphor drastically alters this notion of "access." Hunter (2003: 482–82) writes:

> Viewed through the filter of the cyberspace as place metaphor, computer trespass does not just involve an infringement on my right to use the personal property of my computer system. Instead, the action becomes a trespass against a form of quasi-land that exists online.

In a number of cases, U.S. courts have come to the conclusion that anyone using a publicly accessible website is "entering" a place and should be treated "just like an invitee at common law" (Hunter 2003: 482). Consequently, those who enter without authorization are trespassing. Moreover, much like the real world where conditions of entry may be posted on the doors of private establishments, websites can have digital signs in the form of "Terms of Access" documents that serve the very same purpose. If the person oversteps the bounds of their invitation, then, they too, become trespassers and can be subject to the full force of the criminal law.

Hunter laments that thinking about the Internet in spatial terms has led to "undesirable private control" and the irreversible "tragedy of the digital anti-commons." He suggests that by drawing analogies to the physical environment, a legal framework has been established that imposes notions of private property upon the Internet. This has allowed commercial interests to dominate and "enclose" cyberspace by forcing the courts to recognize and acknowledge online property rights. Thus, much like the real world, property now exists in cyberspace that can be "privately owned, parceled out, and exploited" (Hunter 2002: 446).

In response to Hunter, Mark Lemley (2003) provides an alternate reading of U.S. case law pertaining to the Internet; he offers a far less pessimistic view of the future. While he agrees with Hunter's observations about the courts' reliance on the "cyberspace as place" metaphor and the subsequent consequences of its adoption in law, Lemley suggests that courts and commentators still "have ample room to make reasoned policy decisions" (2003: 523). As Lemley states, it is "easy to be misled by metaphor, but we need not be its slave" (2003: 523).

Lemley, who emphasizes that there is no such place as "cyberspace," elaborates the reasons for his assertion that spatial metaphors about the Internet are highly inaccurate. Pointing to the fact that it is data — in various forms, such as e-mail, downloaded information, MP3 files or viruses — and not people doing the travelling on the Internet, Lemley expresses concern that because courts are relying on these analogies to the physical world, they are thus applying laws to the Internet without a clear understanding of how the technology actually works. Referring to the application of the CFAA on the Internet and publicly accessible websites, he explains that the courts have failed to see that no one "enters" websites: he notes that the defendant in these cases merely sent requests for information to a web server which the plaintiff had, itself, made open to the public, and that the plaintiff's own server sent information in return.

Even if we do decide to adopt these spatial metaphors and accept a one-for-one correspondence between cyberspace and the real world, there are clearly differences that the courts need to take into account. For Lemley, these exceptions are critical. He notes, for instance, that, unlike the physical world where an individual can occupy only one place at a time, the Internet allows you to be everywhere at once. There is also no sense of proximity to one another in cyberspace as there is in the physical world. Nor is there a "public street or sidewalk from which one might observe behaviour that occurs in a particular Internet space" (Lemley 2003: 526).

Despite these concerns, Lemley points out a number of cases where the courts have taken note of these differences without having to completely reject the cyberspace as place metaphor. He suggests that the courts have gotten "these cases right" by using this metaphor as a "point of departure," proving that they can be receptive to the idea that Internet law can use a framework designed for the real world through modifications that account for the peculiarities of cyberspace. For example, the application of personal jurisdiction rules and the metaphors of the physical world have often led the courts to the conclusion that anyone who puts up a website can be sued by anyone in the world, on the basis that they have put their "products" in cyberspace and thus into each and every forum. Although a number of early cases took this position, most courts came to the realization that more criteria were needed. The result has been the development of "interactivity" tests for jurisdiction where a "sliding scale" is established between "passive" and "active" uses of the Internet (discussed in more detail below). Although the tests are still somewhat problematic, Lemley suggests that these cases are clear examples of courts applying traditional standards for determining personal jurisdiction while still being sensitive to the nature of the Internet.

Even with the courts recognizing the limitations of these metaphors and the ways in which cyberspace is decidedly not like the physical world, Lemley still remains rather cautious. Like Hunter, Lemley is concerned that the cyberspatial metaphor has led to the emergence of private property on the Internet. Nevertheless, he believes that the "cyberspace as place" metaphor is not global or inevitable and that, in applying this metaphor, the courts still have to decide whether or not this space should be public or private. According to Lemley, the courts must begin to understand that a metaphor is no substitute for legal analysis.

Dan Hunter and Mark Lemley eloquently illustrate the power of spatial metaphors in influencing legal thinking about the Internet and the drastic implications that this has for bringing private property online. Nevertheless, both scholars share a very deterministic view of the cyberspace-as-place metaphor: they take the position that this has forced judges into viewing the Internet spatially and making legal decisions that promote private property rights online. Judges are seen here as passive recipients who naively accept the cyberspace-as-place metaphor without taking into account many of its limitations. However, this argument rests on a number of implicit assumptions.

First, it is assumed that the cyberspace as place metaphor is the only way that legal actors can think about the Internet. On the contrary, there are certainly different approaches to understanding and conceptualizing this new form of technology. Indeed, one of the most obvious ways is to think about the Internet as a means of communication. Adopting this "Internet as communication" metaphor, and drawing analogies to other mediums like the telephone, seems equally logical and would have a profoundly different impact on legal reasoning and decision making. Thus, if we are to look seriously at the influence of metaphors, then it is important to recognize the plurality of forms of knowledge: we need to consider how certain conceptions of the Internet, which are adopted over others, become dominant in legal thought; alternatively, we need to think about how these conceptions may work in conjunction with other ways of understanding this technology.

The second major assumption is that metaphors only operate in one direction; that is, spatial metaphors directly shape how judges perceive the Internet. In effect, this would suggest that judges take a largely passive role when making legal decisions. On the contrary, one could argue that judges are fully aware of the fact that this notion of cyberspace is simply a metaphor.

And, rather than being slaves to these metaphors, judges are utilizing them as tools to help inform and justify their decisions. Thus, like other social actors, judges "actively" rely upon and mobilize this spatial conception of the Internet to generate particular legal effects.

Despite these criticisms, Hunter and Lemley have greatly contributed to the existing body of research in the area of Internet law by recognizing the importance of metaphors. Using their work as a point of departure, I hope to expand upon this type of socio-legal inquiry in two important ways. Firstly, I consider how courts in Canada have taken up the cyberspace-as-place metaphor by looking specifically at cases where the term "cyberspace" appears. Secondly, I look at the cyberspace-as-place metaphor as one of several ways of conceptualizing the Internet and trace how this particular form of knowledge gets "translated" into legal thought.

The theoretical and methodological approach I take in this chapter is heavily influenced by the general field of Science and Technology Studies (S&TS) and the specific branch of research known as Actor-Network Theory (ANT). In recent years, socio-legal scholars who draw from the work of Michel Foucault and analyze the practices of knowledge and its relation to governance, have borrowed key analytical and conceptual insights from ANT to examine how various forms of scientific and non-scientific knowledges are "translated" into and out of legal settings (Valverde *et al.* 2003; Valverde 2003; Levi 2003). In the section that follows, I provide a brief overview of some of the main analytical concepts of ANT and consider how it has been recently incorporated into socio-legal scholarship.

ACTOR-NETWORK THEORY (ANT) AND SOCIO-LEGAL RESEARCH

Actor-Network Theory (ANT) offers a particular approach to investigating the ways in which scientific facts and technological artifacts come to be produced. Associated with the work of Michel Callon, Bruno Latour and colleagues at the École des Mines, ANT is a relatively new method within the interdisciplinary field of Science and Technology Studies (S&TS). Like many other branches of S&TS, ANT researchers argue that knowledge is a social product rather than something generated through the operation of a privileged scientific method.

ANT also focuses on science and technology "in the making" (Latour 1987: Introduction). Rather than analyzing the final products of a computer, a nuclear power plant, the shape of a double helix or a cosmological theory, ANT researchers follow scientists and engineers in the production of these scientific and technical objects. They start out by rejecting any preconceptions as to what constitutes knowledge or technology and look closely at the ways in which scientific facts and technological artifacts become stable entities, processes or laws, dissociated from the circumstances of their production. Using the language of S&TS, the goal is to examine how it is that science and technology become "black boxed."

ANT researchers do not to look for intrinsic qualities that determine the objectivity or subjectivity of a claim, or the efficiency or perfection of a mechanism. Instead, this type of analysis considers the later transformations that these objects undergo in the hands of others (Latour 1987: 258, see also Chapter 1). As Latour (1987: 29) argues,

> By themselves, a statement, a piece of machinery, a process are lost. By looking only at them and at their internal properties, you cannot decide if they are true or false, efficient or wasteful, costly or cheap, strong or frail. These characteristics are only gained through incorporation into other statements, processes and pieces of machinery. These incorporations are decided by each of us, constantly.

The "black boxing" of facts and machines is thus a collective process. When confronted with a black box, we make a numbers of decisions as to whether or not we take it up, reject it, reopen it or drop it through lack of interest (Latour 1987: 29). These later decisions have direct consequences. If we buy a machine or believe a fact without question, then we make the black box more solid (Latour 1987: 29). But, if we reject the fact or machine, they are weakened and their spread is interrupted.

The goal for those applying an ANT approach is to follow these networks. ANT researchers pay particular attention to the organizing and ordering processes whereby "social action and material and technical elements are brought together — or translated — into a coherent network out of which certain achievements are attained" (Manning 2002: 651; for a detailed discussion on "translation," see Callon 1986; Latour 1987). Contrary to its more contemporary meaning as a method of transport *without* deformation, network within the ANT context refers to the exact opposite process. More specifically, it refers to a chain of *translations* that involves a series of *transformations*.

This notion of translation is central to ANT. The term was originally taken from the work of Michel Serres by Michel Callon (1980): it involves making convergences and "homologies" by relating things that were previously different (Gherardi and Nicolini 2000: 333). It also conveys the mechanical and physical meaning of causing movement in the same direction, as well as the linguistic definition of "undertaking a change from one language to another in which betrayal is inextricably implicated" (Gherardi and Nicolini 2000: 333). As a result, what is passed through the network is never the same at the beginning as it is at the end.

Moreover, these networks are composed not only of people, but also of objects, machines, texts, and so on. All of these actors — both human and non-human — are in constant relation with one another and are capable of action. "Scientific knowledge" is thus the end result of "heterogeneous engineering," in which

Bits and pieces — test tubes, reagents, organisms, skilled hands, scanning electron microscopes, radiation monitors, other scientists, articles, computer terminals, and the rest — that would like to make off on their own are juxtaposed into a patterned network which overcomes their resistance. In short, it is a material matter but also a matter of organizing and ordering those materials. (Law 1992)

If the translation is successful and the heterogeneous materials are stabilized, the network disappears and is replaced by the action itself and the seemingly simple author of that action (Law 1992: 5). Once stabilized, the network can produce ordering effects such as devices, agents, institutions or organizations that represent and stand for something else.

Socio-legal scholars have recently borrowed some of the key insights from ANT to examine practices of knowledge and their relation to governance (Valverde et al. 2003; Valverde 2003; Levi 2003). In particular, these scholars have looked at knowledge claims as the products of translation and heterogeneous networks. Within the legal context, the primary focus of empirical analysis is on the ways in which certain material objects (such as exhibits, precedents, advocacy skills, rhetorical moves and so on) are aligned or "tactically arranged" to achieve certain results (Valverde et al. 2003: 16).

Valverde, Levi and Moore suggest that adopting some of the concepts found in ANT may help lay the groundwork for socio-legal scholarship which goes beyond the dichotomy of studying "law in the books" (as a static and disembodied entity) versus "law in action" (emphasizing struggles and tactics, but usually leaving out law itself) (2003: 16). ANT is particularly useful in this respect as it provides an approach that simultaneously focuses on law in the books and in action (Valverde et al. 2003: 16). From an ANT perspective, the law "in the books" can be viewed both as a network and as an actor. On one hand, it functions as a spokesperson for other objects and texts, taken from other sources that have been ordered and stabilized to allow for their representation as "law." At the same time, however, the law as a non-human entity also provides action as it is constantly taken up as a "black box" and translated into other networks.

Using case studies of Megan's law[1] and community notification practices, case studied from Toronto's Drug Treatment Courts, and the legal discussions regarding the criminalization of soliciting for the purposes of prostitution, Valverde, Levi and Moore (2003) illustrate the interplay between law and risk and the "swapping" of legal and extra-legal knowledges. Contrary to the assertion of certain risk scholars who suggest that the law "absorbs, transforms and dominates" extra-legal knowledges (scientific or otherwise), the authors emphasize the dynamic and interactive nature of this relationship. They argue that it is no longer useful to assume that "expert witness testimony" is epistemologically homogenous (Valverde et al. 2003: 4). They have also found that various legal actors can and do make use of both extra-legal information and the general authority of science to generate legally effective decisions (Valverde et al. 2003: 4).

The focus of the empirical research described above is placed on the translations or movements of knowledges that occur during various legal processes. By taking the position that the term "cyberspace" and other spatial references are more than just metaphors and must be understood as a type of knowledge regarding Internet technology, I adopt a similar socio-legal approach and follow the process by which this knowledge gets "translated" in legal thought. Rather than simply documenting the number of instances where the term cyberspace is taken up in law, I consider the ways in which this form of knowledge is used by judges to inform legal reasoning and decision-making. Particular attention is paid here to the mobilization and movement of this "spatial" knowledge regarding the Internet and how it gets reproduced within legal settings. The court decisions are thus read more empirically, while still bearing in mind the doctrinal and institutional contexts from which they emerge.

THE CYBERSPACE AS PLACE METAPHOR: THE CANADIAN LEGAL CONTEXT

At the time of writing, a search for the term "cyberspace" in Canadian judgements on the Quicklaw Database yielded fourteen matches.[2] This relatively small number may be expected given that the term has only recently entered our lexicon. One could only predict that this number will increase in the near future as it becomes more commonly used in daily language. Nonetheless, the cases that do exist provide an interesting site for examining how this "cyberspace-as-place" metaphor gets taken up in law.

In the majority of the cases examined,[3] judges flippantly use the term cyberspace in comments made in passing. As in other arenas, judges often use "cyberspace" as a spatial metaphor to describe the domain of social interaction and human activity created by Internet technology. In several of these cases, people using the Internet are characterized as "engaging in cyberspace" or having "met others in cyberspace." It has even been used rather facetiously to describe a place where one can "reside." In a family court case involving child custody and access, for instance, the presiding judge describes an absentee father in the following way: "From the children's perspective, [the father] did not just leave their mother; he left them as well when he chose to pursue a relationship with another woman. Even today, they do not know where their father has been living or is now living. He seems to exist, from their vantage point, *in cyberspace* or on the road with his employment" (*Fraser v. McKinlay [2004], O.J. No. 479*, emphasis added). This comment was made in reference to the fact that much of the father's contact with his children was done through e-mail.

In other cases, "cyberspace" is used as a spatial metaphor to describe a type of virtual abyss where digital information gets lost. For example, in

Crisanti v. *Canada* (1996) the Tax Court of Canada dismissed an appeal from an appellant regarding late penalties imposed against him for his 1993 income tax returns, which he had submitted electronically. In dismissing this appeal, the presiding judge remarked, "there is nothing before me which would indicate that the appellant's tax return was transmitted before the deadline and that it was sitting in storage, or *floating in cyberspace*, before being accepted by the Revenue Canada computer..." (emphasis added).

While it may be unwise to read too much into these comments, it is interesting to note that the term cyberspace retains its common meaning as a "virtual" environment made possible by the Internet. It is a place where people meet and interact, and things like tax returns go missing. Another interesting point is that almost all of these judges used the word cyberspace without giving any type of explanation or definition of the term. Instead, it is perhaps somehow assumed that the term is part of everyday language. In only one instance did a judge attempt to provide additional clarification by referring the term to the Internet and computer-mediated communication.

Yet there are other cases where cyberspace and the nature of Internet technology are more central to the decision. In *Braintech* v. *Kostiuk (1999)*, the defendant, Mr. Kostiuk, a resident of British Columbia (B.C.), allegedly posted defamatory messages on a Bulletin Board System (BBS) site about the plaintiff, Braintech Inc. Although Braintech Inc. is also located in B.C. the company sued the defendant in Texas where it has a research facility. A Texas court found in favour of Braintech Inc. and awarded them approximately $400,000 in damages. The company then attempted to have the Texas judgement enforced in B.C. While the trial court in B.C. held in favour of Braintech Inc., the Court of Appeal reversed the decision and held, among other things, that Texas had improperly asserted its jurisdiction in this matter.

One of the key legal questions in this case was whether or not the defendant, Mr. Kostiuk, had committed a tort in Texas by transmitting and publishing defamatory and disparaging untruths. More specifically, does posting a message on an Internet BBS constitute "real and substantial presence" in Texas? The B.C. Court of Appeal ruled against the plaintiffs, reasoning that:

> In these circumstances the complainant must offer better proof that the defendant has entered Texas than the mere possibility that someone in that jurisdiction might have reached out to cyberspace to bring the defamatory material to a screen in Texas. There is no allegation or evidence Kostiuk had a commercial purpose that utilized the highway provided by Internet to enter any particular jurisdiction. (*Braintech* v. *Kostiuk (1999)*: at para. 62)

This decision rested largely on the Court's adoption of the "interactivity" test established in *Zippo Manufacturing Co.* v. *Zippo Dot Com, Inc. (1997).* The critical finding here was that the jurisdictional analysis in Internet cases should be based on the "nature and quality of the activity conducted on the Internet" (Geist 2002: 24). Consistent with well-developed principles of personal jurisdiction, a sliding scale is used to distinguish between "passive" and "active" uses of the Internet.

Personal jurisdiction is proper only in cases where the defendant "clearly does business over the Internet" or "enters into contracts with residents of a foreign jurisdiction that involve the knowing and repeated transmission of computer files over the Internet" On the other end of this spectrum are instances where a defendant has "simply posted information on an Internet Web site which is accessible to users in foreign jurisdictions." These "passive web sites" do "little more than make information available to those who are interested": they provide no grounds for the exercise of personal jurisdiction (*Zippo Manufacturing Co.* v. *Zippo Dot Com, Inc. [1997]*). In adopting this approach, the B.C. Court of Appeal made this suggestion:

> The allegation of publication fails as it rests on the mere transitory, passive presence in cyberspace of the alleged defamatory material. Such a contact does not constitute a real and substantial presence. On the American authorities this is an insufficient basis for the exercise of an *in personam jurisdiction* over a non-resident. (*Zippo Manufacturing Co.* v. *Zippo Dot Com, Inc. [1997]*, cited in *Braintech* v. *Kostiuk (1999)*, para. 65)

But what is perhaps most striking about this decision concerning legal jurisdiction is how the Court relied on this concept of cyberspace.

In both of the passages presented above, cyberspace refers to an intermediary place where electronic data are posted. The alleged defamatory messages made by the defendant on an electronic BBS do not "enter" Texas or remain in B.C., but are present in a type of digital "middle-ground." The fact that the message had a "mere transitory, passive presence *in cyberspace* [my emphasis]" is used as a basis for denying the Texas court's assertion of jurisdiction. The use of the term "cyberspace" is particularly relevant here. By invoking this term, cyberspace gets translated into legal thought and is understood as the place where data transmitted over the Internet "exists." Regardless of whether or not this was a conscious decision on their part, the fact that the judges thought about the Internet spatially and legally, placing these messages "*in* cyberspace," gave the Court even more reason and justification for adopting the interactivity test as a way to determine personal jurisdiction.

The "spatial quality" of cyberspace as an intermediary place for data and information, coupled with these tests for interactivity, also sets it apart from other forms of communication and broadcasting. For the B.C. Court of Appeal, the fact that information posted on a BBS could possibly be read by someone in Texas was not enough to "constitute a real and substantial presence" in that state. Rather, the defendant's messages were said to have a "mere transitory, passive presence in cyberspace" and, consequently, did not qualify them as a form of publication. Therefore, it is not simply the fact that the material gets transmitted via the medium of the Internet that determines its status, but the nature of what is being broadcasted or communicated that is taken into consideration. In taking this position, the Court also recognized and made mention of the "crippling effect on freedom of expression" that this would create, if the simple viewing of material on the Internet alone could be used as the basis for a country to claim jurisdiction.

The legal precedent set in *Braintech* v. *Kostiuk (1999)* regarding jurisdiction on the Internet is later taken up in a civil trial heard by the Ontario Superior Court. In *Pro-C Ltd.* v. *Computer City Inc. (2000)*, the plaintiffs, Pro-C Ltd., sought damages against the defendants, Computer City Inc., for trademark infringement. Pro-C Ltd. is a company based in Waterloo, Ontario that merchandises software and provides consulting services. The company owns the trademark WINGEN in Canada, produces software under this name, and has registered the website URL address: www.wingen.com. Computer City, a Delaware-based computer superstore chain with retail locations throughout the U.S., Europe and Canada, marketed computers under the name WINGEN. These computers were sold over the company's website and stores in the US. While Computer City was aware of Pro-C's trademark and had ample time to change the WINGEN name, the company sold the computers under this name. Consumers seeking information about the WINGEN computers caused havoc with Pro-C's business by crashing its website and overflowing its e-mail capability. Pro-C Ltd. contacted Computer City about these problems and, while Computer City offered their assistance, they proposed no solutions and continued to market these computers.

At the very outset of the written decision, the presiding judge begins by describing cyberspace in relation to Internet technology. Whitten J. writes:

> The Internet, in reality a network of networks, has created a whole new territory independent of conventional geography. The conceptual location of this electronic interactivity available to us through our computers is oft referred to as "cyberspace." Unlike a "real" territory with fixed borders, the Internet is constantly growing and at a phenomenal rate. (*Pro-C Ltd.* v. *Computer City Inc. 2000*, para. 1)

> The Internet has become an immense mass of information or data. Again, in contrast to a real territory, it is not mapped in the sense of its limits and features being charted. The cartographers of the net are the various directories and search engines but they are

hampered by the sheer immensity and growth rate of the Internet. The search for any "site" is keyword driven. (*Pro-C Ltd.* v. *Computer City Inc. 2000*, para. 2)

A distinction is thus made between the "reality" of the Internet as a "network of networks" and the "conceptual location" of electronic interactivity referred to as cyberspace. The judge goes on to further describe cyberspace as a "whole new territory independent of conventional geography" and sets it apart from "real territory" with fixed borders. This separation from the "real world" and the reference to cyberspace as a "conceptual location" implies an understanding that it is not like a "physical place."

The descriptions provided by the judge are rather telling. They not only reflect the ways in which this technology is viewed and understood, but also serve to illustrate how certain types of knowledge are imported from other sites. In making these claims about the Internet, the judge refers to an article on the jurisdiction of cyberspace published in *Wake Forest Law Review* that was cited by another judge in the U.S. It is this particular way of thinking about cyberspace and the Internet, more generally, that gets taken up and translated into legal reasoning. As the presiding judge explains, it is "against this backdrop" that the matter takes place.

At issue in this case was whether or not Computer City's "use" of the WINGEN trademark comes within the jurisdiction or scope of the *Canadian Trademarks Act*. The presiding judge states:

> "Use" in Canada is the jurisdictional paradigm. The *Act* can only confer the property right within Canada and likewise can only protect the right from unsanctioned usage in Canada. Consequently, any liability in Canada from a breach of this statutory regime has to be based on unsanctioned usage in Canada. The "use" by Computer City of the WINGEN trademark must be in Canada. (*Pro-C Ltd.* v. *Computer City Inc. 2000*, para. 85)

If it does, and if this use offends the provisions of the statute, the court may award damages. Although the computers bearing the WINGEN name were never sold in Canadian stores, they were marketed on the Computer City website and accessible to those in Canada, thus posing the following question: Is the fact that Canadian residences can access a particular website originating from outside Canada sufficient to constitute "use" in Canada?

In making its determination regarding "use," the court relied upon the legal precedent set forth in *Braintech* v. *Kostiuk (1999)* and its adoption of the interactivity test for jurisdiction on the Internet, originally established in the Zippo case. Whitten J. states:

> Both Zippo and Braintech illustrate the conceptual problems with Internet use and jurisdiction, the latter of which under the *Trade-*

marks Act translates into "use" in Canada. The basic issue is invariably, does the website remain "out there" in cyberspace or is there a connection established with a particular geographical entity or state of such a magnitude that the entity could claim jurisdiction. The degree of interactivity between the website and the state is in the absence of other traditional indicia, for example a physical presence within the state, a helpful starting point for any such analysis. (*Pro-C Ltd.* v. *Computer City Inc. 2000*, para. 117)

It is interesting to note here is that the judge not only adopts the same legal approach to determining jurisdiction, but takes up the concept of cyberspace as well. As in the *Braintech* case, cyberspace is used as a spatial metaphor to describe a digital place "out there" where websites and "online" advertising can exist. As a result, cyberspace and the notion of interactivity are both "translated" into this new context of trade-mark law. The same legal test used to decide "clear and substantial presence" is now being applied to address the question of trademark "use."

Although the court ruled that www.computercity.com was a "passive" website, it argued that the interactivity test was not the only basis for deciding what constituted a trademark use in Canada. Noting that "invariably Canadians will reach out into cyberspace and access the webpage" (*Pro-C Ltd.* v. *Computer City Inc. 2000*, para. 132), the presiding judge determined that the site must also be "seen in the context of the overall merchandising strategy of Computer City" (*Pro-C Ltd.* v. *Computer City Inc. 2000*, para. 135) to target Canadian consumers. The court found that Computer City's use of the WINGEN trademark on its website was "a use" in Canada under the *Trade-mark Act* and in accordance with principles of jurisdiction and tort law, and subsequently ordered the company to pay Pro-C Ltd. $750,000 in punitive damages.

FROM "PLACE" TO "SPACE": CYBER-SPATIAL METAPHORS AND THEIR IMPLICATIONS FOR ONLINE JURISDICTION

There are currently very few cases in Canada where the word "cyberspace" is used and even fewer where it plays a central role in legal reasoning and decision making. Interestingly enough, the two cases in which this term figures most prominently deal with the question of jurisdiction on the Internet. In both *Braintech* v. *Kostiuk (1999)* and *Pro-C Ltd.* v. *Computer City Inc. (2000)*, the courts take up and subsequently "black box" cyberspace as a spatial metaphor to describe the domain of social interaction created by the Internet. One presiding judge clearly describes cyberspace as a "conceptual location" of "electronic interactivity" and a "whole new territory independent of conventional geography."

Some critics (see Johnson and Post 1996a; 1996b; Post 1997; Barlow 1996) have taken this notion of cyberspace as being a separate place that is far different from the "real world" as a basis for rejecting any form of government intervention on the Internet. They claim that cyberspace should be treated like any other territory and must be recognized as its own sovereign nation. To these cyber-libertarians, any attempt by an existing nation-state to impose its law on "citizens of the Internet" is viewed as an "extra-territorial power grab" and a "form of colonialism" that is to be met with strong opposition (Johnson and Post 1996b; Post 1997).

John Perry Barlow, former lyricist for the Grateful Dead and co-founder of a cyber-libertarian organization called the Electronic Frontier Foundation (EFF) makes this sentiment quite clear in his famous "Declaration of the Independence of Cyberspace." Echoing the U.S. Declaration of Independence, he writes:

> Governments of the Industrial World, you weary giants of flesh and steel, I come from Cyberspace, the new home of Mind. On behalf of the future, I ask you of the past to leave us alone. You are not welcome among us. You have no sovereignty where we gather.... You have no elected government, nor are we likely to have one, so I address you with no greater authority than that with which liberty itself always speaks. I declare the global social space we are building to be naturally independent of the tyrannies you seek to impose on us. You have no moral right to rule us nor do you possess any methods of enforcement we have true reason to fear. (Barlow 1996)

Many of these same critics (see Johnson and Post 1996a) also argue that the very nature of this technology makes centralized control and the enforcement of rules "from above" virtually impossible. As data over the Internet regularly travel across national borders, laws determined by a certain geographic jurisdiction become extremely difficult to apply on this network "designed precisely to make geography irrelevant and indeterminate" (Post 1997; but see also Johnson & Post 1996a; 1996b; Johnson 1996).

Yet this very American-centric conception of cyberspace as a "new frontier" is strikingly different from the one employed by the Canadian courts. The judges in these cases do not view cyberspace as an autonomous nation-state populated by Internet users or "netizens." On the contrary, it is largely perceived as a digital wasteland that lies somewhere in-between the traditionally recognized borders of sovereign territories. The courts understand cyberspace less as a "place" and more as an intermediary "space" where data and information transmitted via the Internet "exist" (or, in some instances, "go missing"). Material posted on a website or a BBS does not automatically "enter" a jurisdiction, where it is viewed, nor does it reside in its place of origin. Nor can it be located "inside" a specific Internet server. Instead, it is believed to be somewhere "out there" in cyberspace.

Thus, while the technical reality is that the Internet operates more like a traditional communications medium whereby data is immediately sent back and forth between two computers, this particular view has been largely ignored in favour of a more spatial understanding of the technology. It is this more common or lay knowledge about the Internet that the courts in Canada have taken up and translated into legal thought when dealing with the question of online jurisdiction. This vision of cyberspace adopted by the courts not only provides a way of thinking about the Internet, but also allows for the traditional practice of connecting jurisdiction with physical territory to still be legally relevant in these cases.

As discussed earlier, some American scholars (see Hunter 2003; Lemley 2003) have argued that the adoption of the "cyberspace-as-place" metaphor has led to the increasing privatization and "enclosure" of this new medium. However, it is equally important to consider what one might perceive to be a more positive implication in taking this approach. By recognizing cyberspace as a digital "no man's land" that is positioned somewhere in-between the territorial borders of the two parties involved, the Canadian courts were forced to realize that, while the general practice of linking jurisdiction with territory could still be applied, it could not generate an adequate solution. As a result, one could argue that the courts had no other choice but to rely on another framework for establishing jurisdiction on the Internet.

Instead of assessing jurisdiction based on the mere presence of material posted on a BBS or a website, the courts in both *Braintech Inc.* v. *Kostiuk (1999)* and *Pro-C Ltd.* v. *Computer City Inc. (2000)*, relied upon the interactivity test established in the Zippo case as a way of distinguishing between "active" and "passive" uses of the Internet. The courts thus moved away from a territorial conception of jurisdiction to one that is more relational and takes into account the quality and nature of the online communication. In doing so, the courts have avoided determining legal forum on the sole basis of the material "crossing" into the place where it is viewed; they have also precluded the possible application of jurisdiction on anyone, anywhere. Yet these decisions may have only been reached by first thinking about the Internet in spatial terms and placing the material in question "out there" in cyberspace.

MAKING CYBERSPACE A LEGAL "REALITY"

Richard Ford argues that "territories are made, not found" (2003: 151; see also 1999). Although it may appear to be something that has evolved naturally, Ford views territorial jurisdiction as a "technology that was 'invented' or 'introduced' in a given social setting at a particular time." He explains its emergence as the "product of the coincidence of two innovations": the science of cartography and the ideology of rational, humanist government (2003: 151).

In a much similar vein, the Internet only "becomes" cyberspace because we make it so (Ford 2003: 151). One way cyberspace is "made real" is by having others accept it as more than just a spatial metaphor. So, while Internet enthusiasts like John Perry Barlow and Howard Rheingold would certainly have us believe that "cyberspace" is truly a "real" place where "real" people reside, it is important for us to consider whether or not this particular view of the Internet is being adopted in other settings. Drawing again on some of the key concepts in ANT, I reiterate that the success of an idea or technical invention is highly dependent on "chains of translation" and on how other external actors take up these objects for their own "network building purposes" (Valverde et al. 2003: 15–16). Objects that are successfully taken up and acknowledged without question become "black boxes."

As I have attempted to illustrate in this chapter, the courtroom is one specific site where cyberspace is being "black boxed" and translated from a spatial metaphor to a legal reality. But, while the technology is still thought about and described spatially, the different actors that have transported and mobilized the concept of cyberspace into law have been relatively unfaithful to the work of early Internet "pioneers." In cases regarding online jurisdiction, the Canadian courts have not seen cyberspace as a sovereign territory whose autonomy must be respected. Rather, the courts have taken up this concept in a way that suits their needs and have perceived it as a digital middle ground that exists somewhere outside the cartographic borders of any territorial jurisdiction. Put simply, much of what these Internet enthusiasts envisioned for cyberspace has been "lost in translation." Nevertheless, by taking this view and adopting it into judicial decision-making, the courts have transformed cyberspace into a legal construct, which, in turn, has had a very "real" and direct impact for how they approach the question of jurisdiction on the Internet.

CONCLUSION

This chapter has examined the use of the term "cyberspace" in Canadian court judgements and illustrated how it has been translated into legal thought. Rather than viewing "cyberspace" as a spatial metaphor or linguistic device used to simply describe the virtual world of human activity and social interaction made possible by the advancements in computer-mediated communications, it is considered here as one type of "black-boxed" knowledge of Internet technology that gets taken up by judges in their decision making, and directly influences how they have approached the issue of online jurisdiction.

Unlike other legal cases where the nature of a technology is brought into question, the courts in both *Braintech Inc.* v. *Kostiuk (1999)* and *Pro-C Ltd.* v. *Computer City Inc. (2000)* do not rely upon technical knowledge or expertise to help inform their decisions. Instead, the spatial metaphor of cyberspace and a more common or lay understanding of how the Internet operates are employed. Ironically, viewing the Internet "spatially" appears to have helped Canadian judges to re-examine claims of jurisdiction as a matter of territorial boundaries and to consider more complex questions regarding the quality of the communication. At the same time, the importation of this spatial discourse into law has turned cyberspace from a literary device used to describe the technology of the Internet to a legal "reality."

NOTES

1. Megan's Law refers to the various state laws in the U.S. that require local law enforcement agencies to notify the public at large, through various media, about the presence of certain sex offenders in their areas. The law was named after seven-year-old Megan Kanka of Hamilton Township, New Jersey. In 1994, she was kidnapped, raped ad murdered, allegedly by a neighbour who was a twice-convicted sex offender. All fifty states do not have a form of Megan's Law.
2. The Canadian Judgements Plus (CJP) database was used here. As of May 15, 2004, only fourteen cases were found that included the term "cyberspace."
3. For this chapter, only cases where the term "cyberspace" figured prominently in the case and where it had some bearing on the decision were selected for analysis.

REFERENCES

Barlow, J.P. 1996. "A Declaration of the Independence of Cyberspace." In N. Spiller (ed.), Cyber_Reader: Critical Writings for the Digital Era. New York: Phaidon Press.

Callon, M. 1980. "Struggles and Negotiations to Define what is Problematic and what is Not: The Sociology of Translation." In K.D. Knorr, R. Krohn and R.D. Whitley (eds.), The Social Process of Scientific Investigation: Sociology of the Sciences Yearbook. Boston: Reidel.

_____. 1986. "Some Elements of a Sociology of Translation: Domestication of the Scallops and Fishermen of St. Brieuc Bay." In J. Law (ed.), Power, Action and Belief: A New Sociology of Knowledge? London: Routledge and Kegan Paul.

Castells, M. 1996. The Rise of the Network Society. Malden, MA: Blackwell Publishers.

Ford, R. 1999. "Law's Territory: A History of Jurisdiction." Michigan Law Review 97: 843.

_____. 2003. "Against Cyberspace." In A. Sarat, L. Douglas and M. Umphrey (eds.), The Place of Law. Ann Arbor: University of Michigan Press.

Geist, M. 2001. "Everybody Wants to Rule the Web." Globe and Mail, 18 January. Available at <http://www.globetechnology.com/archive/gam/E-business/20010118/TWGEIS.html>. (Accessed October 11, 2001.)

_____. 2002. "Is There a There There? Toward Greater Certainty for Internet Jurisdiction." Available at <http://aix1.utoronto.ca/~geist/geistjurisdiction-us.pdf>. (Accessed April 22, 2004.)

Gherardi, S., and D. Nicolini. 2000. "To Transfer is to Transform: The Circulation of Safety Knowledge." Organization 7(2): 329–48.

Gibson, W. 1984. Neuromancer. New York: Ace.

Graham, S. 1998. "The End of Geography or the Explosion of Place? Conceptualizing Space, Place and Information Technology." Progress in Human Geography 22 (2): 165–85.

Gutstein, D. 1999. E.con: How the Internet Undermines Democracy. Toronto: Stoddart.

Herbert, S. 2000. "Zoning Cyberspace." In A. Sarat and P. Ewick (eds.), *Studies in Law, Politics, and Society, Vol. 20*. Stanford, CT: Jai Press.

Hunter, D. 2003. "Cyberspace as Place and the Tragedy of the Digital Anticommons." *California Law Review* 91 (2): 439–519.

Johnson, D. 1996. "Let's Let the Net Self-regulate." Available at <http://www.cli.org>. (Accessed May 1, 1999.)

Johnson, D., and D. Post. 1996a. "Law and Borders: The Rise of Law in Cyberspace." *Stanford Law Review* 48 (5): 1367–402.

———. 1996b. "And How Shall the Net be Governed? A Meditation on the Relative Virtues of Decentralized, Emergent Law." Available at <http://www.cli.org>. (Accessed May 1, 1999.)

Koppell, J. 2000. "No There There: Why Cyberspace isn't Anyplace." *The Atlantic Monthly Online*. Available at <http://www.theatlantic.com/issues/2000/08/koppell.htm>. (Accessed April 28, 2004.)

Latour, B. 1987. *Science in Action: How to Follow Scientists and Engineers through Society*. Cambridge, MA: Harvard University Press.

Law, J. 1992. "Notes on the Theory of the Actor-Network: Ordering, strategy and heterogeneity." *Systems Practice* 5: 379–93.

Lemley, M. 2003. "Place and Cyberspace." *California Law Review* 91(2): 521–42.

Levi, R. 2003. *Governing Crime, Governing Community: The Constitution of Community in Legal Sites*. University of Toronto, Faculty of Law, SJD Thesis.

Manning, N. 2002. "Actor Networks, Policy Networks and Personality Disorder." *Sociology of Health & Illness* 24 (5): 644–66.

McChesney, R. 1999. *Rich Media, Poor Democracy: Communication Politics in Dubious Times*. Urbana: University of Illinois Press.

Oxford English Dictionary. 2004. Available at <http://dictionary.oed.com>. (Accessed April 23, 2004.)

Post, D. 1997. "The Cyberspace Revolution." Keynote address at Computer Policy and Law Conference, July 9, Cornell University. Available at <http://www.cli.org>. (Accessed May 1, 1999.)

Rheingold, H. 1993. *The Virtual Community: Homesteading on the Electronic Frontier*. Reading: Addison-Wesley.

Serres, M. 1982. *Hermes: Literature, Science, Philosophy*. Baltimore, MD: Johns Hopkins University Press.

Statistics Canada. 2004. "Internet Use in Canada." Available at <http://www.statcan.ca>. (Accessed April 23, 2004.)

Sunstein, C. 1993. "On Analogical Reasoning." *Harvard Law Review* 106: 741–91.

Valverde, M. 2003. *Law's Dream of a Common Knowledge*. Princeton, NJ: Princeton University Press.

Valverde, M., R. Levi and D. Moore. 2003. "Legal Knowledges of Risks." Report to the Law Commission of Canada, presented at the joint session of the Canadian Association of Law Teachers and the Canadian Law and Society Association, Halifax, NS, June 2.

Watson, N. 1997. "Why We Argue About Virtual Community: A Case Study of the Phish.Net Fan Community." In S.G. Jones (ed.), *Virtual Culture: Identity and Communication in Cybersociety*. London: Sage.

Wyatt, S. 2004. "Danger! Metaphors at Work in Economics, Geophysiology, and the Internet." *Science, Technology & Human Values* 29 (2): 242–61.

Cases Cited

Braintech v. *Kostiuk (1999)*, 171 D.L.R. (4th) 46 B.C.C.A.

Crisanti v. *Canada (1996)*, T.C.J. No. 329 Tax CC TCJ 6333.

Fraser v. *McKinlay (2004)*, O.J. No. 479.

Pro-C Ltd. v. *Computer City, Inc. (2000)* 7 C.P.R. (4th) 193 OntSupCtJus CPR 117.

Zippo Manufacturing Co. v. *Zippo Dot Com, Inc. (1997)* 925 F. Supp. 1119 (W.D. Pa. 1997).

Legislation

Computer Fraud and Abuse Act (CFAA) of 1986, 18 U.S.C. Section 1030 (1996).

CHAPTER 6

WHO'S THE BEST ABORIGINAL?:
AN "OVERLAP" AND CANADIAN CONSTITUTIONALISM

SIGNA DAUM SHANKS[1]

A PRESENT CONFLICT IN THE NORTH, A FUTURE TREND IN CANADA

In an area of Canada overlapping the Northwest Territories, Saskatchewan, Manitoba and Nunavut, various physical images braid together to form a single isolated landscape called the "tundra" (Thorpe et al. 2001: 11). An occasional bluff containing coniferous trees appears beside flat, often boggy, terrain. Skies are reflected in small creeks and rivers that wriggle beside trees and granite. When spring arrives, fields of wild grass surface between clumps of treeless soil. The diversity does not end with the flora. The largest group of caribou in this region, dubbed the "Beverly herd," migrate based on how the land functions and how other animals accepts its presence (Macdougall 2002: 14). Unless the caribou live in tandem with other species, they do not live at all (Brody 1981: 18 and 279).

This chapter is about how humans fit into the Beverly herd territory (hereinafter "BHT") (Echohh 1997: 5). As I hope to describe, there has been a history of human occupants emulating how the land naturally functions (Taylor 1998: 11). Today, however, this pattern has ended and a rather stressful conflict exists about how the land should be managed and what rules should govern this management (Bussidor and Bilgen-Reinhart 2002: 13). The rules are part of Canada's current legal system. My focus is about how an earlier balance has been replaced by a situation that is, in my mind, extremely imbalanced in how it benefits people.

Why use Canadian law as the way to describe a story about caribou? My choice is based on one observation regarding different opinions of the BHT. The views of various participants are dissimilar; their goals are often also quite oppositional. However, the commonality shared by all the parties is their belief that their own actions are completely legal. But, as their means and goals clearly conflict, at least one party must understand Canadian law better than the other(s). My reflections, while specific to BHT, are generally applicable to Aboriginal-Crown (and Aboriginal-Aboriginal) relations in Canada. In other words, the BHT example exposes some general concerns that I contend are underexplored and misunderstood. The ramifications of this ignorance and inaccurate analysis are stressful and ultimately challenge our assumptions about what values our laws should enforce. The BHT's overlap of natural conditions (which in fact demonstrates a type of balance) is still called an "overlap" but here the context carries a negative connotation. Since it would appear that examples of law-based overlaps will continue, it is imperative to provide discussion about the true nature of such a situation.

By providing details about how a constitutionally-based overlap develops, analyzing such a story's legalistic nature and providing some observations about the impact Canadian law has on a conflict in the BHT, fundamental assumptions about the success of Aboriginal-government relations become worth challenging. Moreover, conclusions about how historical data is used in Canadian law are uncovered. BHT was a place of relative calm before the rule of (Canadian) law was imposed. Now, it is a place where activities considered constitutional actually stop the proper application of fundamental legal tenets. This contradiction — involved in assuming that constitutionalism improves lives, but observing that it actually hurts some members of society — is imperative to understand if the rule of law is to be justified. Today, some Aboriginals become the best they legally can be by terminating other groups' legal rights. Whether such a situation is truly legal (and just) is what I want to question in examining the story of the BHT.

CHANGING TIMES, CHANGING THE RULES ABOUT OVERLAPPING IDENTITIES

In addition to the caribou, families from two indigenous cultures have lived off of this land since time immemorial. Part of the Dene culture and members of the eastern Inuit can trace their cultural, economic and legal heritage to BHT: their norms have been enforced by the caribou's activities and the land's natural conditions. Their histories, over time, show a true reverence for what the land can provide and what limitations the land demands (McMillan and Yellowhorn 2004: 239–60, 273–79, 284).[2]

Through understanding BHT as one land space, one learns that the Dene and the Inuit both understand their own autonomy and their realistic co-existence with another nation. The Dene, more active in the south and western parts of BHT, understand their past in a more inland and less winterly way than their Inuit neighbours (Bussidor and Bilgen-Reinhart 2002: 30). The Inuit, in comparison, recollect aspects of the land which demonstrate a culture with a maritime and more northern location (Purich 1992: 28). Both cultures, whether in technology, linguistics or economic relations, demonstrate internal independence and recognition of interrelations (Bennett and Rowley 2004: 137–42; McCormack 1988: 17; Ray 1996: 28–29; Bussidor and Bilgen-Reinhart 2002: 5). The caribou herd plays a vital part in the definition of each culture's norms. The caribou make Dene people Dene and the Inuit people Inuit. As the Royal Commission on Aboriginal

Peoples explains, the Inuit culture live "in conditions demanding great resourcefulness, inner strength and quiet patience.... [They have] a technology more complex than that of any other preindustrial culture" (1996: 78–79). The Beverly herd teaches skills, provides staples and demonstrates respect for the land: if this is not reinforced by the Inuit and Dene, their survival is not ensured (Pryde 1972: 178–92; Tester and Kulchyski 1994: 237).

This existence of two cultures in a stable relationship, respecting each other's need for survival, is not only an indigenous phenomenon. British exploration, followed by Canadian national policies, impacted indigenous life conditions in ways that non-Aboriginals and academics are only now beginning to appreciate. While the Dene and Inuit did experience variations of colonialism, they mainly did so much later than other southern indigenous nations. Their experiences with treaty making illustrate this point.

The history of treaty making occurred during the last three centuries. The goals of the treaties vary among the agreements' signatories. Trade, peaceful relations and land settlement for immigrants often influence government officials when drafting the treaties' contents. Due to the location of the Dene and Inuit, and the fact that their land was not essentially useful for achieving many Crown priorities, government agents largely left agreements for regions occupied by Inuit and Dene families alone. But when land value came to include below-soil exploration, Dene territory suddenly seemed important. When mining techniques became more successful, Dene leaders were eventually approached. Chiefs were not averse to treaty making. They understood that a nation's self-understanding included the determination of criteria for belonging to their culture. What Dene chiefs opposed, however, was the Crown strategies for achieving settlement. Encounters in what is now southern Saskatchewan, between First Nation communities and newcomers, were not positive. Chiefs were, in many cases, forced to sign agreements in order to keep their community members alive. As well, documents had a normative assumption of land surrender that was not explained fully to signatories (Venne 1997: 173). Dene leaders, upon learning what happened to their southern neighbours, assertively rejected Crown proposals. Unless they could be assured that Dene lives would continue after treaty making as they did before, chiefs were uninterested (Buckley 1992: 28; Francis, Jones and Smith 1992: 64).

Crown agents repeatedly reassured chiefs that the Dene way of life would not be jeopardized. This promise not only reassured the Dene; it also soothed government officials in Ottawa. If the Dene were self-sufficient, Canada would need to provide less assistance to this isolated and hard-to-reach part of Canada.[3] If the Dene could hunt the Beverly herd, it wouldn't need the provisions that other First Nation bands regularly received through treaty details and Indian Act provisions. In a sense, maintaining a pre-treaty Dene identity was beneficial to all treaty parties. After deciding that the documents did not jeopardize their economic, cultural and legal practices, some Dene leaders became signatories to Treaty 8 in1899. Other chiefs signed Treaty 10 in 1906 (Miller 1989: 106; Van Kirk 1999: 89). The caribou hunt represented the reinforcement of a traditional activity: it was a way to observe what was then modern treaty adherence (McCormack 1988: 16, 81; Ray 1996: 274; Macdougall 2002: 20).[4]

In comparison, the Inuit of BHT have no historic treaties with the Crown (Tester and Kulchyski 1994). Perhaps because their natural resources seemed more difficult to access, or because the land's remote location made it less important to settle as a way of demonstrating Canadian sovereignty, the colonizers allowed Inuit communities to function essentially as they had prior to any contact with Europeans. Colonizing policies undoubtedly impaired Inuit communities in many other devastating ways. But Inuit families persevered courageously: they have proven incredibly resilient in maintaining traditional knowledge (Purich 1992: 28–37). Thus, even though the Dene had a treaty and the Inuit did not, each culture successfully reinforced an activity in which they jointly participated prior to contact with Europeans. Into the twentieth century, hunting the caribou in BHT continued as it always had (*Re. Eskimos* 1939; see also Backhouse, 1999).[5]

Although many moments between Aboriginals and non-Aboriginals during the twentieth century were certainly not particularly just, some events helped achieve better conditions for Aboriginals in Canada. Many of these improvements occurred as a result of arguments presented in courtrooms: their implications are still experienced today. In 1973, the *Calder* v. *A.G.B.C.* (1973) case detailed how the Supreme Court of Canada decided arguing for "Indian title" was possible. Crown officials had a fiduciary obligation to protect this title due to the responsibilities explained in the Royal Proclamation of 1763 (*St. Catherines Milling and Lumber Co.* v. *the Queen 1888*).[6] Canada quickly invented a policy as a means to avoid losing future litigation. Called the "comprehensive claims" policy, it described how if an indigenous community believed it had enough evidence to prove it had legal land title to a region, it could approach the federal government to negotiate a settlement (Canada 1981). Many Aboriginal political organizations, and non-Aboriginal sympathizers, helped protest the Trudeau government's "White Paper." After the Prime Minister made his constitutional ideals known, lobbyists continued to support Aboriginal calls for any future Canadian constitution to make mention of Aboriginals in its contents (see Department of Indian Affairs and Northern Development 1973). The Prime Minister and Premiers, originally against this idea, changed their minds after deciding that a section about Aboriginals would limit, rather than expand, Aboriginal rights in the future.

Section 35 of the *Constitution Act* (1982) explained that Aboriginal peoples would receive constitutional protection for Aboriginal and treaty rights (Walkem and Bruce 2003: 11).[7] This legislation triggered another policy-making move in Canada — the "Specific Claims" policy, which permitted any community believing its treaty rights had been infringed upon to commence negotiations with Canada in order to avoid litigation (see Canada 1982).

Throughout the 1980s, courts were repeatedly asked to explain what "Aboriginal right" and "treaty right" meant, and how these terms related to the fiduciary obligation in the Royal Proclamation. In perhaps the most famous example, in 1984, then Justice Dickson explained in Guerin that indigenous rights were "sui generis" (meaning "unique" or "sacred") (*Guerin* v. *the Queen 1984*). He connected the interpretation of section 35 to the legal responsibilities created by the Royal Proclamation (*Guerin* v. *the Queen 1984*: 385, 387). With this development, it seemed that the Dene and Inuit were in good constitutional stead. The Dene treaty rights were constitutionalized; as well, the Inuit had a strong argument for a "comprehensive claim" that would, when implemented, achieve constitutional protection. Historic relationships could be given modern status, and modern agreements could acknowledge the importance of the past. This sense of optimism was brought to a sudden halt in 1989, when the Dene received word from the Department of Indian Affairs and Northern Development (hereinafter "DIAND"), that the federal government wanted them to end hunting the caribou in BHT, effective immediately.[8] Incensed by such a demand, the Dene filed a Specific Claim. This application was quickly rejected: at this point the Dene commenced traditional court proceedings and filed necessary documents for a lawsuit in the Federal Court of Canada (Purich 1992: 15–16; see also, *Fond du lac band* 1993).[9]

While the Dene considered their options, other legal questions were under scrutiny. In 1990 the Supreme Court brought a ruling, explained by then Chief Justice Dickson in *Sparrow* (1990), that "Aboriginal title" (replacing the phrase "Indian title" in *Calder* v. *A.G.B.C.*) was an example of an "Aboriginal right" as mentioned in s.35. Land title, therefore, became a constitutional concern. He continued to describe how sovereignty was always understood as belonging to the Crown (see Macklem 1991). Moreover, the Crown could ignore claims of s.35 rights if other concerns of the country appeared more important. But if the Crown wished to violate a s.35 right, the point of the violation must be "reasonably justified" (*Sparrow* 1990: 1087) and "compelling and substantial" (*Sparrow* 1990: 1113).

These legal changes happened at the same time as other political tensions were developing. The "Oka Crisis," which emerged after a rejected Specific Claim in Quebec, made Canada and Canadians think more about what issues were actually impacting Aboriginal-government relations (see York 1999). As a result, Prime Minister Mulroney announced two policies aimed at decreasing the distrust between Canada's indigenous peoples and Crown authorities. A Royal Commission would commence a national investigation about historic and modern injustices (*Unfinished Business* 1990: 3). In addition a venue would provide an alternative place for investigating rejected Specific Claims. The Indian Claims Commission (hereinafter the "ICC"), introduced in 1991, would hopefully help all affected parties find reconciliation to conflicts (Orders-in Council 1991-1329 and 1992-1730; Hurley 2002). The emergence of the ICC meant that the Dene had another way to argue for their understanding of Dene treaty rights. The Dene filed an application at the commission on December 1, 1992, requesting an inquiry regarding their Specific Claim (Indian Claims Commission 1993: 161). By this time, the Dene understood why Canada would not want Dene rights to continue. Apparently the agreement currently under negotiation with the Inuit contained sections that conflicted with how the Dene interpreted Treaty 8 and Treaty 10. A version of modern Inuit constitutional rights, when implemented, could not possibly permit Dene hunting to occur in its current form.

Since the early 1970s, the Inuit were part of a larger group that was negotiating a settlement with the Crown. In 1991, the settlement's version was essentially complete and simply needed passage through Parliament. The *Nunavut Land Claims Agreement Act* (hereafter the "*NLCA*") defined the location for a third territory called "Nunavut." This modern treaty, to be implemented as of April 1, 1999, decreed that the Nunavut Inuit would obtain complete ownership of 353,610 square kilometres (18 percent) of the territory.[10] A territorial government would have powers similar to provinces regarding regulatory mechanisms; all boards and commissions would be comprised solely of Inuit people (*NLCA*, 5.2, 12, 13). One board, for example, would hold $1.15 billion (*NLCA*, 25, 31) with a mandate to improve and stabilize economic and cultural aspects of Inuit customs (*NLCA*, 32), through such measures as education grants and government employment (*NLCA*, 23). For the Dene, the most notable part of the *NLCA* was the fact that the future territorial government gained the right to determine who would hunt in the territory (Burrows 1998: 448–49). Although other individuals and groups could obtain permission to hunt in Nunavut territory, the territorial government would ultimately decide which non-Inuit people these would be.[11] As parts of BHT where the Dene hunted would be located in Nunavut, the *NLCA*'s implementation directly conflicted with the application of Treaty 8 and Treaty 10.

When the Dene filed their application at the ICC, the federal government protested, claiming that the ICC was not authorized to evaluate the request. On April 1, 1993, the ICC ruled against Canada, and concluded that the application kept to the instructions governing the ICC, as explained in *Outstanding Business* (Canada 1982). Canada disagreed with the ICC's findings; it filed a second protest, arguing the Dene were asking for a "declaration of rights," and that ICC commissioners were being asked to interpret the Constitution, which was outside the ICC's legal realm. By finding that Canada did not know the definition of "lawful," the federal government replied that the ICC could easily remark about the matter without reference to constitutional issues, and that investigations would commence the following month (May 1993).[12]

While the House of Commons and the Senate passed the Nunavut Land

Claims Agreement Act *NLCAA*, ICC commissioners listened to presentations in communities located in Saskatchewan's most northern region. By
December 1993, after the *NLCAA* became law, the ICC concluded that the
federal government had a legal responsibility to permit and promote the
Dene hunt (Indian Claims Commission, 1993: 11). The ICC found that "the
very identity of the Dene people is inextricably linked to that portion of
their traditional territories north of the 60th parallel known as the 'barren
lands'" (Indian Claims Commission 1993: 10 and 63). How the Dene wanted
to hunt (and how they interpreted their treaty rights) protected this link
(Indian Claims Commission 1993: 62–63, 68 and footnote 166). As the ICC
states, if "the claimants be denied the existence of their rights, as provided
by treaty and law, there would be a 'non-fulfillment' of a treaty.... Part of
Canada's 'lawful obligation' is to ensure that doesn't occur" (Indian Claims
Commission 1993: 69).

As the ICC did not have the authority to write legally-binding decisions,
its report included "recommendations" only. Commissioners concluded
with two suggestions:

> The parties should remain mindful of the spirit and intent of the
> Policy and process, which is to encourage and support the fair
> negotiation of outstanding claims. This is best done without the
> application of technical court rules and procedures. ([1995] 3 ICCP
> 3 at 67)

> Outstanding Business does not strictly allow for the negotiation
> of this claim. However, other processes for negotiation of similar
> issues have been established by Canada, one of which is described
> as "Administrative Referral." As soon as possible, the parties should
> commence negotiation of the claimants' grievance pursuant to that
> process. (Indian Claims Commission 1993: 70)

When Canada chose not to enforce the recommendations, it was not breaching a judicial decision, so the Crown simply ignored the Dene and the ICC's
recommendations. The Dene had the ICC's favour, but was left in the same
legal place they were before the inquiry started.

The ICC reacted by releasing a second report about the BHT hunt ((1996)
4 ICCP 177 at 187). Not only did the ICC continue to support the Dene, but it
now concluded that Canada was breaching its obligations further by delay-
ing its reinstatement of the hunt (Indian Claims Commission 1996: 183).
According to the ICC, Canada's refusal to enforce the Dene hunt had created
"an absurd result" (Indian Claims Commission: 184). The Commission
repeated,

> the Ministers of Indian Affairs and Justice (must) formally recog-
> nize that the Athabasca Denesuline have unextinguished rights to

hunt, fish, and trap throughout their traditional territories pursuant to Treaties 8 and 10. In the alternative, if Canada is not prepared to recognize the existence of Denesuline treaty rights north of 60*, we would recommend that Canada provide litigation funding to the Denesuline to facilitate a resolution of the issue in the Federal Court. (Indian Claims Commission 1996: 187–88)

Although being careful not to directly interpret s.35, the effect of the ICC's position was clear: the Denes' treaty rights were violated.[13] Keeping to its previous position, Canada chose to ignore this second report as well.

During the 1990s, the *NLCAA* was regularly promoted as a template for future Crown-Aboriginal settlements. It garnered national and international attention as a document that actually balanced indigenous values with Crown prerogatives. Dene protests, in comparison, went largely ignored by the general public. Despite having provincial and national support for their plight from other indigenous organizations, and despite the constantly evolving condition of treaty rights jurisprudence, Canada did not recognize ICC findings and Dene calls for negotiations. Interestingly, Inuit leaders originally supported Dene outcries, but as soon as it became apparent that the *NLCAA* would need modification in order to aid Dene problems, that sympathy quickly ended. In 1999, the *NLCAA* became law, Nunavut's boundaries were enforced, and the territorial government's agenda was implemented. To this day, while Canada and Nunavut contend that the *NLCAA* is valid, the Dene continue to believe that it ignores their view about the hunt; they contend that the ICC's response does not take into account the fact that the Beverly herd moves back and forth across the human metes and boundaries that define two territories and two provinces. Currently organizing the documentation necessary for litigation, the Dene vow that the caribou's fundamental influence upon Inuit culture must be considered in context with Dene claims. Treaty 8 and Treaty 10 are not followed in the way they were prior to 1989.

THE NEW RULES' LEGAL IMPLICATIONS

After learning about this story, it is now important to determine the strength of each party's constitutive position. Currently, Nunavut and Canada agree with implementation of the *NLCAA* as politically appropriate and legally justified. In comparison, the Dene and the ICC view the *Act*'s contents as a clear violation of Treaty 8 and Treaty 10. Therefore, thinking about rights and responsibilities means imagining what would happen if this conflict actually did go through the current Canadian legal regime (as the Dene plan it will).

Three norms must be evaluated in order for the story's constitutional form to be exposed. One of them received regular mention during the ICC inquiry. The other two have influenced recent actions by the indigenous communities, but it was not possible to include them in ICC analysis in any overt fashion. It becomes clear that, although each has a separate function, they are as intertwined as the various land conditions in BHT. By thinking about which ones favour which party, we might more easily arrive at suggestions for resolution. After observing which party truly has the strongest constitutional foundation, I have developed reflections about the practicality of modern Crown-Aboriginal relations. Predictions about how future overlaps can be avoided have thus become less impossible to envision.

I consider the BHT conflict between Dene and Inuit relations with the Crown an example of a constitutive "overlap." This labelling is, however, more expansive than any included in previous mentions of overlaps. Before the BHT conflict, overlaps were mentioned as a potential problem between First Nation groups involving Aboriginal title (Sterritt 1998/1999; *Delgamuukw v. British Columbia* 1997: 9 and 185).[14] But referring to the BHT dispute as an overlap means that I am, in effect, arguing that an overlap can happen when any Aboriginal group clashes with another indigenous culture regarding the implementation of s.35 rights. This change is not, I think, legally unreasonable nor politically unrealistic. The more cultures envisage modern settlements, the more clashes with other Aboriginal groups must be imagined as possible. My use of overlap is therefore a call to consider problems in every Crown-Aboriginal relationship. This expanded definition has constitutional merit. This conflict of law is not about one section challenging another part's purpose, but is about the internal workings of one part of one document. Since Aboriginal title is a combination of Aboriginal rights and treaty concepts, the previous understanding of overlaps arguably already described treaty and activities rights. Including the Inuit and Métis in potential understandings of overlaps is simply a more proper inclusion of all indigenous groups (*Hunter v. Southam* 1984: 155; *R. v. Blais* 2003: 40).[15]

If my expanded understanding of "overlap" is justifiable, I now need to explain what norms are relevant for this discussion. The three notions, "fiduciary obligation," "treaty rights" and "Aboriginal rights," all influence how various parties acted. But they also reveal who would find true solace in Canadian law should litigation happen. Determining the strengths and weaknesses helps parties decide whether their positions are truly worth promoting.

"Fiduciary Obligation"
Throughout the BHT inquiry all parties referred to the "fiduciary obligation." This notion represents a protectorate relationship where the government ensures indigenous peoples' success within a non-indigenous created country. The guidance in *Calder v. A.G.B.C.* is vital, as it helps judges and the Crown realize that an arrangement is not just another contract with a group of people. It helps justify historically contextualized treaty agreements and understandings about issues that are not yet part of treaties. But it also

stands independent of constitutional interpretation. In short, the fiduciary obligation is an autonomous condition and a tool for comprehending other juridical concepts. Its nature, over the past twenty years, has also taken on two forms. The "best interest" obligation occurs when the Crown must do what it legally can to protest a matter which is in the indigenous party's best interest. As this condition does not yet have constitutional protection, it might not be a treaty right or Aboriginal right according to judicial review. But, should other national concerns seem more important than a best interest matter, the Crown can contend that the interest needs to be ignored. Should that claim be valid, the Crown must demonstrate the obligation's second version — the "duty to consult." Governments must communicate this lack of protection to the affected indigenous party. The duty's form will depend upon what will not be protected (see Rotman 1996). A "sliding scale" approach has been enforced by the Supreme Court of Canada in order to ensure that the ramifications of a violated best interest are fully understood (see Lawrence and Macklem 2000; *Haida Nation* v. *British Columbia (Ministry of Forests)* 2004: 38).

Examining the Dene's role in the BHT conflict reveals that they have experienced a breached fiduciary obligation of some type. Clearly, Canada's actions did not protect the Denes' best interests. But the Crown could contend that settling the NLCAA had national importance and that this act is a better interpretation of conservation and harvesting issues. It could, in other words, either claim it is in the Dene's best interests that the historic treaties be violated or that the violations were necessary: in that case the federal government needs only to demonstrate that consultation in the proper form was undertaken.

The Dene's dependence upon the BHT herd makes the first Crown argument incredibly weak. Due to the Dene's location, and the historic references to the hunt, little exists which could benefit the Dene as much as the hunt. Canada's first position, then, seems unlikely to succeed. But Canada's second position would, I think, be just as flawed. The hunt is not only important to the Dene, but arguably completely necessary. Moreover, how the Crown informed the Dene and the conditions of the termination were extremely harsh. Notification was the form of "consultation" here, and the notice demanded immediate termination. Dene views were not included in the Crown's decision-making, nor were the Dene given time to readjust to this policy change. Upon reviewing the norm's two types, I submit that Canada is likely in constitutional trouble and will owe damages to the Dene.

However, it will be difficult to create damages that do not breach Crown obligations owed to the Inuit. If, as the treaties support, the court orders the recommencement of the BHT hunt, either the Inuit's best interests will be violated or the duty to consult will be in question. If the BHT hunt is proven not to impair the Inuit's own hunt, perhaps the best-interest violation can be avoided. But if Canada does not inform the Inuit about how this litigation process usually happens, and what possibilities could occur, the Inuit could arguably contend that they have not experienced fair consultation. If so, the Inuit could easily claim that their ignorance about this possibility constitutes a breach.

The courts will need to demonstrate important creativity to end the triggering function of this component of the overlap. If a resolution does not take into account potential ramifications for all the indigenous nations, a decision's implementation simply continues the norms' conflicting roles. Informing parties that future arguments cannot happen due to a concern for legal stability will conflict with other jurisprudence regarding the un-constitutionality of "extinguishment clauses" (Burrows 2002: 108–10).[16]

Understanding that the story has fiduciary-obligation breaches by Canada in the form of DIAND is not, however, a complete understanding of this term's role. Besides analyzing the various forms "obligation" can take, this discussion also must include remarks about varieties of meanings of the term "Crown." Besides cabinet portfolios, other parties involved in overlaps could have a legal responsibility to ensure the obligation is enforced.[17]

In his evaluation of administrative tribunals, Sossin (2003) notes that the executive (cabinet) branch and the judicial branch of Canada's govern-mental system are inexorably linked. Their interaction, and interdepend-ency, is clear when one observes how a passed law influences jurisprudential possibilities, and how a decision, conversely, dictates what bills and acts are considered legal. This reality is not a negative trait. Instead, it is an unavoidable and helpful part of our democratic system. This realization of the connectedness of the cabinet and the judiciary, however, is a reminder that the legal roles of each branch must be regularly recalled and applied to entities which are invented to enforce parliamentary procedure. The point of truly understanding legal places is particularly vital when evaluating fiduciary obligations. These obligations must be demonstrated by the execu-tive branch but are not owed by the courts. An entity's actual form might or might not include a responsibility to enforce fiduciary obligations. The Supreme Court warns us that underappreciating the application of fiduciary obligations has unconstitutional and unjust effects (*Paul* v. *A.G.B.C.* 2003: 9, 22).

If a body participates in a legal problem, and it is unclear whether the body is akin to the Crown or is, instead, like the judiciary, how is the body's role determined? Certain Supreme Court decisions help answer this question. For instance, *Baker* v. *Minister of Citizenship and Immigration* (1999) includes many ways for evaluating legal roles of various parties. Here the Court concludes that an entity's role is only understood when both its legislative source and its daily activities are evaluated (*Baker* v. *Minister of Citizenship and Immigration* 1999: 53). When Aboriginal peoples are involved, the Court further concludes (in *C.P.R.* v. *Matsqui* (1995), that evaluating the source and activities is even more relevant: because their roles are sui generis, they must be is properly understood (*U.E.S., Local 298* v. *Bilbeault* 9088).

This distinction is considered important so as to appreciate a tribunal's or judiciary's impartiality and independence.

This concern about an entity's mandate and actual functions typically reveals data about a particularly helpful trait — partiality. Should a body not have impartiality, but instead enforces a "reasonable apprehension of bias," it cannot be considered judicial in nature (*C.P.R.* v. *Matsqui* 1995: 43). In Committee for *Justice and Liberty* v. *National Energy Board* (1978), the Court explains how to determine if the bias exists:

> what (would) an informed person, viewing the matter realistically and practically — and having thought the matter through — conclude [sic]. Would he think that (an evaluator)... whether consciously or unconsciously, would not decide fairly [sic].

Besides its bias (or lack thereof), another factor helps determine a body's proper categorization. If an entity's actions include the potential to produce "binding" decisions, it is functioning like the judiciary. It has replaced the first level of inquiry in a court of law. The party displeased with the results must appeal the findings. In *Paul* v. *A.G.B.C.*, a tribunal ceased to be judicial in nature because it did not have the power to analyze legal questions (*Paul* v. *A.G.B.C.* 2003: 41; see Sossin 2004: 111).[18] Bindingness, also mentioned in *Baker* v. *Minister of Immigration and Citizenship* (1999: 54) and Provincial Court Judges, (*Manitoba Provincial Judges Assn.* v. *Manitoba (Minister of Justice)* 1997: 140) means that the body is not political in its functions (*2727-3174 Québec Inc.* v. *Quebec (Régie des permis d'alcool)* 1996: 70).

But the Court has also found that an entity's failure to positively demonstrate similarities to one category does not mean it automatically defaults to the other branch. In other words, a body must have traits of one area as much as it does not emulate the other part of parliament. This finding was written in *Vancouver General Hospital* v. *Stoffman* (1990: 513), and reaffirmed in *2727-3174 Québec Inc.* v. *Québec (Régie des permis d'alcool)*.[19]

How does this jurisprudence impact the BHT story? Here, I contend that recalling how the ICC participated in the conflict should give reason for expanding who exactly must reinforce the fiduciary obligation owed to the Dene. The Commission's legislative source and its functions make it more like the Crown than a court, and such a categorization means that the ICC must also keep true to the Royal Proclamation.

The ICC's statutory reference is the *Inquiries Act* (1985). This federal legislation permits the Crown to propose an investigative authority to examine a specific issue or event. In either case, the inquiry's legal role is also specific to each proposed body. An entity can be invented which replaces a court and writes binding decisions. Alternatively, a commission can merely present final results which are consultative in nature. Procedures can be those of another inquiry or administrative body, or completely new rules can be created. A body can be very temporary with a time or budgetary limit. Alternatively, it can function until an issue is investigated in its fullest form, or until the government decides to create a body to either investigate a specific event or, alternatively, a specific topic. In short, an administrative body originating from the *Inquiries Act* can be whatever the Crown desires and the House of Commons supports. Orders-in-Council are used to detail the framework of an inquiry, and these Orders are passed in the same way that other legislative bills are forwarded.

The Orders-in-Council detailing the ICC make the Commission devoted to the investigation of failed Specific Claims according to standards explained in *Outstanding Business* (Canada 1982). The ICC is ordered to determine,

> a) whether a claimant has a valid claim for negotiation under the Policy where that claim has already been rejected by the Minister; and
>
> b) which compensation criteria apply in negotiation of a settlement, where a claimant disagrees with the Minister's determination of the applicable criteria.

The Chief Commissioner and other commissioners have decided that these orders require that inquiry sessions occur in locations easily accessible to indigenous participants. Since they are not permitted to listen to, or remark about, issues of constitutionalism, commissioners' findings are not binding. Hence the ICC has regularly called its resolution ideas "recommendations." When an inquiry is complete, and recommendations are made, the ICC is directed to the following:

> (i) to submit their findings and recommendations to the parties involved in a specific claim where the Commissioners have conducted an inquiry and to submit to the Governor in Council in both official languages an annual report and any other reports from time to time that the Commissioners consider required in respect of the Commission's activities and the activities of the Government of Canada and the Indian bands relating to specific claims, and
>
> (ii) to file their papers and records with the Clerk of the Privy Council as soon as reasonably may be after the conclusion of the inquiry.

Should an indigenous party be displeased with ICC results, it must pursue traditional Canadian legal proceedings and file a Statement of Claim in the Federal Court of Canada.

The first Chief Commissioner needed to invent procedures which enforced the principles in *Outstanding Business*. Therefore (then) Chief

Commissioner Harry Laforme decided that traditional court proceedings were not helpful for analyzing rejected Specific Claims. Certain differences between standard litigation and ICC processes are, therefore, very obvious. Laforme announced that indigenous communities would be the assumed locations of inquiry. Indigenous participants could also speak in their own languages. Community members would be important experts for understanding problems. Information provided by experts, furthermore, might be considered "hearsay" in a regular trial, but, as oral history was a vital part of any inquiry, that data was permitted in an ICC investigation (Indian Claims Commission 2001: 14). Laforme concluded that these ICC procedures were legally justified due to the nature of the Royal Proclamation (*Order in Council P.C. 1991-1329*, 1 September 1992; *Order in Council P.C. 1992-1730*, 27 July 1992; *Order in Council P.C. 1991-1329*, 15 July 1991)

But, besides these announcements by the ICC itself about its daily functions, other events help shed light on the Commission's actual legal form. First, the ICC has publicly criticized the federal government for budget cutbacks to the ICC during the last ten years. The ICC's funding originates from DIAND's annual budget. Unlike the courts, it is not funded by the Department of Justice. The financial cuts, most explicitly criticized by former Chief Commissioner Phil Fontaine, have arguably impaired the ICC's potential to provide the assistance which the Commission has acknowledged it is legally required to enforce (Hurley 2002). During a presentation to the House of Commons Standing Committee on Aboriginal Affairs (2002), Fontaine even concluded that the inadequate conditions at the ICCs would ultimately increase the number of indigenous communities which would pursue litigation (See Royal Commission on Aboriginal Peoples 1996: 592–96). The ICC's mandate could not, in short, be enforced due to the decreased financial support from DIAND (Hurley 2002).

The federal government has never publicly agreed with the ICC's findings on this point. Yet recent Crown actions in other circles address the Commission's concerns. For example, the *Specific Claims Resolution Act* (the "*SCRA*") received Royal Assent on November 7, 2003. When it becomes law, the *SCRA* will permit the Crown to create a tribunal devoted to investigating failed specific claims and rendering binding decisions. This tribunal's panelists will be able to remark upon any legal matter they believe relevant to an inquiry, (*SCRA* 46(c), 65, 74) and they may even include conclusions about compensation for aggrieved parties (Hurley 2002: 13). In order to avoid "irreconcilable decisions" by a tribunal, a panel can adjourn an inquiry until all affected parties are notified and given some form of tribunal standing (*SCRA* 2003: 66). Mary Hurley (2002: 25–26), a researcher at the Library of Parliament, concluded that the *SCRA* was born out of the ICC's failure to have political or legal resonance.

Yet another change has also influenced the legal role of the ICC. During its first ten years, the ICC reported to Parliament as a whole with a written Annual Report and presentations to whatever parliamentary committee seemed relevant. Now, it is only responsible to address DIAND officials.

Certain aspects of the ICC seem judicial in nature. Commissioners remark about one legal norm (fiduciary obligation), and they can openly criticize DIAND policies. But I argue that the ICC overwhelmingly illustrates Crown-like qualities. If such a categorization is correct, it then follows that the ICC has a legal responsibility to enforce the fiduciary obligation on its own accord. The question then becomes whether it has done so.

When ICC activities are recalled, its specific treatment of the Dene is extremely admirable. The ICC supported the Dene's request, proceeded more quickly than court proceedings often do, and agreed with the Dene's understanding of the hunt's legality. Commissioners directly challenged some of DIAND's beliefs. The second report, with the goal of further reproaching Canada, was yet another way of demonstrating how strongly the ICC supported the Dene. This support is not necessarily Dene-specific. But the ICC's actions could also be understood as specific examples of how its independence, in the form of procedures appropriate for the issue at hand, can be observed. In that sense, these events might not be considered evidence of the ICC acting as an extension of the Crown.

These challenges to DIAND, however, do not trump other ICC characteristics, nor can they overtake the increase of DIAND connections over the past ten years. An apprehension of bias, in the sense used to recognize a judicial institution, is evident in ICC procedures about inquiry locations, languages and oral testimonials. An inquiry's "recommendations" are clearly not equal to a court ruling. Budget decisions are not made by the Attorney General but, instead, by the Minister of Indian Affairs. What becomes arguable, then, is that the ICC might have demonstrated proper obligations to the Dene specifically, but changes over time threaten or breach those obligations to other indigenous parties. Fontaine's reflections are particularly revealing. If the ICC does not believe it is performing properly, why would its indigenous applicants?

If my argument about the ICC being the Crown for the sake of fiduciary obligations is arguable but not completely accepted, another trend in jurisprudence makes the connection between the obligation and the ICC important to evaluate. Recently the Supreme Court of Canada found that a corporation did not have a duty to consult in the form of accommodation (*Haida Nation* v. *British Columbia* 2004: 53; *Taku River Tlingit First Nation* v. *British Columbia* 2004). The Court decided that this scenario did not merit an entity obtaining the duties which are part of the Crown's obligation. This decision is important when we look at the process by which the Court determines this conclusion. It concludes that "accommodation" is only one version of consultation. Furthermore, this most onerous form cannot be expected of a business that has, in this case, been performing the activity it did long before the legal problem arose. So the question then becomes, what if the entity in question is not a business? Additionally, what if its functions are specific to the matter at hand? (*Haida Nation* v. *British Columbia* 2004:

18, 25). As well, what if the form of consultation is less demanding than "accommodation"? I contend that the Courts have created space for a body such as the ICC to be considered a third party responsible for enforcing Crown legal responsibilities. The fullest application of this decision (*Haida Nation*) suggests that a government-affiliated body, potentially enforcing a less participatory form of consultation, will be found liable for the obligation. In *Haida Nation*, the Chief Justice concludes that "the stakes are huge," when parties debate legal issues pertaining to Aboriginal peoples. By supporting views of then Chief Justice Lamer in *Delgamuukw* (1997) that an obligation must be appropriately demonstrated in order to ensure the Royal Proclamation is properly applied (1113), the Chief Justice demonstrates fears that an indigenous people's "heritage will be irretrievably despoiled" if the obligation's potentially is not fully explored (*Haida Nation* 2004: 7). Thinking about the ICC (or the Crown itself) as a third party demonstrates such an exploration. Again, while the Dene's treatment is noteworthy and admirable, the ICC's systemic conditions are likely not legally valid.

In the end, Canada should prepare itself to be found in breach of at least one form of the obligation to the Dene. Should it not experience creative evaluation regarding the restoration of the obligation, it could be found in breach of its obligations to the Inuit as well. The ICC, in the meantime, is strongly attached to the Crown and could easily share in this responsibility as either the Crown proper or, alternatively, a third party. Consultation has definitely not proven evident to the Dene in order for best interest violations to be considered justified.

"Treaty Rights"

"Treaty rights," while supposedly part of Canadian law before 1982, received little interpretative attention prior to modern constitutional talks. The nature of this norm is extremely influential upon most Crown-Aboriginal relations, as nearly all of Canada is treatied. As well, a modern land claim agreement, for constitutive purposes, transforms into a treaty upon implementation. So while parties may not refer to treaty rights in an obvious way when communicating their positions, they are keenly aware that this term founds their very (argued for) legitimacy.

In the past, courts were not favourable to First Nations who demanded better treatment from the government by using treaty references. Reactions included the interpretation of phrases, literally or without historical context. Crown imperatives, if a conflict existed between a treaty's contents and another government policy, were found more proper. But due to the inclusion of treaty rights in the constitution, and the evolution of fiduciary obligation discourse, interpretive times are not as tough as they were. Today, courts regularly mention that treaties are sacred documents that need more than standard contractual interpretation methods. Their sui generis role obligates the Crown to adhere to the documents' conditions (*Nowegijck* v. *the Queen* 1983: 26).[20] The spirit and intent of treaty negotiations must influence the treaty's modern interpretation. (See generally D. Arnot, "The Honour of the Crown.") The spirit and intent of treaty-making should influence a document's interpretation. Any ambiguities in interpretation must be interpreted in a way favourable to the indigenous adherents. Crown policies with important national interest can place a treaty's implementation in question (*R.* v. *Cote* 1996; *R.* v. *Sundown* 1999).[21] But if such a change is necessary, the Crown must either explain how this change is in the indigenous parties' "best interests," or the Crown must demonstrate a proper "duty to consult" (See *R.* v. *Badger* 1996; *R.* v. *Cote* 1996; *R.* v. *Gladstone* 1996; *R.* v. *Fox* 1994).[22] As Justice Binnie wrote in *R.* v. *Marshall* (1999: 21), "a deal is a deal." Fiduciary-obligation discourse, as I have just included, helps enforce this historic and modern reality when governments attempt to renege on their legal responsibilities.

Treaty 8 and Treaty 10, since their appearance, have not stopped the Dene from hunting the Beverly herd. Crown agents promised that part of the treaty's purpose was to protect Dene cultural and economic ways which existed prior to treaty-making. The Dene understood the hunt as a reinforcement of their values and as a demonstration of treaty enforcement. During the twentieth century, government officials actually promoted the hunt. Its legitimacy, in short, was never challenged until 1989. These facts make it evident that the Dene have a very strong claim of violated treaty rights. The Crown could argue that the violation is justified due to larger overarching national interests. But, just as Canada has no evidence that a breach of a best-interest fiduciary obligation was justified, it does not have any proof that a violation is valid here either. Even if it, retroactively, re-called a concern that seems applicable, the Crown did not demonstrate its consultation duty. So either a treaty rights violation exists, or the duty to consult is again violated.

How can this constitutive problem be resolved? If we consider a principle of contract law, we see that treaty rights decisions which favour the indigenous adherents often mention that the Aboriginal parties involved should be placed in a position as though the treaty violation had never occurred. This conclusion typically means that damages must enforce the treaty principles but that other reparations represent what would have occurred during the violation's time had the violation not happened. Sometimes, some indigenous parties have approved receiving a completely monetary settlement, or another item (such as a land tract) for the violation. But it is unlikely that such a settlement would be approved by the Dene. The hunt is so important to the Dene cultural foundation that it arguably needs reinstatement.

If the hunt were to be reinstated, a court would have to take one of two actions. It would either have to "read" Articles 5 and 40 of the NLCA as permitting the caribou hunt for the Dene. Alternatively, it would have to find the two articles unconstitutional. As other sections of the NLCA arguably conflict with a broader reading, it is likely that the latter choice would be more appropriate. The moment such a finding is rendered, I argue that the Inuit have either a breached best-interest or duty-to-consult obligation, depending upon how their communication with Canada has evolved during this litigation. Moreover, they could also have a strong argument for a treaty violation. The Crown could respond to Inuit claims by maintaining that the Dene hunt does not jeopardize Inuit cultural conditions and that the litigation process was completely accessible and understandable to the Inuit. A favourable decision for the Dene would challenge many different sections of the NLCA. In fact, it would challenge one of the fundamental principles of the act — that the Inuit control what happens in Nunavut. Permitting the Dene hunt contradicts more than merely the hunting aspect of the NLCA. Should the Inuit then choose to pursue legal action, the circular nature of the fiduciary obligation is repeated in treaty rights jurisprudence. Unless and until a court formulates a test or a settlement which is acceptable to all participating nations, Aboriginal peoples will be capable of challenging any proposed solutions to the violated treaty rights in an overlap. The Crown, again, must be prepared to provide significant reparations.

"Aboriginal Rights"

Another term in s.35, "Aboriginal rights," is not an obvious part of an overlap if a modern land settlement or a historic treaty is involved. Treaties are, after all, supposed to represent arrangements about Aboriginal rights. So appreciating the conflict as a non-treaty disagreement is not the main way a problem might be envisaged. Why Aboriginal rights discourse is important, however, is in how it influences the other two terms' natures and how an Aboriginal rights argument could be forwarded as an alternative argument by an indigenous party (should its view about treaty rights be rejected). Aboriginal rights jurisprudence, therefore, is an influential part of any overlap analysis.

What is an Aboriginal right? Earlier, I described how it can be a protective label for a variety of subjects. Courts describe how site-specific activities to complete land title are part of this constitutive category. The decision which has influenced parties' strategy the most is the 1996 *Van der Peet* ruling. Then Chief Justice Lamer explained that three standards must be successfully presented. The subject must be one which existed prior to contact with Europeans, it must be "integral" to the indigenous party's cultural identity and that same subject must have continuity since contact occurred. The test was (and is) regularly reproached for its unjustly harsh standards and for its contradiction to principles explained in other s.35 decisions (Barsh and Henderson 1997; Borrows 1998a; *R. v. Van der Peet* 1996). Since its appearance, however, the *Van der Peet* test has evolved somewhat. A subject's continuity can include moments of pause, if the matter's stoppage occurred due to government policies disapproved by the indigenous community. The integrality should not be measured using non-indigenous priorities. Finally, pre-contact can mean prior to sovereignty or European control of a region (*Delgamuukw* v. *British Columbia* 1997: 83; *R.* v. *Powley* 2003: 10, 35).[23]

As I have already mentioned, then Chief Justice Dickson wrote in *Sparrow* that an Aboriginal right can be violated. This violation, however, must keep to standards influenced by fiduciary obligations. The violation must be justified by the Crown in ways that demonstrate that the reason is "compelling and substantial" and that the affected indigenous parties are properly informed. The Crown's sovereignty is never questioned. But that sovereignty is only legitimate when Aboriginal sui generis roles are properly protected (*Delgamuukw* v. *British Columbia* 1997: 82; *R.* v. *Van der Peet* 1996: 49).

The overlap story here is, first and foremost, an example of conflicting treaties. But if parties believe their treaty rights arguments are not strong, they could include Aboriginal rights interpretations in their positions. Doing so means explaining how the treaties' applications are, in fact, not constitutionally proper. In other words, an indigenous party is arguing that the treaty be forgotten and the subject in question be re-understood as an Aboriginal right. Should the Dene choose this strategy, they must explain how the conditions of Treaty 8 and 10 are unjust due to the limitations they demand which were not properly explained. If the hunt is not permitted when the treaties are applied, but the Dene understood that it would continue, they could contend that the treaties are not valid. The hunt then could become a site-specific activity worthy of constitutional protection. It is possible if this position is favoured, however, the Dene might jeopardize the implementation of other treaty conditions. It is unclear whether the Dene is willing to accept such a potential effect.

The Inuit, as well, could decide to contend that they never learned of the *NLCA*'s actual implications. In other words, the *Act*'s implementation is not a positive experience and Canada failed to fully inform them. This breached consultation, then, potentially leads to the Inuit calling for its hunting pattern to be considered a site-specific activity as well. By withdrawing their support of the *NLCA*, they would be representing a strong Aboriginal title argument. Perhaps the Inuit who are historically attached to BHT might approve this strategy. But whether Nunavut would approve it is extremely unlikely, as arguing for Aboriginal rights outside of the *NLCA* could jeopardize the entire agreement's validity (and the territory's actual existence).

So the influence of Aboriginal rights discourse is not necessarily a direct one. What it does, instead, is help provide context for why some activities are worth mentioning in a historic treaty or modern agreement. Another overlap, involving activities or land title to a non-treated part of Canada, would involve this norm as the primary tool and treaty rights jurisprudence as the alternative. Either way, fiduciary obligations are always part of the story, as a violation of either right likely does not represent either best interests or proper consultation.

AN OVERLAP'S APPEARANCE, AN OVERLAP'S RESULTS, AN OVERLAP'S END

The above comments about various constitutive norms provide some observations about how an overlap starts, how it will evolve, and what choices parties have to eliminate the stresses an overlap creates. Certain conclusions seem particularly evident in the BHT story, and these aspects likely have resonance in other overlaps as well.

First, it does not appear that either the Dene or Inuit imagined that their separate pursuit of modern constitutionalism would ultimately challenge each others' cultural conditions. This point is important to flag as it illustrates how some information about Aboriginal-Crown relations is still not accessible to Aboriginals themselves. Some aspects of talks and relationships are arguably confidential, but appreciating what others pursue seems a logical topic to ascertain. Whether this point is evident due to communities' less capable pursuit of access or the Crown's substandard notification efforts is unclear. Likely the uninformed state can be considered as constituting both general conditions and events specific to an overlap.

As well, an overlap might appear to be a "conflict of law," which, as an event, does happen regularly in the evolution of legislation and jurisprudence in any legal system. Such a conclusion is, however, an incomplete understanding. Conflicts of law typically arise when at least two separate norms collide. This state has happened to Aboriginals in Canada (See *Corbiere* v. *Canada* 1999).[24] An overlap, however, is about the internal components of one legislative source, s.35. The interplay of fiduciary obligations with this section complicates the determination of overlaps in a way that has less in common with "conflicts of law" discourse. Concluding that an overlap is simply about competing jurisprudence is an incomplete analysis.

Third, when an overlap is evident, one juridical conclusion is obvious. The Crown has breached its fiduciary obligation to at least one party. The scenario's specific details will reveal whether the violation is of the best-interest or consultation form, but it could also be in both forms. Furthermore, treaty rights violations are also possible, and, if they are proven, the breached obligations happen again. As the ICC concluded, the Crown's hesitance to settle an overlap in an early stage only hurts the Crown's legal legitimacy and increases what reparations it will invariably need to provide.

Fourth, no juridical response has yet to provide guidance about what to do when an overlap happens. Mentions about overlaps have appeared, but judges have not created a tool that would directly address the problems an overlap represents. Here, the BHT can be helpful. In my view, one part of the story is important to recall. At some time in the story, it is reasonable to assume that Canada became aware that the historic treaties' interpretation and the modern agreement's contents would clash. Yet the Dene were not informed of this point by Canada, and it is unclear whether Canada clearly stated this conclusion to the Inuit of the eastern Arctic.

What does this mean when we imagine how to solve the tensions the overlap creates? When interplayed with modern legal discourse, one recommendation is possible. When Canada decided the two rights would conflict and one set of the rights (the Denes') needed to end, a breached fiduciary obligation (and likely a treaty violation) occurred. But the notification of the hunt's end is not where the legal problems really begin. The standards in Haida Nation demand that we determine the moment the Crown learned that a conflict might arise. At that moment, an obligation was triggered. Clearly, such an obligation was not reinforced. Had it been, it is likely that Dene views would have influenced the nature of the NLCAA. Their participation would have, arguably, created dialogues that would not have permitted the conflict between the Act and the historic treaties to develop. In other words, the concerns which found an overlap would be eliminated, as the recognition of overlapping cultural practices would be part and parcel of the NLCAA's legal application. When a constitutive overlap is exposed, therefore, a fiduciary obligation breach has automatically happened. It is not necessary for the protesting indigenous communities to present data about their separate experiences. Courts should easily observe that an overlap, on its own accord, acknowledges a breached obligation of one or both forms. When this conclusion is immediately noted, talks leading to legislative creations or modern treaty interpretation must be halted in order that the core breached obligation be addressed. Talks can continue afterward, and obligations and treaty rights violations are still possible, but they will be separate from overlap concerns. This pause, while an overlap's separate normative form is evaluated, permits an appreciation of the interrelatedness among various indigenous cultures. Negotiations, therefore, will then better reflect the reality of inter-indigenous relations that Crown officials have either ignored or not even noticed.

As a final reflection, it is also vital to consider the role of these inter-indigenous relations on their own accord. They are a part of Canada's current political state. Various Aboriginal organizations discuss, debate and disagree about numerous issues. Sometimes a certain pan-Aboriginal voice can appear from these talks. But more often, different viewpoints are the norm. The relations among Aboriginal groups in modern Canada are rarely studied and are not appreciated enough by society. But it influences how relations with Aboriginals and the Crown evolve.

What, then, do Dene-Inuit relations represent? They illustrate agreement about the importance of strong and respectful treatment from the Crown. They are both fully aware of the dependence upon the Beverly herd. Finally, they acknowledge each other's existence as a way to explain their own internal cultural autonomy. A Dene is Dene due to Dene traits. But she also has such an affinity because she is not part of an Inuit community. The other, in short, helps define the self. This definition existed prior to Europeans arriving; it is vital to the two cultures' integrity; and it continues on today with changes only evident when Crown policies interfere with it. In sum, it matches the conditions espoused in *Van der Peet*. The interrelations can, I conclude, have a constitutional form and hold the key to imagining how an overlap is terminated. If the right to interrelate (including discussions about survival) is a constitutional right, that would mean the Dene and the Inuit could determine BHT concerns without Crown influence before talks with the Crown commence. Furthermore, the Crown must protect this process, as it is in both nations' best interests. Just because the two nations disagree about BHT today does not mean they always will. Their disagreements, furthermore, worsened when they used non-indigenous processes. Recognizing the legal role of inter-nation relations permits us to envisage political arrangements between the Dene and Inuit that would never let an overlap form. Providing the normative space for such a relationship is politically prudent and constitutively warranted. If only Canada had recognized that part of history, they would not need to provide reparations for breached obligations today.

When the Beverly herd moves back and forth in its territory, it clearly pays no heed to modern metes and bounds. The caribou move where food and warmth can be had, and where the land is not used in ways which jeopardize future visitations. The Inuit and Dene, after many years of observing the habits of the herd, have framed their values and actions around the caribou's ways. Current Canadian laws do not make room for balance, since each nation is forced to discuss constitutional matters separately with the Crown: however, I want to suggest that constitutionalism actually demands that we recognize this inter-indigenous relatedness. Until this legal point is integrated into modern Crown-Aboriginal relations, overlaps will continue to appear, and the Crown will be found responsible for breached obligations every time. Whether considered as a way to integrate traditional indigenous law, to fully apply Canadian constitutionalism or to save the Crown from experiencing financial woes during litigation, giving inter-indigenous relations legal recognition resolves many of the traumas an overlap creates. It recognizes that an overlap, when properly understood, is not ultimately illegal (*Delgamuukw* v. *British Columbia* 1997: 158). It is an admission that Aboriginals are the best they can be when their interdependence is recognized by all of Canadian society.

POSTSCRIPT: A MOOTIST PROPOSAL

One more matter about the BHT story is helpful to know. While not necessary for a complete constitutive analysis, it reveals some issues that are difficult to integrate into regular academic analysis, but are, I believe, vital to appreciate when attempting to form solutions for overlaps. My exposure to this story illustrates certain nuances not mentioned in case law, ICC proceedings or court documents. I learned about the struggle in BHT during a "mooting" event in law school. (Mooting events are mock legal events used by law schools to teach adversarial methods to students.)

In 1998, during the second term of my second year at Osgoode Hall Law School, I participated in an activity which had existed for ten years. Students from across the country could apply for permission to be a mooter in "Kawaskimhon." This time, the weekend of law students pretending to be parties involved in a legal dispute, the moot was in my home town. With written submissions provided by different teams, students were prepared to debate the issues that were at stake when ICC recommendations were ignored by Canada. I was the only student from Osgoode, and I pretended to be the Inuit organization which negotiated the NLCAA with Canada.

This moot is different from other mooting events at law schools. It is not considered a "competition." Best oralists and best written submissions, for example, are not announced. For two days, students attempt to negotiate resolution. Typically, a supervising "coach" provides assistance to team members during the event and then marks the team's submission. My experience, as a mooter in 1998 and as a coach in 2001, 2002 and 2005, is that the first day includes remarks that seem similar to traditional litigation. After a night's rest, however, participants return, eager to show their negotiation strategies. These techniques, however, clearly deviate from my experiences at officially learning negotiating strategies from lawyers who specialize in negotiations. Concessions are more easily imagined; representation of the goals of a party is sometimes actually withdrawn. In short, the Kawaskimhon moot demonstrates an atypical legal training. In 1998, I learned of a strategy that has resurfaced time and again when I have coached (or even worked) in the field of indigenous peoples and Canadian law. Aboriginal parties find agreement by themselves, but then realize that this resolution suddenly disappears when Crown concerns are remembered.

In 1998, this realization happened while joking with people on breaks, while walking to the banquet and while grabbing a coffee outside the room used for the moot. Even though I was representing a side that was not particularly empathetic to historic treaty interpretation, I could still discuss resolution with students representing the Dene. This possibility was, I think, founded on us trying to answer one question: what are we doing? The "doing" was letting the Crown govern us. Constitutive norms were not, ultimately, leading to indigenous improvement. We were fighting among ourselves: government parties could simply watch our disputes and wait until we jointly invented some position.

Why is this memory important to me? Having seven years to rethink its role, the recollection of resolution without the participation of the Crown has great potential. At the moot, I was a novice: my neophyte exposure to section 35 discourse did not let me articulate my dream of telling the Crown representatives to leave the room and let us negotiate without them. I thought the negotiations would lead to a legal resolution: I did not realize that such an outcome would ultimately fail to be anything but a political possibility. Why would the Crown let us do that?

Today, I have decided that this proposal about which some of us joked (but which we then sadly discarded) is not so unattainable anymore. I am willing to highlight its political and social benefits. But now, hopefully more aware of section 35 trends, I have greater optimism in its legal nature. I have already argued that negotiations among the Dene and Inuit have constitutional merit. The more I learn about the history of inter-nation relations and compare those histories to trends in other legal subfields, the more it becomes clear to me that understanding ourselves is partially based on distinguishing ourselves from others. Non-Aboriginals regularly confirm this norm when they build a fence, use a passport or enforce a national boundary. We have important internal traits, but we are also different — recognizing that each Indigenous Nation has its own set of internal characteristics that sets it apart from other Nations. One arrangement, which would recognize these differences, could be sharing a specific region for the purposes of hunting or land tenure. If the norms which define these arrangements are pre-contact, integral and demonstrated continually, they have constitutional merit. It should not matter that these values and actions are not what non-Aboriginals enforce. They are sui generis. They are also the key to stopping an overlap before it starts.

I remember that, when I was daydreaming about having the Crown leave the mooting circle, I was also thinking that resolution could not be that simple. After all, we were just a bunch of law students looking for a free trip to make our second term of second year pass more quickly. We were not experienced lawyers.

But, when I compare my recollection of this event with the situation today, I am aware that no resolution among the Crown, Dene and Inuit exists: Canada denies the legal responsibility that I (and others) think it has; the Inuit are nervous that their years of negotiations will be for naught if they acknowledge Dene claims; and the Dene wonder whether they have enough money to begin litigation. It seems no one has peace with this problem.

In the meantime, the annual hunt is not enforced, as it had been for centuries, in its traditional ways. Indigenous cultures do not have the freedom to reinforce ideas that ensure their survival. Perhaps, in the end, we indigenous peoples can only stop being a burden by ending whatever form we need to take in order to continue indigeneity into the twenty-first century. Overlaps might represent a constitutive impasse but, in the end, they allow the Crown to be "beneficial to the public" in a way that erases indigenous identities. If Canada contends that "the present situation of affairs is utterly impossible by all the methods hitherto proposed," we need to make new proposals. Maybe our problem is not our ideas. Maybe the problem is, as Jonathan Swift suggested in 1729 in *A Modest Proposal*, that they are not permitted to be the ideas they can be.

NOTES

1. Doctoral candidate, Department of History, University of Western Ontario. This award was received while a graduate student at the University of Toronto, Faculty of Law. Generous guidance about this issue was provided by Sylvia Bashevkin, Karen Knop, Brenda Macdougall, Patrick Macklem, Sheila Purdy, Bob Rae, John Whyte and Norman Zlotkin. Steven Bittle of the Law Commission of Canada went above and beyond any obligations he had in organizing this piece's appearance. Finally, I am particularly indebted to Lorne Sossin.

2. Future uses of "Dene" and "Inuit" refer only to the members of these cultures who describe their families' past in relation to BHT. The communities of each culture with affinity to BHT are arguably part of larger groups of Dene and Inuit cultures.

3. See NA RG-10, vol. 3848, file 75, 236-1, Walker, J. (Officer NWMP) to Clifford Sifton, Minister of the Interior and Indian Affairs, 30 November 1897. Walker states, "no time should be lost by the Government in making a treaty with these Indians for their rights over this Territory. They will be more easily dealt with now than they would be when their country is overrun with prospectors and valuable mines must be discovered. They would place a higher value on their rights than they would before these discoveries are made and if they are like some of the Indians of the Saskatchewan they may object to prospectors or settlers going into that country until their rights are settled."

4. This arrangement, with the idea of hunting outside treaty boundaries, was understood by the Dene as a fully accepted condition by Crown representatives. Citing RG 10, vol. 6759.

5. In an interesting and racially-centric interpretation, the Inuit were considered "Indians" for the purpose of the *Indian Act* in *Re: Eskimos*.

6. The Supreme Court of Canada recognizes "Indian title" as a legal norm, and it justifies this recognition by using *St. Catherines Milling and Lumber Co.* This decision, written by the British Privy Council, permitted the Crown to define what indigenous title meant, whereas *Calder* suggests that indigenous descriptions of land title help determine indigenous title.

7. For the purpose of this chapter, the relevant parts of s. 35 state "the existing aboriginal and treaty rights of the (A)boriginal peoples of Canada are hereby recognized and affirmed" and "Aboriginal peoples" is defined as "includes the Indian, Inuit and Métis peoples of Canada."

8. Letter from John F. Leslie, Chief, Treaties and Historical Research Centre, Indian and Northern Affairs Canada, to Ralph Abramson, Director of TARR, Manitoba, 8 June 1989.

9. See *Fond du lac band* for a failed attempt at an interlocutory injunction. The matter, as it did not involve provincial legislation, was commenced at the Federal Court of Canada.

10. The NLCAA approved the passage of the *Nunavut Land Claims Agreement* (hereinafter the "NLCA"). The following references to the NLCA: Arts 17, 18, 19, and 21 explain the territory's physical location.

11. Article 40 of the NLCA describes "Other Aboriginal Peoples": it mentions the Dene in particular at Art. 40.5 and describes how the Dene, if given permission to hunt in Nunavut, must keep to standards equal to those of the Inuit, with an "allowable harvest" predetermined by the Nunavut government.

12. This entire stage of the challenges to the ICC's authority by Canada is also

published by the ICC in (ICCP 2003: 5–9).

13. Vice-Chief Dantouze to Commissioner Corcoran, ICC, 19 June 1995. The Dene did file a statement of claim in the Federal Court of Canada on December 19, 1991 seeking a declaration that the Dene have existing treaty and/or Aboriginal rights in lands north of the 60th parallel. They have, however, chosen not to seek relief on this matter while participating in the ICC process.

14. Some of the best discussion regarding the evidence a protesting First Nation can have about another nation's pursuit of constitutional protection is Neil Sterritt et al.'s criticism of the Nisga'a Final Agreement. Supreme Court of Canada justices have also remarked about the existence of overlaps impacting relations among First Nations regarding land title (1998).

15. The Supreme Court, as written in *Hunter v. Southam Inc.*, regularly mentions that constitutional rights are to be understood as part of a "continuing framework." Recently this conclusion was reiterated in the s. 35 case of *R. v. Blais*.

16. Modern agreements can no longer state that the subject matters contained therein can never be renegotiated in the future. But this finding is not retroactive, so nearly all historic treaties and some modern agreements include "extinguishment" clauses. For a critical analysis of this point, see Borrows 2002.

17. Lorne Sossin (2003: 129) has provided important guidance about this point.

18. This case also shows that there may be a blurring between the legislative branch and judiciary. For the purposes of determining fiduciary obligations, however, Lorne Sossin explains how leaping from non-judicial to Crown interpretations provides a more realistic understanding of Aboriginal roles, as Aboriginals will always be considered to be a group needing more than simply legislative analysis. Sossin (2003) notes how the judiciary and the executive have a "fluid and reinforcing nature," in which each one verifies its functions by demonstrating it is not the other.

19. As explained by Lorne Sossin, one of the inherent principles an administrative body is supposed to demonstrate is equity. Equity is an extension of the concern with procedural fairness that the Supreme Court has concluded must be enforced. By ensuring equity, parties must take on the responsibilities of certain legal norms if they are willing to take on the rights of that type of legal roles. The ICC may not openly state it is part of the Crown, but it proceeds in a manner which ultimately enforces Crown views, and that enforcement must undergo juridical scrutiny. See *Baker v. Canada* (1999: 23–27) in particular for details about noting the statutory scheme of a tribunal to evaluate its legitimacy to make any decision.

20. *Nowegijck* includes the sui generis notion for treaty interpretation.

21. *R. v. Cote* and *R. v. Sundown* [1999] both discuss the scope of how a right can be interpreted. The most common justification for limiting the scope of a treaty right has been when the treaty may conflict with conservation purposes of other legislation.

22. See *R. v. Badger* [1996], *R. v. Cote* [1996], *R. v. Gladstone* [1996]. "Safety" has also been an issue in the courts when discussing a treaty's scope, but this word has also not been defined clearly in the decisions. See, for example, *R. v. Fox* [1994] 3 C.N.L.R.

23. *Delgamuukw* looks at how post-contact commences after Crown sovereignty is established; *R. v. Powley* [2003] describes how the Métis can meet the prior contact part of the test if post-contact occurs after Europeans have effective "control" of a region.

24. This case explains the delicate balance of interpreting individual rights explained in the *Canadian Charter of Rights and Freedoms* and group rights protected by s. 35.

REFERENCES

Backhouse, Constance. 1999. *Colour Coded: A Legal History of Racism in Canada, 1900–1950*. Toronto: University of Toronto Press.

Barsh, R., and J.Y. Henderson. 1997. "The Supreme Court's *Van der Peet* Trilogy: Native Imperialism and Ropes of Sand." *McGill Law Journal* 42, 993.

Bennett, John, and Susan Rowley (compilers and editors). 2004. *Uqalurait: An Oral History of Nunavut*. Montreal and Kingston: McGill-Queen's University Press.

Brody Hugh. 1981. *Maps and Dreams*. Vancouver and Toronto: Douglas and McIntyre

Burrows, J. 1998. "Frozen Rights in Canada: Constitutional Interpretation and the Trickster." *American Indian Literature Review* 22, 37.

_____. 2002. *Recovering Canada: The Resurgence of Indigenous Law*. Toronto: University of Toronto Press.

Burrows, John J., and Leonard I. Rotman. 1998. *Aboriginal Legal Issues: Cases, Materials and Commentary*. Toronto: Butterworths.

Buckley, H. 1992. *From Wooden Ploughs to Welfare*. Montreal and Kingston: McGill Queen's University Press.

Bussidor, Ila, and Ustun Bilgen-Reinhart. 2002. *Night Spirits: The Story of the Relocation of the Sayisi Dene*. Winnipeg, MB: University of Manitoba Press, 4th printing.

Canada. 1981. *In All Fairness: A Native Claims Policy, Comprehensive Claims*. Ottawa: Ministry of Supply and Services.

_____. 1982. *Outstanding Business: A Native Claims Policy — Specific Claims*. Ottawa: Minister of Supply and Services.

_____. 1990. January–21 February *Unfinished Business: An Agenda for All Canadians in the 1990s*. Minutes of Proceedings and Evidence. Issue No. 20, 31.

Department of Indian Affairs and Northern Development. 1973. *Communiqué*. "Statement Made by the Honourable Jean Chrétien, Minister of Indian Affairs and Northern Development on Claims of Indian and Inuit Peoples." 8 August.

Echohh, Victor (Acting Chief, Black Lake Denesuline Nation, Treaty 8). 1997. 4 November. Treaty Elders Forum, Black Lake, Saskatchewan (translated from Dene). Cited in Cardinal, Harold and Walter Hildebrandt. 2000. *Treaty Elders of Saskatchewan: Our Dream is that Our Peoples Will One Day be Clearly Recognized as Nations*. Calgary: University of Calgary Press.

Francis, R. Douglas, Richard Jones and Donald B. Smith. 1992. *Destinies: Canadian History Since Confederation*. Toronto: Holt, Rinehart and Winston.

House of Commons Standing Committee on Aboriginal Affairs, Northern Development and Natural Resources. 2001. *Evidence*. May. Meeting No. 18, 29.

Hurley, Mary C. 2002. Law and Government Division. "Bill C-6: The Specific Claims Resolution Act." Legislative Summary LS-431E, Library of Parliament, Parliamentary Research Branch. Footnote 3-4, 9. 10 October.

Indian Claims Commission. 1993. "Interim Ruling: Athabasca-Denesuline Treaty Harvesting Rights Inquiry." 7 May.

_____. 2001. *Annual Report 2000–2001*. Ottawa: Minister of Public Works and Government Services Canada.

_____. 2001. *Annual Report.* Ottawa: Minister of Supply and Services Canada.

_____. 2002. "Brief Presentation to the House of Commons Standing Committee on Aboriginal Affairs." 26 November.

_____. 2003. "Special Issue on Interim Rulings." 16 ICCP 5-9.

Lawrence, S., and P. Macklem. 2000. "From Consultation to Reconciliation: Aboriginal Rights and the Crown's Duty to Consult." *Can. Bar Review* 70.

Macdougall, Brenda. 2002. "Power and Co-Management Agreements: The Beverly Qumanirjuiq Caribou Management Board and the Role of Aboriginal People." Unpublished article manuscript.

Macklem, P. 1991. "First Nations Self-Government and the Border of the Canadian Legal Imagination." *McGill Law Journal* 36, 382.

McCormack, Patricia. 1988. *Northwind Dreaming: Fort Chipewyan, 1788.* Edmonton: Provincial Museum of Alberta.

McMillan, Allan D., and Eldon Yellowhorn. 2004. *First Peoples in Canada.* Toronto and Vancouver: Douglas and McIntyre.

Miller, J.R. 1989. *Skyscrapers Hide the Heavens: A History of Indian-White Relations in Canada.* Toronto: University of Toronto Press.

Pryde, Duncan. 1972. *Nunaga: My Land, My Country.* Edmonton: Hurtig.

Purich, Donald. 1992. *The Inuit and Their Land: The Story of Nunavut.* Toronto: Lorimer.

Ray, A. 1996. *I Have Lived Here Since the World Began.* Toronto: Key Porter.

Rotman, L. 1996. *Parallel Paths: Fiduciary Doctrine and the Crown-native Relationship in Canada.* Toronto: University of Toronto Press.

Royal Commission on Aboriginal Peoples. 1996. *Restructuring the Relationship.* Vol. 2, Part 2, Recommendations 2.49- 2.4.33. Ottawa.

_____. 1996. *Report of the Royal Commission on Aboriginal Peoples, Vol. 1, Looking Forward, Looking Back.* Ottawa: Minister of Supply and Services.

Sossin, Lorne. 2003. "Public Fiduciary Obligations, Political Trusts, and the Equitable Duty of Reasonableness in Administrative Law." *Saskatchewan Law Review* 66, 129.

_____. 2004. "The Rule of Policy: Baker and the Impact of Judicial Review on Administrative Discretion." In David Dyzenhaus (ed.), *The Unity of Public Law.* Oxford and Portland Oregon: Hart Publishing.

Sterritt, N. 1998/99. "Competing Claims Ignored!" *BC Studies* 120, 73.

Sterritt, Neil J. Susan Marsden, Robert Galois, Peter R. Grant and Richard Overstall. 1998. *Treaty Boundaries of the Nass Watershed.* Vancouver: University of British Columbia Press.

Taylor, David. August 1998 "Tracking Caribou from the Elders to High-tech." *Americas* (English Edition) 50, 46, 11.

Tester, Frank James, and Peter Kulchyski. 1994. *Tammarniit (Mistakes): Inuit Relocation in the Eastern Arctic 1939–63.* Vancouver: University of British Columbia Press.

Thorpe, Natasha, Naikak Hakongak, Sandra Eyegetok and Kitikmeot Elders. 2001. *Thunder on the Tundra: Inuit qaujimajatuqangit of the Bathurst Caribou.* Ikaluktuuittiak, Nunavut: Tuktu and Nogak Project.

Van Kirk, Sylvia. 1999. *Many Tender Ties: Women in Fur Trade Society 1670–1870* Winnipeg: Watson and Dwywer.

Venne, S. 1997. "Understanding Treaty 6: An Indigenous Perspective." In M. Asch (ed.), *Aboriginal and Treaty Rights in Canada: Essays on Law, Equity and the Respect for Difference.* Vancouver: University of British Columbia Press.

Walkem, Ardith, and Halie Bruce. 2003. "Introduction." In Ardith Walkem and Halie Bruce (eds.), *Box of Treasures or Empty Box? Twenty Years of Section 35.* Vancouver: Theytus Books.

York, Geoffrey, and Lorena Pindera. 1999. *People of the Pines: The Warriors and the Legacy of Oka.* Toronto: McArthur.

Statutes

Inquiries Act RSC *1985*, c. I-11.

Nunavut Land Claims Agreement.

Order in Council PC 1991-1329, 15 July 15.

Order in Council PC 1992-1730, 27 July 27 1992.

Royal Proclamation of 1763 , R.S.C. 1985.

Specifics Claims Resolution Act, R.S.C. [2003, c.23].

The Constitution Act, 1982, Schedule B to the *Canada Act 1982* (U.K.), c.11.

Cases

2727-3174 Québec Inc. v. *Québec (Régie des permis d'alcool)* [1996], 3 S.C.R. 919.

Baker v. *Canada (Minister of Citizenship and Immigration)* [1999], 2 S.C.R. 817.

Calder v. *A.G.B.C.* [1973], S.C.R. 313.

Corbiere v. *Canada (Minister of Indian and Northern Affairs)* [1999], 2 S.C.R. 2003.

Committee for Justice and Liberty v. *National Energy Board*, [1978], 1 S.C.R. 369.

C.P.R. v. *Matsqui* [1995], 1 S.C.R. 3 at p. 24.

Delgamuukw v. *British Columbia* [1997], 3 S.C.R. 1010.

Fond du lac band v. *Canada* [1993], 1 F.C. 195.

Guerin v. *the Queen* [1984], 2 S.C.R. 325.

Haida Nation v. *British Columbia (Minister of Forests)*, 2004 SCC 73.

Hunter v. *Southam Inc.* [1984], 2 S.C.R. 145.

Indian Act in *Re: Eskimos* [1939], 80 S.C.R. 44.

Manitoba Provincial Judges Assn. v. *Manitoba (Minister of Justice)* [1997], 3 S.C.R. 3.

Nowegjick v. *the Queen* [1983], 1 S.C.R. 29.

Paul v. *A.G.B.C.* [2003], 2 S.C.R. 585.

R. v. *Badger* [1996], 1 S.C.R. 771.

R. v. *Blais* [2003], 2 S.C.R. 236.

R. v. *Cote* 138 D.L.R. (4e) 385.

R. v. *Fox* [1994], 3 C.N.L.R. 132 (Ont.C.A.).

R. v. *Gladstone* [1996], 2 S.C.R. 723.

R. v. *Marshall* [1999], 3 S.C.R. 456.

R. v. *Powley* [2003], 2 S.C.R. 207.

R. v. *Sundown* [1999], 1 S.C.R.

R. v. *Van der Peet* [1996], 2 S.C.R.

Re Eskimos (sub nom. Re Term "Indians"), [1939], S.C.R. 104.

Sparrow [1990], 1 S.C.R. 1075.

St. Catherines Milling and Lumber Co. v. *the Queen* (1888), 14 App. Case (P.C.).

Taku River Tlingit First Nation v. *British Columbia (Project Assessment Director)* 2004 SCC 74.

U.E.S., Local 298 v. *Bibeault*, [1988], 2 S.C.R. 1048.

Vancouver General Hospital v. *Stoffman* [1990], 3 S.C.R. 483 at 513.